Stalin's Revenge

Stalin's Revenge

Operation Bagration and the Annihilation of Army Group Centre

Anthony Tucker-Jones

Pen & Sword
MILITARY

First published in Great Britain in 2009 by
Pen and Sword Military
an imprint of
Pen and Sword Books Ltd
47 Church Street, Barnsley
South Yorkshire S70 2AS

ISBN 978-1-84415-866-9

A CIP catalogue record for this book is available from the British Library.

Typeset in 10pt Palatino by
Mac Style, Beverley, East Yorkshire

Printed and bound in the UK
by the MPG Books Group

Pen and Sword Books Ltd incorporates the imprints of Pen and Sword
Aviation, Pen and Sword Maritime, Pen and Sword Military,
Wharncliffe Local History, Pen and Sword Select, Pen and Sword
Military Classics, Leo Cooper, Remember When, Seaforth Publishing
and Frontline Publishing.

For a complete list of Pen and Sword titles please contact
PEN and SWORD BOOKS LIMITED
47 Church Street, Barnsley, South Yorkshire, S70 2AS, England
E-mail: enquiries@pen-and-sword.co.uk
Website: www.pen-and-sword.co.uk

Contents

Contents

List of Illustrations

Maps

Preface and Acknowledgements

Commencing at 0500 on 23 June 1944, General Hans Traut's 78th Sturm (Assault) Division, guarding the vital Smolensk–Minsk–Moscow Highway, endured over two hours of heavy artillery bombardment and aerial attack. His men sat in their protective bunkers, weapons on their knees or resting between their legs, as the earth shook violently about them. Dust and clods of earth fell from the roof boards as they prayed they would avoid a direct hit. Operation Bagration, Joseph Stalin's revenge for Adolf Hitler's rape of the Soviet Union, had begun.

The Soviet Union's German-occupied north-western frontier republic of Byelorussia, or White Russia, was like a land of Norse legend, inundated with lakes and swamps, with great swathes blanketed in dense, impenetrable forests (much of it infested by hostile Soviet partisans), bisected by large rivers. All this was ideal for defence, though it was an inhospitable landscape, and provided many lonely and miserable places to die.

Traut's men sheltering from death had glazed expressions; sweat beaded on their foreheads. Soon, those that survived this deluge of angry metal would have to face the oncoming Soviet tanks and infantry. They had no way of knowing it, but they were in fact at the very forefront of the steel storm being unleashed on Generalfeldmarschall Ernst Busch's Army Group Centre. Their job was to hold the highway and the city of Orsha at all costs – the question was whether they would withstand the Red Army's steamroller now bearing down on them.

'The Great Russian summer offensive started a little over a fortnight after D-Day in the West,' recalled American war correspondent Alexander Werth, 'and, somewhat symbolically, on 23 June, the day after the third anniversary of the German invasion of the Soviet Union. The roles had now been reversed.'

Famed *Red Star* war correspondent Vasily Grossman, who was with the Red Army during Bagration said, 'To Bobruisk led the road to revenge!…A cauldron of death was boiling here, where the revenge was carried out – a ruthless, terrible revenge.'

A sense of unease, even dread, permeated Hitler's high command by the summer of 1944. There was no hiding the fact that the Soviets outnumbered the Germans, were out-producing them and on the whole were outfighting them. A growing Soviet confidence born of bitter experience was also matched by a growing technological edge over Germany. The combination of all these factors ultimately meant defeat for Adolf Hitler on the Eastern Front.

There could be no denying the impact of growing Red Army competence coupled to resources that Hitler simply could not match. His refusal to face up to the harsh reality of the situation was exemplified by his dismissal of Generalfeldmarschall Erich von Manstein, one of his most outstanding generals, who had the temerity to point out that Hitler could not win a straight fight.

By 1943 Stalin had wrested the initiative from Hitler at Stalingrad and Kursk, heralding a turn in the tide. The following year Stalin's retribution for the German violation of the Soviet Union began to gather full momentum. In total he launched ten separate offensives with the revitalized Red Army along various sectors of the 2,000-mile-long front, made possible through Mother Russia's abundant labour reserves and the unrelenting toil of her factory workers.

During January 1944 Stalin had secured Leningrad and the Leningrad–Moscow railway. Then in February and March the Red Army moved to eject German forces from the southern and eastern parts of Ukraine, and the Soviets reached the River Bug. A third offensive liberated the Crimea and cleared the Germans from the Black Sea ports of Odessa and Sevastopol.

In the far north Stalin then sought to punish the Finns for their alliance with Hitler, and in early June his forces attacked along the Karelian isthmus. Within just two days the Finnish-German defences had been broken and the Mannerheim Line had been pierced. Another Red Army thrust was launched north of Lake Onega, and by the end of July the Finns had been driven right back. The fifth offensive, Operation Bagration, was aimed at Byelorussia, and the sixth was to clear western Ukraine and eastern Poland. Following these, attacks would be made into Romania, then the Baltic States, Hungary and finally Lapland.

Operation Bagration annihilated Hitler's Army Group Centre and trapped Army Group North, neutralizing almost a million men. Launched almost three years to the day of the Nazi invasion of the Soviet Union, this was Stalin's retribution for Hitler's Operation Barbarossa. Bagration, in combination with the Lvov–Sandomierz and Lublin–Brest operations launched a few weeks later, saw the Red Army recapture practically all territory within the Soviet Union's 1941 borders, advance into East Prussia and reach the very outskirts of Warsaw after gaining control of Poland east of the Vistula River. In one fell swoop the Wehrmacht lost a quarter of its strength on the Eastern Front.

The vast statistics involved in Operation Bagration are almost beyond comprehension, offering little more than relative totals for the opposing armies. The realities of the losses no matter how exaggerated are almost impossible to grasp; the best analogy perhaps is if you imagine the populations of entire towns and cities simply being wiped off the face of the earth in a matter of weeks or even days.

While Stalin and his generals hold centre stage, this is also the story of the German Führer, Adolf Hitler, and Generalfeldmarschall Ernst Busch, who followed Hitler's orders slavishly to the detriment of his command. Likewise, Generaloberst Georg-Hans Reinhardt, commander of 3rd Panzer Army, was prepared to needlessly sacrifice part of his command in the name of following orders. In contrast, General Kurt von Tippelskirch did all he could to salvage his 4th Army from the Red Army's fatal grasp.

Siegfried von Westphal, one of Hitler's leading generals, summed up Bagration succinctly: 'During the summer and autumn of 1944, the German armies suffered the greatest disaster of their history, which even surpassed the catastrophe of Stalingrad.' There could be no more damning indictment. Alexander Werth called it 'one of the greatest victories of the war'.

While Stalingrad and Kursk paved the way for Soviet victory, Bagration ensured that Hitler would never regain the strategic initiative. Bagration was a much greater death-blow than the defeat of Army Group B in Normandy by the Western Allies, which occurred at the same time. The laurels of victory went to marshals Georgi Zhukov and Konstantin Rokossovsky, while the defeated Ernst Busch was swiftly sacked in disgrace. Only before Warsaw was Generalfeldmarschall Model able to retrieve the disastrous situation.

All seemed lost for the Nazi cause, and yet the bloodletting was to drag on interminably. Bagration was a staggering blow to Hitler's military effort, yet the exhausted Wehrmacht managed to fend off the advancing Red Army for almost a year. In the face of determined resistance on the part of the Germans, Stalin was obliged to launch another four major offensives to drive them out of Eastern Europe and reach Berlin. Ultimately Soviet manpower proved a major problem, as the Red Army had peaked by the end of 1944.

Even more remarkably, in the spring of 1945, after Hitler's abortive winter counter-offensive on the Western Front, he was able to launch a massive counter-attack in Hungary. This was unsuccessful, wilting in the face of well-prepared Soviet defences and a subsequent counter-offensive, yet it showed the Germans never lost the ability or will to resist, despite Bagration.

During the 1980s I spent a considerable time monitoring the Soviet threat, based in part on the overwhelming superiority of their ground forces, particularly the Soviet groups of forces stationed in Eastern Europe and the other armies of the Warsaw Pact. The myth of the Red menace had arisen from those very achievements of the Red Army in 1944–45, and even by this late stage in the Cold War still shaped Western conventional strategic thinking. Bagration had shown just what the Soviets were capable of.

What follows is an account of a military disaster of epic proportions. That Hitler and his generals did not give up seems almost beyond reason. Even though this assessment focuses on the fighting in Byelorussia, in itself a vast geographical region, it cannot simply be considered in isolation if true justice is to be paid to the Soviet military effort in the summer of 1944.

While this book is primarily concerned with the quite remarkable opening two weeks of Operation Bagration, culminating in the liberation of Minsk and the destruction of Army Group Centre, it also covers the related Lvov–Sandomierz offensive to the south in Ukraine. This took the Red Army over the Vistula and was effectively the second part of Stalin's general summer offensive, forming the left hook to clear the Soviet Union of German troops.

Finally it assesses Bagration's natural high water mark before Warsaw, by which time Hitler's forces had recovered sufficiently to temporarily halt Rokossovsky in his tracks. This fighting is usually overshadowed by the controversy surrounding the Warsaw rising and the subsequent brutal extermination of the Polish Home Army by Hitler. In fact it was largely a separate battle intended to stem the Soviet tide.

A series of key military factors contributed to Stalin's successful revenge, most notably the introduction of ever more powerful armour, the creation of his massive tank armies and the revitalization of the Red Air Force into an effective ground support arm. In order not to sidetrack the narrative with such detail, these developments along with Hitler's military weaknesses in the air and on the ground are considered separately in the appendices.

Internationally a number of people were kind enough to assist with research as I sought to grasp the complexities of such a huge battlefield as the Eastern Front. In America at West Point US Military Academy I must thank Lieutenant Colonel Kevin W. Farrell, professor and Military History Division chief, and Frank Martini, cartographer, for their assistance and permission to draw on West Point maps of the campaign. Likewise my thanks go to Kendall D. Gott, chief, Research and Publications Team, US Army Combat Studies Institute, Fort Leavenworth, Kansas, for tracking down various out-of-print publications.

In Canada my thanks go to photographer Scott Pick for making his superlative Eastern Front collection available to illustrate this work. The bulk of the photographs in this book have never been published before, and I am very indebted to him for his generosity and time. Likewise fellow Eastern Front historian Nik Cornish of Stavka Military Image Research in the UK and Rene Chavez in America were kind enough to support my work through the provision of images from their private collections. I offer my gratitude to military historian Tim Newark, for fostering my fascination with Stalin and his generals, and to Preston Isaac, for letting me experience first-hand the creature comforts of the famed T-34/85. Also my thanks go to my editor, Rupert Harding, whose sound advice helped make this a much better book, as well as Merle Read and Pamela Covey. I am likewise grateful to artist and cartographer Dennis Andrews, for making sense of a vast and complex battlefield and producing the maps with such clarity.

Readers will note that I refer to the 'Russians' as Soviets: this is in acknowledgement and tribute to the vast numbers of other ethnic groups (such as the Armenians, Byelorussians, Georgians, Tajiks, Ukrainians, Uzbeks) that made up the Soviet Union and fought with the Red Army. The Soviet Socialist Republic of Byelorussia did not become the Republic of Belarus until 1993, hence the use of the former spelling.

Finally this book is for my parents.

Anthony Tucker-Jones
Barnstaple, Devon
2008

Dramatis Personae

Senior Soviet Commanders
First deputy supreme commander and Stavka special representative to the 1st and 2nd Byelorussian Fronts
Marshal Georgi Zhukov

Chief of staff and Stavka special representative to the 1st Baltic Front and 3rd Byelorussian Front
Marshal Aleksandr Vasilevsky

1st Baltic Front
General of the Army I.Kh. Bagramyan

4th Assault Army
General Lieutenant P.F. Malyshev

6th Guards Army
General Lieutenant I.M. Chistyakov

43rd Army
General Lieutenant A.P. Beloborodov

3rd Air Army
General Lieutenant N.F. Papivin

3rd Byelorussian Front
General Colonel I.D. Chernyakovsky

11th Guards Army
General Lieutenant K.N. Galitsky

5th Army
General Lieutenant N.I. Krylov

31st Army
General Lieutenant V.V. Glagolev

39th Army
General Lieutenant I.I. Lyudnikov

5th Tank Army
Marshal P.A. Rotmistrov

1st Air Army
General Lieutenant T.T. Khryukin

2nd Byelorussian Front
General Colonel G.F. Zakharov

33rd Army
General Lieutenant V.D. Kryuchenkin

49th Army
General Lieutenant I.T. Grishin

50th Army
General Lieutenant I.V. Boldin

4th Air Army
General Colonel K.A. Vershinin

1st Byelorussian Front
General of the Army K.K. Rokossovsky

3rd Army
General Lieutenant A.V. Gorbatov

28th Army
General Lieutenant A.A. Luchinsky

48th Army
General Lieutenant P.L. Romanenko

61st Army
General Lieutenant P.A. Bedov

65th Army
General Lieutenant P.I. Batov

6th Air Army
General Lieutenant F.P. Polynin

16th Air Army
General Colonel S.I. Rudenko

Senior German Commanders

Army Group Centre
Generalfeldmarschall Ernst Busch

3rd Panzer Army
Generaloberst Georg-Hans Reinhardt

VI Corps
General der Artillerie Georg Pfeiffer

IX Corps
General der Artillerie Rolf Wuthmann

LIII Corps
General der Infanterie Friedrich Gollwitzer

4th Army
General der Infanterie Kurt von Tippelskirch

XII Corps
Generalleutnant Vincenz Müller

XXVII Corps
General der Infanterie Paul Völckers

XXXIX Panzer Corps
General der Artillerie Robert Martinek

9th Army
General der Infanterie Hans Jordan

XXXV Corps
Generalleutnant Kurt-Jürgen Freiherr von Lützow

XXXXI Panzer Corps
General der Artillerie Helmuth Weidling

LV Corps
General der Infanterie Friedrich Herrlein

2nd Army
Generaloberst Walter Weiss

VIII Corps
General der Infanterie Gustav Höhne

XX Corps
General der Artillerie Rudolf Freiherr von Roman

XXIII Corps
General der Pionere Otto Tiemann

CHAPTER 1

Debate, Deception and Deployment

Marshal Georgi Zhukov, first deputy supreme commander, saviour of Stalingrad, was summoned to Moscow to see Soviet leader Joseph Stalin on 22 April 1944. Zhukov was a survivor and the rising star of the Red Army. He and his fellow generals had every reason to feel quietly confident, for after almost three years of horrendous bloodletting the Red Army was slowly but steadily turning the tables on Adolf Hitler's armed forces, the Wehrmacht.

Zhukov was indeed in an ebullient mood: over the last three months he had overseen the expulsion of the Wehrmacht from the rest of Ukraine west of the Dnepr, culminating in the Kamenets-Podolsk Pocket, and Soviet forces pushing into Romania north of Jassy. For the past month he had played a direct role in the liberation following the death of the 1st Ukrainian Front commander. Byelorussia was next to be liberated.

Zhukov recalled with satisfaction:

Aboard a Moscow-bound plane I studied the latest reports furnished by the Fronts. Once again they confirmed my belief that the Stavka [Soviet high command] had made the correct decision on 12 April 1944, when routing the German forces in Byelorussia was given top priority. To draw a maximum of German strategic reserves from Byelorussia, it was first necessary to deliver a series of powerful blows against other sectors.

Success here was certain: first, the operational deployment of the troops against Army Group Centre, whose front lines were bent outwards towards our troops, created advantageous conditions for deep enveloping blows at the foundations of the bulge; second, we were now in a position to muster overwhelming superiority over the enemy in the directions of the main blows we had contemplated.

I was very familiar with Byelorussia, especially those areas held by Army Group Centre.

Once in Stalin's office, Zhukov found gathered chief of operations of the general staff and first deputy chief of the general staff General A.I. Antonov; the commander of Soviet armoured forces, Marshal Ya.N. Fedorenko; commander of the Red Air Force, Colonel General A.A. Novikov; and deputy chairman of the Council of People's Commissars, V.A. Malyshev. Chief of Staff Marshal

Aleksandr Vasilevsky was not present as he was in the Crimea overseeing the destruction of German forces trapped there.

First Stalin was briefed by Antonov on the Wehrmacht's options for the coming summer and on the rejuvenated Red Air Force and his burgeoning tank armies. Afterwards he said: 'Now let's hear what Zhukov has to say.'

Zhukov began to discuss possible problems for the summer when Stalin interrupted him: 'These will not be the only problems. In June the Allies intend to finally conduct a major landing in France. Our allies are in a hurry. They are afraid we will rout Nazi Germany without them.' The Stavka must have felt that the Allies' landings were not before time after they had spent so much time clearing the Mediterranean.

While Stalin puffed on his pipe, Zhukov recalled with some finality: 'In outlining my suggestions for the plan for the summer campaign of 1944, I made the point of drawing Stalin's notice to the enemy group in Byelorussia; once it was defeated, the enemy defences on the entire western strategic direction would collapse.' Stalin asked Antonov what he thought (he agreed), and then ordered Vasilevsky and his front commanders to report to him.

On 1 May 1944 Stalin publicly announced:

> But our tasks cannot end with the clearing of enemy troops from within the bounds of our motherland. The German troops today are reminiscent of a wounded beast, which has to creep away to the border of its own lair, Germany, to lick its wounds. But a wounded beast that goes off to its lair does not stop being a dangerous beast. If we deliver our country and those of our allies from the danger of enslavement, we must pursue the wounded German beast and deliver the final blow to him in his own lair.

Even at this stage it was clear that beyond Byelorussia, Stalin had his heart set on Berlin.

Eleven days later Vasilevsky informed Stalin that German resistance in the Crimea had collapsed. All of the southern Soviet Union had been liberated save a pocket south of Kishinev. To the north Hitler's forces clung on to western Ukraine in the Lvov, Brody and Kovel regions, most of Byelorussia and the Baltic States, Estonia, Latvia and Lithuania.

Debate in the Lair of the Red Tsar

On 20 May Stalin summoned Zhukov, Vasilevsky and Antonov to finalize their plans for the destruction of Army Group Centre and the liberation of Byelorussia. Stalin instructed his three main front commanders, generals Ivan Bagramyan, Ivan Chernyakovsky and Konstantin Rokossovsky, to report their suggestions. On the 22nd Stalin, accompanied by Zhukov, Vasilevsky and Antonov, saw Bagramyan and Rokossovsky. Chernyakovsky was seen three days later.

Rokossovsky, whose 1st Byelorussian Front would play a key role in the coming battle, saw Stalin with Central Committee secretary Georgi Malenkov and Vyacheslav Molotov on the night of the 22nd. For the southern part of the offensive Stalin advocated a single thrust towards the city of Bobruisk, which offered the shortest route to the Byelorussian capital, Minsk. Veteran soldier Rokossovsky saw this as madness; there had already been enough senseless bloodletting within the Red Army.

Rokossovsky wanted a two-pronged attack on German positions: against the 9th Army at Bobruisk, west of the Berezina, and the 3rd Panzer Army at Vitebsk this would create a wide gap for the drive on Minsk, followed by the encirclement of the 4th Army to the east of the city. He also wanted to attack from both sides of the Berezina river, whereas Stalin envisaged a single thrust toward Bobruisk from the north-east, from the Dnepr bridgehead held by Rokossovsky's 3rd Army.

Rokossovsky saw that this would expose his right flank to possible counter-attack by the Germans, who were on both sides of the Dnepr, and leave the rest of the German 9th Army a free hand. If his 28th and 65th Armies attacked on the left up the west bank of the Berezina, 9th Army would be tied down and the whole of his 3rd and 48th Armies could be committed on the right flank.

Hardened by war and the Gulag, Rokossovsky was more than prepared to stand up to Stalin. A tense argument ensued.

'The defence must be breached in one place,' Stalin insisted.

'If we breach the defences in two places, Comrade Stalin, we shall gain many advantages.'

'What advantages?'

'If we breach the defence in two sectors, we can bring more forces to the attack, whereupon we deny the enemy the possibility of transferring reinforcements from one sector to another. In addition, Comrade Stalin, a success achieved even in one of these sectors will place the enemy in a difficult position, while guaranteeing to our Front a successful development of the operation.'

'And that's what you call advantages?' said Stalin.

'Go out and think it over again,' said the Soviet leader at 2220 hours. The general was given time to stew next door, perhaps contemplating his nail-less fingers, a gift from the Gulag. Rokossovsky was made to wait outside the conference room for two hours.

'Have you thought it through, General?' asked Stalin later.

Rokossovsky eyed the 'yes-men' who filled the room and replied: 'Yes, Sir, Comrade Stalin.'

'Well then…a single thrust?'

'Two thrusts are more advisable, Comrade Stalin.'

'Will we not thereby dissipate our forces from the very beginning?'

'A certain dissipation of forces will occur, Comrade Stalin,' replied Rokossovsky. 'But we do this while taking into account the forested and swampy terrain of Byelorussia and the disposition of enemy troops.'

Whether or not the Soviet leader agreed, this was a public test of his authority that he could not or would not tolerate.

'Go out and think it over again.' Stalin paused, then added: 'Don't be stubborn, Rokossovsky.' The threat must have been implicit: Operation Bagration was only a month away and it seemed it was about to lose one of its key commanders.

Malenkov and Molotov were sent next door to try to make Rokossovsky see sense. 'Don't forget where you are and with whom you're talking, General,' said Malenkov. 'You're disagreeing with Comrade Stalin.'

Molotov joined in: 'You'll have to agree, Rokossovsky. Agree – that's all there is to it!'

If they thought they could browbeat a man who had endured three years in the Gulag and torture, they were wrong. Rokossovsky returned to the meeting.

'So which is better?' asked Stalin.

'Two strong blows are better than one strong blow,' replied Rokossovsky in a steady tone. The others waited in silence, expecting the inevitable axe to fall.

Stalin was not satisfied, and pressed Rokossovsky further.

'But which of them should be primary, in your opinion?'

Rokossovsky, pressing his luck, said, 'They should both be primary.'

'Can it be that two blows are really better?' said Stalin, after a moment's worrying silence.

In truth he already knew the answer – perhaps he had just been testing the general. The guiding council of Zhukov on Stalin's strategic thinking is clear: he had helped Stalin see the sense in the wider two-pronged attack; Stalingrad and Kursk had shown the way for the two-pronged attack for Rokossovsky's front. Stalin would have replaced a lesser general, so clearly Rokossovsky was the man of the moment. Stalin would not regret his decision.

Zhukov later recalled:

> It must be pointed out that the version prevalent in certain military circles, i.e., that Rokossovsky had urged the Supreme Commander to accept the idea of 'two main blows' in the Byelorussian direction with the forces of the 1st Byelorussian Front, is without foundation. Both blows planned by the Front had been proposed by the General Staff and were approved by Stalin as early as 20 May, before the Commander of the 1st Byelorussian Front arrived at GHQ.

Stalin selected the operational codename Bagration in honour of Georgian Prince Pyotr Bagration (1765–1812). He was the hero of Hollabrunn in 1805, when, covering the retreat of the Allied army under Field Marshal Mikhail Kutuzov, he fended off the French, who had a five to one superiority. Over a third of Bagration's holding force became casualties, but his action allowed Kutuzov to link up with approaching reinforcements. He also served at Austerlitz, Eylau, Heilsberg and Friedland.

Bagration's place in history was sealed when he was mortally wounded leading the left wing of the Imperial Russian Army at Borodino against Napoleon's Grand Army on 7 September 1812; it took him five days to die. Prince Bagration was descended from the Georgian royal family and it no doubt pleased Stalin, a fellow Georgian, to honour him. He was a national hero and a symbol of resistance.

Borodino had been a turning point in the Tsar's war with Napoleon, signalling Napoleon's last offensive. Stalin intended Operation Bagration to be a turning point in his war with Hitler, although that process had already started twelve months earlier. The Nazi presence in Byelorussia was to be expunged and Army Group Centre wiped from the face of the map.

Stalin was less pleased with the antics of Bagration's descendants. The German Foreign Ministry had organized a conference of émigré leaders from governments in exile in April 1942. About forty people attended, including Count Irakly Bagration, pretender to the Georgian throne, and grandson of the Caucasian bandit Said Shamil.

The Byelorussians were crying out to be liberated, having languished under Nazi oppression for three years. From 1941 to 1944 Generalkommissar Wilhelm Kube, followed by General Kurt von Gottberg, had administered the republic, assisted by the traitor Ivan Ermachenko. According to Soviet sources they had laid waste to Byelorussia, wreaking devastation to the value of 75 billion roubles, which included the destruction of 1.2 million buildings and farms, 8,825 schools, and 5,000 theatres and clubhouses.

The human cost had been appalling. Tens of thousands had been killed, including 90,000 Jews in the Minsk ghetto. Another 388,000 people were deported as slave labour, 260,000 of whom did not return home. At the start of the war there had been 9.2 million people living in Byelorussia; by the end of 1944 a third had gone. Even allowing for post-war Soviet propaganda, clearly Byelorussia suffered terribly under the Nazi yoke.

The Byelorussian cities of Vitebsk and Orsha were strategically important to Stalin and the Stavka because they guarded the 50 mile (81km) wide land bridge between the Dvina and Dnepr rivers. An assault on Army Group Centre would enable the Red Army to skirt the vast Pripyat marshes and push into the Polish plains toward Warsaw.

On 31 May the front commanders received the Stavka directive for Bagration. This envisaged three blows to Army Group Centre; towards the Lithuanian capital, Vilnius, by the 1st Baltic and 3rd Byelorussian Fronts, towards Baranovichi by the 1st Byelorussian Front, and towards Minsk by the 2nd Byelorussian Front in conjunction with the 1st and 3rd Byelorussian Fronts.

The first assault was charged with crushing the German forces in the area of Vitebsk, followed by a westward move to envelop those defending the Borisov–Minsk area. The second was to destroy the Zhlobin–Bobruisk defences and exploit the attack toward Slutsk and Baranovichi with a view to swinging south-west of Minsk. The third attack was to strike the Mogilev–Minsk sector.

Hitler Deceived

After Generalfeldmarschall Günther von Kluge was injured in a car accident on 28 October 1943, the 59-year-old Generalfeldmarschall Ernst Busch, who up to that point had been commanding 16th Army outside Leningrad, was appointed to replace him as commander of Army Group Centre. He handed Army Group North's 16th Army over to General Christian Hansen. Busch was not very dynamic, but as Army Group Centre was expected to be conducting defensive operations throughout the summer of 1944, he seemed a safe pair of hands.

Oberst or Colonel Reinhard Gehlen, head of the general staff's Fremde Heere Ost or 'Foreign Armies East' intelligence branch, was well placed to appreciate just how bad things were. He noted:

By the spring of 1944 the military situation on the Eastern Front was so gloomy that I felt it safe to supply our long-term Intelligence digests only in sealed envelopes to other leading members of the General Staff and to Major Baun [Hermann Baun in charge of espionage operations in the Soviet Union]. I had to ask them not to show the reports to anybody else and to return the documents to me, 'in view of the way the enemy position is viewed therein.'

By the end of March, Gehlen assessed there would be Soviet offensives on every single sector of the front, but emphasized the threat to Army Groups A (which became Army Group South Ukraine on 31 March 1944) and South (which became Army Group North Ukraine on 4 April 1944).

Gehlen reported on 3 May 1944 that there were 1,200 Soviet tanks facing Army Group South Ukraine, 500 opposite Army Group North Ukraine, 423 facing Army Group North and just 41 deployed against Army Group Centre. His report also assessed that this total of 2,164 tanks could swell to 3,400, which, including reserves, meant the Soviets had 8,120 tanks available.

Hitler was misled during May and June by fake build-ups in the 3rd Ukrainian Front and 3rd Baltic Front areas, convincing him that Stalin's major attacks would take place in Ukraine or the Baltic States. Also on 3 May the commander of the 3rd Baltic Front, facing Army Group North's 18th Army, was instructed to mass eight to nine divisions along with tanks and artillery behind his right flank. Way to the south in Ukraine dummy tanks and artillery, as well as anti-aircraft positions, were set up, and fighter patrols were conducted north of Kishinev, the Moldavian capital, in order to confuse the German 6th Army.

By mid-June the assessed number of Soviet tanks opposite Army Group Centre was anything from 400 to 1,800; this continued to compound the poor intelligence estimate as in reality it was in excess of 4,000. Remarkably German intelligence detected Marshal P.A. Rotmistrov's presence near Smolensk opposite 3rd Panzer Army, but no one deduced that his command, the powerful 5th Guards Tank Army, might also be in the area. It was assumed to still be way to the south with the 2nd Ukrainian Front facing Army Group South Ukraine. Alarm bells should have started to ring, but Soviet deception and concealment techniques were such that no tanks were spotted. Concealing the arrival of Rotmistrov's four tank brigades, not to mention his two mechanized brigades and three cavalry divisions, equipped with 524 tanks and self-propelled guns, was some achievement. Stalin's successful deception would cost Hitler dearly.

Zhukov knew that Hitler and Busch had been fooled and that great care had to be taken with the massive build-up for Bagration:

All these movements had to be done with great caution to prevent the enemy from detecting the preparations for the offensive. This was especially important since our reconnaissance reports showed that the German High Command expected us to strike the first blow of the summer campaign in the Ukraine, not Byelorussia. It evidently believed that the wooded and boggy terrain would not allow us to move to Byelorussia and employ to best advantage our four tank armies now located in the Ukraine.

Soviet Deployment

For Bagration the four Red Army fronts gathered 118 rifle divisions, 8 tank and mechanized corps (each roughly equivalent to a panzer division), 6 cavalry divisions, 13 artillery divisions and 14 air defence divisions. These forces including support troops numbered 1.7 million men, more than double those of Army Group Centre.

Most notably for the opening stages of Bagration the Soviets had 2,715 tanks and 1,355 assault guns, about six times the number deployed by Busch. They also had an overwhelming superiority in artillery, with 10,563 guns of 76mm calibre or greater, 2,306 multiple rocket launchers, and 11,514 82mm and 120mm mortars. Nothing could withstand such a steel bulldozer.

Stores were likewise gathered in abundance. 'It was,' said Alexander Werth, 'with the possible exception of Kursk – the most thoroughly prepared of all the Russian operations, with everything worked down to its finest detail, and nothing was left to improvisation.'

Ultimately there could be no hiding the 5,000 trains, each with an average of 50 freight cars, making 90–100 daily trips to the fronts. Some 3,000 trains were used to shift the rations and ammunition, while the rest moved the men. The ever-growing stockpiles included 1.2 million metric tons of petroleum, oil and lubricants, 900,000 metric tons of ammunition and 150,000 metric tons of rations. On top of this Bagration was expected to consume 45,000 metric tons of supplies a day, or 275 metric tons per division per day.

Once at the railheads the Red Army had at its disposal up to 12,000 trucks, deployed in four truck brigades of 1,275 trucks each, with one per front, plus one truck regiment per army with 348 trucks, or 40 trucks per division. These were able to move 25,000 tons of ammunition, fuel and supplies to the front-line troops in a single shipment.

Some freight was also transported by air, though nowhere near on the scale of the railways and roads. Once Bagration was under way, forward units would receive 1,240 metric tons of ammunition, 1,182 tons of fuel and about 1,000 tons of spares and equipment by airlift. Stalin's planners were expecting up to 18 per cent of the force committed becoming casualties, and prepared 294,000 hospital beds. Busch's intelligence officers and the Luftwaffe could hardly miss a build-up of such magnitude.

By 1944 the Red Army was divided into ten fronts running north to south: Leningrad, 3rd, 2nd and 1st Baltic, 3rd, 2nd and 1st Byelorussian, and 1st, 2nd and 3rd Ukrainian. The Soviet use of the term 'front' should not be confused with the front line: this was peculiar to them. Effectively it was a specific theatre of operations where a group of armies, similar to a German army group, were deployed under central command in a specific sector.

Opposite Hitler's Army Group Centre were four Soviet fronts: General of the Army Ivan Kh. Bagramyan's 1st Baltic, General Colonel Ivan Chernyakovsky's 3rd Byelorussian, General Colonel Georgi F. Zakharov's 2nd Byelorussian and lastly General of the Army Konstantin K. Rokossovsky's 1st Byelorussian Front. Utilizing four fronts meant that over 40 per cent of the Red Army was to be committed to Bagration.

To the north-east of Vitebsk, Bagramyan's 1st Baltic Front consisted of the 4th Assault, 6th Guards, 43rd and 3rd Air Armies, totalling 21 guards rifle and rifle infantry divisions, 2 artillery divisions, 3 tank brigades and 7 aviation divisions.

Then Chernyakovsky's 3rd Byelorussian Front, in the Smolensk area, comprised the 11th Guards, 5th, 31st, 39th, 5th Tank and 1st Air Armies. His forces could field 33 infantry divisions, 3 cavalry divisions, 5 artillery and rocket divisions, 10 tank brigades, 2 mechanized brigades and 15 aviation divisions.

South of Chernyakovsky, General Zakharov's 2nd Byelorussian Front contained the 33rd, 49th and 50th Armies, with fighter and bomber support supplied by the 4th Air Army. Zakharov had at his disposal 21 rifle divisions, 2 tank brigades and 5 aviation divisions, which were deployed between Minsk and Bryansk.

Holding the front line north-west of Kiev, Rokossovsky's 1st Byelorussian Front comprised the 3rd, 28th, 48th, 61st and 65th Armies, and the 6th and 16th Air Armies. This excluded the 8th, 47th, 70th, 1st Polish and 2nd Tank Armies held in reserve for the follow-up offensive. The attack formations could muster approximately 44 rifle, 9 cavalry and 5 artillery divisions, as well as 7 tank, 5 mechanized and 3 river brigades, supported by 21 aviation divisions.

The Red Air Force's major effort in the summer of 1944 was also in Byelorussia: the operation would witness the largest tactical concentration of Soviet air power to date. The Red Air Force had 5,327 combat aircraft and another 1,007 bombers under strategic command: a total of 21 fighter divisions, with 2,318 fighters, 14 strike divisions with 1,744 IL-2 Shturmoviks and 8 bomber divisions with 655 medium bombers.

The 3rd, 2nd and 1st Byelorussian Fronts were supported by General Khryukin's 1st Air Army, Vershinin's 4th and Rudenko's 16th. Khryukin had only just taken up his post, having previously, during the liberation of Sevastopol and the Crimea, commanded the 8th Air Army. The latter was disbanded and its resources split between General Slyusarev in the Rava Russkaya sector and General Krasovsky in the Lvov sector, comprising the 2nd Air Army.

These three air armies, plus elements of Papivin's 3rd Air Army on the 1st Baltic Front to the north and elements of Polynin's 6th Air Army to the south, were able to field 6,000 aircraft. One third consisted of Shturmoviks, some 1,100 day and night bombers and 1,900 fighters.

Half this force was from the eleven air corps allocated to the GKO (*Gosudarstvenny komitet oborony* – State Committee for Defence) Air reserve. Khryukin's 1st Air Army, earmarked to play a major role, was augmented with three fighter, one Shturmovik and one bomber corps, giving it a combat strength of 1,881 aircraft comprising 840 fighters, 528 Shturmoviks, 459 bombers and 54 reconnaissance aircraft.

Similarly Krasovsky's 2nd Air Army on the 1st Ukrainian Front grew to three fighter, three Shturmovik, two bomber and one composite corps numbering over 3,000 aircraft ready for the breakthrough into Poland.

Behind Enemy Lines

Stalin, as well as waging war on the front lines, was also waging a brutal guerrilla war in the rear areas of Hitler's armies. In particular, partisan forces attacked the Germans' long and exposed lines of communication, blowing up railway lines, roads and supply dumps on a regular basis. (The Russian War Academy as early as 1940 had made the Bobruisk area the scene of partisan war games under General Kulik.) In Byelorussia this triggered all-out war as Army Group Centre sought to contain the situation.

In some places this struggle verged on civil war, with the partisans murdering collaborators. Local government officials, policemen and militia were liquidated as 'enemies of the state' as the opportunity arose, if they were deemed to have assisted the Nazi occupation in any way.

Zhukov observed: 'Partisan units and detachments were very active in the Byelorussian operation. This was facilitated by the wooded terrain. More Soviet officers and men had been left behind there when our troops retreated in 1941.'

For the first six months following Hitler's invasion of the Soviet Union, the German supply system across Byelorussia and Ukraine functioned largely unhindered. Red Army stragglers caused problems but they were little more than a hindrance. By late 1941 sabotage was becoming more routine and organized, and during the winter the pattern became set.

To make matters worse Army Group Centre was reliant on 110,000 Soviet rail workers, who of course cooperated with the partisans. In mid-1943 the chief of transportation, Army Group Centre, was reporting an average of forty-five demolitions a day.

By August 1943 partisan activity against the railways had increased by 25 per cent, and that month 20,505 individual demolition points were recorded, with 4,528 mines removed. In just two nights, of the 6,000 miles of track in their area the lines were cut in 8,422 places.

In the spring of 1942 Stalin established a partisan staff to coordinate these guerrilla forces, and by December there were 130,000 irregulars under arms who had created numerous no-go areas in the Germans' rear. Most of these men operated in the central area. Even before Hitler had fully occupied Byelorussia, eighty-nine districts of the Gomel, Minsk, Mogilev, Pinsk, Polesie and Vitebsk regions had underground Communist Party committees. Some 13,000 Communist and Komsomol members remained behind at great risk to continue the struggle against Hitler.

The Byelorussian Headquarters of the Partisan Movement, under Pyotr Zakharovich Kalinin, second secretary of the Central Committee of the Communist Party of Byelorussia, was established in September 1942. Kalinin served as chief of staff of the Byelorussian partisan units from 9 September

1942 to 14 November 1944. His HQ liaised with Red Army units, handling recruitment, training and equipping of local partisan forces.

Soviet partisan activity in Byelorussia had become a major problem by mid-1943, when the tempo of operations was increased after Operation Zitadelle to support the late summer offensive to free the Dnepr and Smolensk areas of German occupation.

Army Group Centre under Generalfeldmarschall Günther von Kluge found itself harried by substantial irregular forces operating from the safe areas south of the vast Pripyat marshes. The partisans attacked rail and road communications in order to reduce supplies reaching the 3rd Panzer Army and 4th Army tasked with holding Vitebsk and Smolensk against the Kalinin Front (later 1st Baltic) and the West Front. These operations also served to draw German units from the front as the rear area security forces struggled to contain the escalating situation.

In response von Kluge launched Operation Maigewitter (May Storm) in the area of Vitebsk in May 1943, followed by Kormoran (Cormorant) on 22 May to 20 June, against those enemy forces operating in the Novy Borisov–Minsk railway area. Conducted in central Byelorussia, this helped pin down a major part of the Byelorussian resistance. Kormoran overlapped with the anti-partisan Operation Freischütz (Marksman) north of Bryansk, while Operation Kottbus was carried out in the Polotsk–Borisov–Lepel region behind 3rd Panzer Army during June 1943.

SS-Obergruppenführer and General der Polizei Kurt von Gottberg commanded the German and auxiliary security units in Byelorussia and was widely reviled for his brutality. In mid-1943, 16,662 police under his control killed almost 10,000 people in eastern Byelorussia while trying to eliminate a partisan 'republic'. Just 599 prisoners were taken and 1,000 weapons captured; such actions played into the hands of Soviet propagandists.

In total Army Group Centre conducted 140 operations against the partisans in Byelorussia, during which 5,454 villages were damaged or destroyed; however, by the end of 1943, according to Soviet sources, the partisans controlled over 108,000 square kilometres, some 60 per cent of Byelorussia.

The extent of Soviet partisan control over vast areas of Byelorussia did not go unacknowledged by the Germans and resulted in their scorched earth policy in the spring of 1944 (winter crops were ploughed under and spring sowing was prevented). Alexander Werth recalled:

General Tippelskirch, Commander of the 4th German Army which took part in the Byelorussia retreat, later referred to 'a vast wooded and marshy area from the Dnepr nearly all the way to Minsk which was controlled by large partisan formations, and was never in three years, either cleaned up, still less occupied by German troops.'

Nonetheless, these German operations partially blunted the partisan campaign that opened in early June 1944 to support the launch of Bagration. By this stage the partisans had lost about 25,000 men killed and many more wounded and captured.

According to Belarus archive figures, 373,492 men served the partisan movement in Byelorussia in one way or another. In the summer of 1944 the movement had 143,000 men organized into 150 brigades and 49 detachments. On 8 June these forces were alerted that they must disrupt enemy communications to support a major forthcoming operation.

CHAPTER 2

Red Storm Rising

Hitler's Army Group Centre had first stormed across eastern Poland, evicting the Red Army, and into Byelorussia on 22 June 1941 as part of Operation Barbarossa. The Soviet republic became the scene of bitter fighting, as it was through its territory that Army Group Centre charged toward Moscow. The Red Army's defensive battles in Byelorussia ended in a crushing defeat for Stalin's ill-prepared and ill-lead troops.

Under Generalfeldmarschall Fedor von Block, Army Group Centre (comprising 2nd and 3rd Panzer Groups and 4th and 9th Armies, supported by the II and VIII Fliegerkorps) had been in the forefront of the assault on the Soviet Union and crushed initial resistance in its area of operations in just two weeks.

The Red Army's underlying doctrine had been offensive not defensive, with any future war being waged on an enemy's territory – in this case with Soviet-occupied eastern Poland acting as the battlefield. Hitler struck first and in the south his allies attacked from Slovakia, Hungary and Romania into Ukraine. Only Bulgaria refrained from joining his crusade against Bolshevism.

By October 1943 Army Group Centre was short of 200,000 men. Those replacements it had received von Kluge found severely wanting. While Army Group Centre, and all the other army groups for that matter, were bleeding to death, Hitler assumed the Red Army was suffering the same problem. In a long letter to Hitler written on 14 October, von Kluge pointed out that this was far from the case, as well as highlighting the many difficulties faced by Army Group Centre.

When Busch took charge of a total of seventy-six divisions, the six Hungarian and eight Luftwaffe field divisions were little more than window dressing. Similarly the three German and one Slovak security divisions and the two field training divisions were intended to counter partisan activity, not stand up to the reinvigorated Red Army. Of Army Group Centre's core strength of fifty-five divisions, none were at full strength and twenty-two of these were little more than battle groups of Kampfgruppen.

During the winter of 1943–44 Heinrici's 4th Army managed to beat off four Soviet attempts on Orsha. Similarly Reinhardt's 3rd Panzer Army hung on to Vitebsk. Busch deserved little credit for any of this, as Army Group Centre had been reactive rather than proactive. His refusal to question Hitler's stand-firm order resulted in a 60 mile (96km) gap opening up to the south with Army Group North Ukraine after Model retreated to the Dnepr. In early January, Soviet attacks on Army Group North meant Busch lost contact with this command as well. Clearly things did not bode well for Army Group Centre under his direction.

'44 Red Storm

Alexander Werth was full of praise for the rejuvenated Red Army: 'In the last two years, despite extremely heavy losses in both men and equipment, the Russians had gone on building up a tremendously effective, competent and powerfully equipped army, while Germany's reserves in manpower were now in constant decline.'

By January 1944 the Wehrmacht on the Eastern Front was in tatters. From January to March 1944 the Red Army drove the Germans away from Leningrad and Novgorod. Similarly from December 1943 to May 1944 they were to be expelled from most of Ukraine. While Hitler was expecting an attack he had no way of appreciating the vast scale of Stalin's massive counter-offensive.

Thanks to Soviet deception the Germans were now expecting another assault on Army Group North Ukraine to the south, and had been diverting precious resources there. This army group had already been severely weakened and driven from most of Ukraine by June 1944.

According to Zhukov's intelligence, by early 1944 Hitler and his east European allies had some 5 million men, 5,400 tanks and assault guns, 54,500 guns and mortars, and over 3,000 aircraft deployed against the Red Army. However, Zhukov claimed that the Soviet armed forces had a 230 per cent superiority in aircraft, 70 per cent in artillery and 30 per cent in manpower. He noted: 'This quantitative advantage, coupled with excellent qualitative characteristics of the weapons, was boosted even further by the high morale of our troops and the improved tactical and strategic skills of the command echelons.'

Zhukov recorded in his memoirs:

After an in-depth and comprehensive analysis, the Supreme Command decided in the winter campaign of 1944 to mount an offensive on a front running from Leningrad all the way down to the Crimea.

According to our plan, the major offensive operations were to be launched in the South Western theatre of war in order to liberate the entire Ukraine west of the Dnepr, and the Crimea. It was decided to totally smash the siege of Leningrad, and to push the enemy out of the entire Leningrad Region. On the North-Western Direction the troops were to reach the boundaries of the Baltic Republics. The Western Direction was ordered to liberate as much of Byelorussia as possible.

When the actions of Soviet forces in the winter of 1944 were planned, it was also decided to concentrate the principal effort on the 1st, 2nd, 3rd and 4th Ukrainian Fronts so as to build up a greater superiority over the enemy in those sectors and to swiftly smash the forces of Army Groups South and A.

Visiting Stalin, Zhukov pressed him on encirclement operations, to which the Soviet leader responded: 'We are now stronger, and our troops more experienced.

Now we can and must carry out operations aimed at encircling the German forces.' The first half of 1944 was to be dominated by such operations.

The tide had turned against Hitler in 1943, but what of Stalin's strategic setting for Bagration? Firstly he threw the Leningrad, Volkhov and 2nd Baltic Fronts, supported by the Baltic Fleet, long-range aircraft and partisans, at Army Group North on 14 January 1944. These forces totalled 1.2 million men, 1,475 tanks and 21,600 field guns and mortars. To ward off this onslaught Army Group North, consisting of 18th and 16th Armies under Feldmarschall Georg von Küchler, could muster 741,000 men, just 385 tanks and 10,070 field guns.

Well-prepared defences, including concrete bunkers, minefields and barbed wire, protected von Küchler's troops. Nevertheless, hampering his defensive efforts were some 35,000 Soviet partisans who set about his communications around Gdov, Pskov, Strugi Krasniye and Luga. They also derailed over 130 troop trains by blowing up 58,000 rails and 300 bridges.

Leningrad: The 900 Days

On 13–14 January 104,000 shells fell on the positions of the 9th and 10th Luftwaffe Field Divisions. The Germans resisted bitterly, but on the 20th Novgorod was liberated and forces from the Leningrad and Volkhov Fronts linked up at Luga at the end of the month. The attacking Baltic Front pinned down the 16th Army. In addition the revitalized Soviet Air Force threw itself at Army Group North. The 13th and 14th Air Armies flew almost 13,000 sorties, while airmen from the Baltic Fleet flew another 4,500. By the 28th the 18th Army had suffered 40,000 casualties. Army Group North, though avoiding encirclement, was thrown back up to 175 miles (280km).

From mid-January to the beginning of March the Soviets drove the Wehrmacht steadily westward away from the city of Leningrad, heralding the end of the 900-day siege. The Soviets spent six weeks clearing the Germans out of the region west of Leningrad and Lake Ilmen, and east of lakes Chud and Pskov.

By March the Germans were holding a defensive line running southwards anchored on the eastern banks of lakes Chud and Pskov, and just east of the towns of Pskov, Ostrov, Pushkinskie Gory and Novosokolniki, although the Soviets had forced a bridgehead on the western bank of Lake Pskov.

Küchler lost three whole divisions and another seventeen were severely mauled. This victory cost the Soviets an appalling 313,953 casualties, including 76,886 dead, captured or missing. While the Wehrmacht had managed to stem the Soviet tide in the northern sector, way to the south things were to quickly unravel.

Victory in Ukraine

At the end of 1943 the Red Army also fought to liberate the Ukraine west of the Dnepr. The 1st, 2nd, 3rd and 4th Ukrainian Fronts massed 2.3 million men, 2,040 tanks and self-propelled guns, 28,800 field guns and mortars, and 2,370 aircraft with which to smash Manstein's Army Group South and Kleist's Army Group A, which could muster some 1.7 million troops, with 2,200 panzers, 16,800 field guns and 1,460 aircraft. Once again Soviet partisans, numbering 50,000 in

Ukraine, the Crimea and Moldavia, played their part; the Soviets claimed they tied up 10 divisions and 30 police battalions.

Soviet intelligence indicated that thirty German divisions confronted General N.F. Vatutin's 1st Ukrainian Front, including eight panzer and one motorized, under General Raus. They also knew that Hitler still harboured hopes of smashing the Red Army by capturing a bridgehead west of the Dnepr and Kiev.

In late November 1943 Lieutenant General Nikita Khrushchev recalled upon his arrival at Kiev:

> After Kursk I was connected first with the Voronezh Front, then with the 1st Ukrainian Front. We were pushing hard toward Kiev. It was a triumphal hour when we reached the west bank of the Dnepr. We were fighting for the liberation of the capital of the Ukraine, the mother of Russian cities. Everyone felt tears of joy welling up inside him. Since 1941 we had been thrown back all the way to Stalingrad. And now, tomorrow or the next day, we would be in Kiev!
>
> While we were outside the city, Zhukov arrived from General Headquarters [he was coordinating the 1st and 2nd Ukrainian Fronts]. An underground bunker was prepared for him and me to sleep in. During the day we sat around joking and discussing the situation. On the second or third day we didn't even bother to use the dugout any more. We had driven the Germans into the woods, and our troops were skirmishing on the outskirts of the city. We were fighting from our bridgehead west of the city in order to prevent the enemy from breaking out on the Zhitomir-Kiev road.

In December 1943 the Stavka ordered the 1st Ukrainian Front to prepare to destroy 4th Panzer Army with the Zhitomir-Berdichev Operation. In preparation it was assigned the Soviet 1st Tank Army, 18th Army, and the 4th Guards and 25th Tank Corps. This followed the Germans having exhausted themselves capturing Zhitomir and by their attempts on Kiev the previous month.

By the time of the attack Vatutin's 1st Ukrainian Front could field sixty-three infantry divisions, three cavalry divisions and six tank and two mechanized corps. These were organized into the 1st Guards, 13th, 18th, 27th, 38th, 40th and 60th field armies, and the 1st and 3rd Guards Tank Armies. The offensive commenced on 24 December and within six days had forced a breakthrough 187 miles (302km) wide and 62 miles (100km) deep.

To assist Army Groups South and A, Army Groups Centre and North were stripped of twelve divisions. In the meantime Zhitomir was liberated again on 31 December, though the Germans clung on to Berdichev until 5 January 1944. They concentrated their forces in the Vinnitsa and Uman areas and then counter-attacked the 38th, 40th and 1st Guards Tank Armies. Although the Soviets were thrown back about 19 miles (30km), the 1st Ukrainian Front had advanced 125 miles (200km), liberating the Kiev and Zhitomir regions, and by mid-January lay in a line through Sarny, Slavuta, Kazatin and Ilintsy.

The Soviet breakthrough south-west of Kiev forced the 4th Panzer Army back over 100 miles (160km), exposing the 8th Army's right flank. The latter was dangerously vulnerable because it remained with a foothold on the southern banks of the Dnepr in the Kanev area, and it was not long before the Red Army attempted to surround it. This was dubbed by the Soviets the Korsun-Shevchenkovsky salient, also known as the Cherkassy pocket.

Death in the Korsun Pocket

According to Soviet intelligence the 1st Panzer and 8th Armies had nine infantry, one panzer and one motorized division in the Korsun-Shevchenkovsky salient. This had to be eliminated because it sat on the junction of the 1st and 2nd Ukrainian Fronts. Including forces from the latter the Soviets directed twenty-seven rifle divisions, four tank, one mechanized and one cavalry corps armed with 370 tanks and self-propelled guns and almost 4,000 guns and mortars at the salient. According to Zhukov this gave them 70 per cent superiority in infantry, 140 per cent in guns and 160 per cent in armour.

The attack was opened by the 2nd Ukrainian Front on 24 January 1944, though it was hampered by an unwelcome thaw. The German high command ordered a counter-attack with the 3rd, 4th and 11th Panzer Divisions moved to the Novo-Mirgorod area on the 27th, followed by 13th Panzer two days later. The 16th and 17th Panzer Divisions were also assembled in the Rizino area.

The Soviets' second envelopment attempt succeeded on 3 February when the 1st and 2nd Ukrainian Fronts linked up near Zvenigorodka, trapping 56,000 men of the XI and XXXXII Corps in the Cherkassy or Korsun pocket. The plan was for a two-pronged relief, with 1st Panzer Army's III Panzer Corps driving from the south-west and 8th Army's XXXXVII Panzer Corps striking from the south.

Despite their losses of transport aircraft at Stalingrad, the Luftwaffe was expected to provide an air bridge to Korsun. As far as Hitler was concerned the Demyansk airlift of 1942 would be repeated. Road conditions were such that the two relief corps had to be resupplied by air as well. The Red Air Force shot the Luftwaffe out of the sky as it struggled to keep the trapped troops provisioned. In addition XXXXVII Panzer Corps was reduced to just sixty-one panzers and assault guns, and could do little more than conduct local attacks.

Hitler told the surrounded corps to stay put while four panzer divisions tried to cut their way through. The 16th and 17th Panzer Divisions of III Panzer Corps attempted to reach them, pushing northward on 4 February. In the meantime General Wöhler flew out, leaving General Stemmermann to direct the defence.

Hitler signalled Stemmermann, saying: 'You can rely on me like you would on a wall of stone. You will be freed from the ring. For the time being hold on.'

Stemmermann had no intention of holding on; he rejected an offer to surrender on the 9th and Zhukov signalled Stalin:

According to information received from PoWs, during battles in encirclement enemy troops have sustained heavy losses and their officers and men are now in a state of confusion bordering on panic.

According to intelligence reports surrounded enemy forces have concentrated [the] bulk of their troops in [the] Steblev-Korsun-Shevchenkovsky area. The enemy is apparently preparing for [a] last attempt to break out towards Panzer group advancing on Malaya Boyarka.

The German counter-attack quickly bogged down, so the 1st SS and 1st Panzer Divisions struck south, getting as far as Lysyanka, just 5 miles (8km) from the pocket. Unfortunately for those trapped, III Panzer Corps just did not have the strength to make the final push. By 10 February the pocket was just 6 miles by 7 (9.6 by 11km).

The breakout order was finally transmitted to Stemmermann on the 15th, informing him that he could expect no further help:

Capabilities of III Panzer Corps reduced by weather and supply difficulties. Task Force Stemmermann must accomplish break-through on its own to line Dzhurzhentsy-Hill 239 where it will link up with III Panzer Corps. The breakout force will be under the command of General Lieb [XXXXII Corps] and comprise all units still capable of attack.

The 5th SS Panzer Division led a desperate attempt to break out on the 16th only to be met by the 4th Guards and 27th Armies. In the bitter fighting that followed the Germans lost 20,000 killed and 8,000 captured. The Soviets claimed the battle for Korsun-Shevchenkovsky cost the Germans a total of 55,000 killed or wounded and 18,200 captured. The Germans maintained that 30,000 men managed to escape the pocket.

Although the XI and XXXXII Corps escaped they were severely depleted and had to be pulled from the line. This had a great impact on the ability of Army Group South to fend off attacks in the Uman area. Thus it was at Cherkassy that the last German offensive strength in Ukraine was drained away, creating the conditions for the victorious Soviet advances into Byelorussia, Poland, Romania and the Balkans in the summer and autumn of 1944.

The Kamenets-Podolsk Pocket

Vatutin had been mortally wounded, so Stalin directed Zhukov to finish off Manstein's Army Group South. His intention was to trap the 1st and 4th Panzer Armies, along with 200,000 men. The Soviets received 754 tanks, giving them a five to two superiority in armour. The German collapse in the south was swift.

Zhukov struck on 4 March 1944, covering 100 miles (160km) in a matter of days. Once the 1st Ukrainian Front had reached the Tarnopol-Proskurov line and the 2nd Ukrainian Front had cleared Uman and forced the Southern Bug near Dzhulinka, the 1st Panzer Army was threatened with encirclement. The road to Uman was littered with 200 Tiger and Panther tanks, 600 field guns and 12,000 lorries.

Way to the south, in the Bereznegovatoye-Snigiryovka area, thirteen divisions of the German 6th Army were threatened by the 3rd Ukrainian Front. In the battle to escape westward it lost eight divisions between the Ingulets and the Southern Bug. The Black Sea ports of Nikolayev and Odessa were soon liberated.

To the north some twenty-two German divisions under General Hans Hube's 1st Panzer Army were caught in the Kamenets-Podolsk pocket in late March. Manstein and Hube were determined they would not sacrifice their troops in another fruitless Stalingrad gesture.

'After the Orel offensive was over,' recalled Nikolai Yakovlevich Zheleznov, serving with the 63rd Brigade, 4th Tank Army, 'we were pulled back for reorganisation. We received new equipment and crews, and in February–March 1944 our army took part in the Proskurov-Chernovitsy offensive operation.' Following that he was involved in the battle for Kamenets-Podolsk.

Zheleznov remembered the horror of the fighting vividly:

We got held up for two and a half to three hours at that village, but entered Kamenets-Podolsk in the evening. We lost two tanks on the outskirts, destroyed by a battery of anti-aircraft guns. Their crews burned. I saw them when they were buried – grown men reduced to mummies the size of a twelve-year-old child. The skin on their faces was reddish bluish brown. It was scary to see them and it's very disturbing to recall now.

Our reconnaissance team reported German trucks on the outskirts of the town. We went to have a look. There were so many trucks there! Probably around 3,000, if not more! Apparently, these were the supply columns of the enemy's Proskuriov group of forces. The trucks were stuffed with sausage, ham, various cans of food, chocolate, cheese. There was also plenty of alcohol – French cognac, Italian wine. I especially remember Amaretto. I remember the taste of that liqueur as one of the pleasures of the war.

Evgeni Bessonov was serving as a tank rider company commander, in a motor rifle battalion with a mechanized brigade in the 4th Guards Tank Army. He fought for two long years, covering 2,356 miles (3,800km), and also saw the chaos in Kamenets-Podolsk:

At dawn on 25 March 1944, we reached Kamenets-Podolsk. Our company on three tanks bypassed the city from the west and approached the outskirts from the south…the streets were filled with trucks parked next to each other. It was not only hard to drive – it was hard to walk, so tightly were the abandoned trucks parked. Later we learned that these trucks with all their commodities and food belonged to the rear units of a large German formation that had retreated west. However, our Brigade cut their retreat routes and they had to stop in the city. There were very many trucks, at least 1,000 to 1,500 of them, and there were all kinds of booty in them!

The following day Bessonov and his men celebrated, throwing a party using the captured German food and wine. Two days later he narrowly missed being killed.

Constantly on the move, Hube's forces were sustained by an effective Luftwaffe air bridge. Zhukov expected Hube to fight his way southward to the bridges over the Dniester and into Romania; instead he headed westward to Buchach. The II SS Panzer Corps was sent to cut its way through to Hube, and by 9 April his forces had been rescued. Hitler, though, was not grateful, instead lamenting that so much ground had been given up. Efforts to save 4,000 men trapped at Tarnopol were tragically not successful. Army Group South then fell back into Romania.

Sensing that Admiral Miklós Horthy of Hungary was losing the stomach to fight, on 19 March 1944 Hitler occupied his ally. He initially proposed garrisoning Budapest with Romanian and Slovak troops; such nonsense would have created immediate internecine war among the Axis allies. German troops drove from Vienna, and Budapest's surrounding airfields were seized by German paratroops. Publicly Horthy remained compliant while privately trying to abandon Hitler.

By then von Manstein was lamenting that 'the scale and quality of the Hungarians' weapons did not meet the requirements of warfare against Soviet armoured units'. He was horrified that by this stage of the war the Hungarian chief of staff and the commander of the Hungarian 1st Army had the cheek to complain about their lack of preparedness and lack of anti-tank weapons. He wanted to know just how they had been spending their time!

In April the war came to the streets of the Romanian capital, Bucharest. Romanian writer Mihail Sebastian (pen name of Iosif Hechter) remembered: 'Four days after the bombing, the city is in the grip of madness…Everyone is fleeing or wants to flee…Half the city is without electricity. There is no water supply. The radiators do not work…The number of dead is not known…Rosetti said 4,200 – but that isn't certain either.'

Only now did Hitler dispatch any significant numbers of tanks to Romanian leader Marshal Ion Antonescu, consisting of 100 panzers and 114 assault guns. The Romanian 1st Tank Division was re-established along German panzer division lines in April; once equipped with German tanks it returned to the Eastern Front and continued to resist the Red Army.

Defeat in the Crimea

'Hitler's decision to hold the Crimea was one of his most insane inspirations,' commented American correspondent Alexander Werth. He saw the liberation of the Crimea as a clear indication that German morale was faltering:

> It will remain one of the great puzzles of the war why, in 1941–42, despite overwhelming German and Romanian superiority in tanks and aircraft, and a substantial superiority in men, Sevastopol succeeded in holding out for 250 days and why in 1944, the Russians captured it within four days…Was there not something lacking in German morale by April 1944?

With the Red Army sweeping west General Erwin Jänecke's 17th Army, cut off in the Crimea since the end of 1943 by the 4th Ukrainian Front and North

Caucasian Front, now faced destruction. The fate of his command was almost a repeat of 6th Army's at Stalingrad.

Hitler forbade a sea evacuation because he thought the Soviets would use the Crimea to launch air attacks against Romania's vital oil refineries. He also argued, not unreasonably, that 17th Army would be a thorn in the Soviets' flank; his delusion was that the Red Army would be thrown back and the Wehrmacht would link up with it again. He consigned 17th Army to a cruel and chaotic fate.

Despite the strength of their formidable defences the prospect for the German and supporting Romanian forces – totalling around 230,000 men, equipped with 215 panzers, 3,600 guns and mortars, and 148 aircraft – was little short of grim. The German XXXXIX Mountain Corps, commanded by General Rudolf Konrad, defended the northern Crimea, with the German 50th Infantry Division blocking the Perekop isthmus and the German 336th Division south of the Sivash Sea. The German V Corps, commanded by General Karl Allmendinger, was deployed at Kerch to the east, consisting of the German 73rd and 98th Infantry Divisions and the Romanian 3rd Mountain and 6th Cavalry Divisions.

The 4th Ukrainian Front attacking from the north and the Separate Maritime Army striking from the east could field 470,000 men, 559 tanks and self-propelled guns, and almost 6,000 field guns and mortars, supported by 1,250 aircraft. The Germans claimed 604 Soviet aircraft over the Crimea in the six months leading up to their evacuation, with remarkably one pilot from II/SG 2 claiming 247 of the kills.

The push into the Crimea started on 8 April 1944, just as Odessa was being entered. The fall of Kerch three days later sealed the fate of the defenders, and once it became clear that the northern Perekop defences would not hold the Germans began to evacuate, regardless of Hitler's dictates. During mid-April to mid-May almost 121,000 men managed to escape the developing trap (half of whom were Germans), thanks to the bravery of the Romanian Royal Navy operating out of Constanta, some 220 nautical miles away. This success, though, came at a heavy cost.

Soviet submarines and warships intercepted those trying to flee across the Black Sea. In the first stage of the evacuation two German submarine hunters, a tanker and a lighter were damaged. One Romanian destroyer, two armed transport pontoons and several transport ships were also damaged.

During the second stage the Germans lost five ships, three tugs and two lighters, and another vessel was damaged. Four German submarine hunters were sunk, as were three motorboats. Another six submarine hunters were damaged. Three large Romanian transport ships were sunk and two warships were damaged. Also, two Hungarian transport ships were damaged.

During the subsequent fighting retreat to Sevastopol, the Germans lost 12,221 men and the Romanians 17,652, along with most of their armour. The 17th Army held out in Sevastopol until 9 May; resistance at the Kherson bridgehead, though, did not cease for another three days, when the last 3,000 troops were overwhelmed, Soviet artillery having prevented their evacuation by sea. Some 25,000 German personnel surrendered at noon on the 12th.

While about half of the 17th Army escaped across the Black Sea, approximately 117,000 men were killed, wounded or captured. The Germans lost 65,100 casualties and their Romanian allies 31,600; some 20,000 local Soviet 'volunteers' suffered an unknown fate. Soviet casualties during the offensive amounted to some 84,800 men, 171 tanks, 521 pieces of artillery and 179 aircraft.

The Soviet authorities claimed that, during their offensive west of the Dnepr in Ukraine and in the Crimea, the Red Army destroyed ten divisions and forced the Germans to dissolve another eight, while a total of sixty-eight German divisions lost 50 to 60 per cent of their effectives. It seemed impossible to conceive that the Wehrmacht could weather such bloodletting. In the aftermath Army Group A was re-designated Army Group South Ukraine, and Army Group South became Army Group North Ukraine. The Bulgarians, Hungarians and Romanians now all sought to abandon Hitler.

At the end of April Zhukov noted:

Even though throughout the winter and spring campaign, the actions of our forces had resulted in signal victories I felt the German troops were still strong enough to put up a stiff defence on the Soviet-German front. As far as the strategic proficiency of their High Command and the local army group commands were concerned, after the disaster in the Stalingrad area and particularly after the Kursk battle it had drastically declined.

Unlike the first phase of the war, the Nazi Command had become sluggish and lacked ingenuity, particularly in critical situations. Its decisions betrayed the fact that it was unable to correctly assess the capacities of either its own troops or those of the enemy. The Nazi Command would often be too late in withdrawing its forces from under the threat of flanking blows or encirclement – and this, of course, placed these in a hopeless situation.

Finland's Punishment

The Finns, who had found themselves at war with Stalin over a boundary dispute in 1939, had thrown their lot in with Hitler two years later. The Finnish army, supported by just three battalions of captured Soviet tanks, got to within 30 miles (48km) of Leningrad, while other Finnish forces supported by a German division struck north of Lake Ladoga.

To coincide with D-Day, the Western Allies' invasion of France, Stalin launched a major offensive against Hitler's Finnish allies north of Leningrad along the Karelian isthmus and in the Lake Ladoga area on 9 June 1944. Although Finland had opened negotiations in February, the unforgiving Stalin threw half a million men, 800 tanks, 10,000 artillery pieces and 2,000 combat aircraft at the Finnish army. The Finns mustered 268,000 men, supported by just 110 tanks, 1,900 guns and 248 combat aircraft. Their armoured division was outnumbered and their elderly T-26s were no match for the battle-hardened T-34s.

The Soviet offensive was preceded by a bombardment of over 80,000 shells. On the second day the Soviets broke through the Finnish lines and made gains that threatened Finland. Soviet troops liberated Petrozavodsk on the 28th. The Finns requested six German divisions, and although Hitler sent the 122nd Infantry

Division, an assault gun brigade and anti-tank weapons, the Finns were driven back with the loss of 36,000 casualties.

Hitler dispatched reinforcements and a Luftwaffe fighter-bomber unit to temporarily stabilize the situation on the condition the beleaguered Finns did not sue for peace. With this aid the Finns were able to handle the crisis, and halted the Soviets in early July.

At this point, the Finnish forces had been driven back about 62 miles (100km), bringing them to approximately the same line of defence they had held at the end of the Winter War. Finland finally made peace with Moscow in August and, monitored by Finnish armour, the Germans withdrew into northern Norway to continue the war.

CHAPTER 3

Where Will Stalin's Blow Fall?

Everything pointed to Stalin attacking the Kovel-Lvov area with a push on Warsaw or an offensive in the Baltic. Also as part of the Allied D-Day deception plans for the invasion of Normandy, Operation Bodyguard resulted in German intelligence picking up rumours of Soviet-American planning in Novorossiisk for a naval attack on the Romanian coast in the Black Sea. Such cooperation was nonsense in light of the difficulties experienced by the American shuttle bombing campaign, but to Hitler it was another threat that could not be dismissed out of hand.

While German intelligence estimated the Soviet summer offensive would strike south of the Pripyat marshes through Romania, Hungary and Slovakia, they were alert to troop build-ups in the Kovel-Tarnopol area. In response General Friedrich Hossbach's powerful LVI Panzer Corps on Busch's right was reinforced with a view to creating a reserve army.

Hitler and his staff were convinced that Stalin's blow would fall in northern Ukraine: the republic's vast steppes had provided few defensive barriers for the German army groups in the south. If this happened Hitler reasoned Army Group Centre could strike south and cut the Red Army off. Unfortunately for him, Stalin had every intention of striking again in Ukraine, but this was not scheduled to commence until three weeks after the start of Operation Bagration. In effect Stalin was planning to destroy two entire German army groups in one go.

An assault on the Baltic States could cut off Army Group North and Centre, but the geographical advantage in this region lay with the defenders, and the Baltic States were of little strategic importance. Similarly Byelorussia favoured the defenders as it was heavily forested and swampy, and the roads were poor. Army Group Centre had successfully withstood everything that the Red Army had thrown at it since January 1942.

'Fatherland' and 'Panther' Lines

Hitler's defensive positions indicated that Stalin would opt to strike in Ukraine. His position was quite secure in the northern zone, with the Pskov–Ostrov fortifications on the left and the 'Panther Line' running from Ostrov to Opochka and further south to Idritsa. In the Baltic States even if the 'Panther Line' was pierced, Latvia with its dense forest, marshy streams and in places major hills was ideal for defensive and delaying tactics. Likewise in the central zone Hitler could fight a delaying action while a new defensive system was established along the line of the Niemen–Narev–Vistula. In the southern zone there was not much that Model could do to improve his position between Kovel and the upper Dniester.

It was clear to Hitler and his generals that the northern zone required forces only for passive defence. The going was always much better in the winter when the frozen ground offered the Red Army much firmer purchase on the terrain, so attack was expected there and in the central zone only during the cold weather.

Sure enough, during the Soviet operations of December–January 1944 Vitebsk had been threatened, with the Red Army capturing Gorodok, an advanced strong-point of Vitebsk; they also cut the Vitebsk–Polotsk railway and approached Vitebsk along the northern bank of the Dvina. But the extremely bad weather and German counter-attacks forced the abandonment of the Vitebsk operation.

The northern edge of the central defensive zone had originally been anchored on Nevel, but since its loss to the Soviets Army Group Centre had turned its attention to fortifying Vitebsk itself and the surrounding region, an area ideally suited for defence, with the local countryside dotted with small lakes and blanketed in thick forest on the northern side of the Dvina. To the south the Luchesa, the Dvina's marshy tributary, protected it. Between Vitebsk and Orsha the defensive lines were some of the strongest the Germans had ever constructed on the Eastern Front. They were dubbed the 'Fatherland Line' as they covered the gap between the Dvina and Dnepr.

Stretching from Orsha to Rogachev, the valley of the middle Dnepr presented a vast and impassable network of swamps, small rivers and streams. If the Red Army managed to contend with all these barriers and crossed the Dnepr it would be confronted by the Berezina and Drut, again heavily forested and dotted with swampy ground fed by rivers. Also, German engineers had heavily fortified the Bobruisk–Rogachev–Zhlobin triangle.

To the south things were not so rosy: following all the Red Army's activity the Germans had not been given the opportunity to prepare elaborate in-depth defences. The Soviets crossing the Dnepr at many points between the Ukrainian capital, Kiev, and Dnepropetrovsk had compromised the 'Dnepr Line'. Such defences that had been prepared were not comparable to the 'Panther' and 'Fatherland' lines to the north. In particular the Znamenka–Kirovograd gap provided good operational ground for the Soviets, as did the Volynian tableland.

The Exposed Byelorussian Balcony

Many of Hitler's commanders were uneasy about maintaining the 'Byelorussian Balcony', as the bulge in Army Group Centre's line was nicknamed. Alexander Werth noted Hitler had a sound strategic reason for this:

> Hitler's remaining allies were becoming more and more unreliable and their governments were hoping to get out of the war at the first convenient opportunity. It is ironical that one of the reasons Hitler was determined to cling on to the Vitebsk–Mogilev–Bobruisk Line at the east end of the great 'Byelorussian Bulge' penetrating deep into Russia was that its loss would have a demoralizing effect on the Finns who, since the loss of the Karelian

Isthmus and Viipuri earlier in the month, were sorely tempted to resume their armistice talks with the Russians.

To no avail Generalfeldmarschall Busch, commanding Army Group Centre, had been pleading with Hitler to pull out of Byelorussia, or at least to 'shorten the line'.

General F.W. von Mellenthin, serving with the XXXXVIII Panzer Corps, Army Group North Ukraine, supported the view that Army Group Centre should be pulled back:

> Despite persistent attacks Army Group Centre had retained a considerable part of White Russia, including Vitebsk and the important railway junction at Orsha. The Eastern Front was still too long for an effective defence, and we would have gained much by evacuating Estonia and White Russia and withdrawing to the line Riga–Lemberg–mouth of the Dniester. But with Hitler in command, that was too much to hope for.

Hitler was now obsessed with strongpoints upon which the Red Army could founder. His Führer Order no. 11 defined designated 'fortified areas' (*feste Plätze*), and 'local strongpoints' (*Ortsstützpunkte*). With this he confused the chain of command and inadvertently signed the death warrants of many senior generals by ordering:

> Each 'Fortified Area Commandant' should be a specially selected, hardened soldier, preferably of General's rank. He will be appointed by the Army Group concerned. Fortified Area Commandants will be personally responsible to the Commander-in-Chief of the Army Group.
>
> Fortified Area Commandants will pledge their honour as soldiers to carry out their duties to the last.
>
> Only the CinC of an Army Group in person may, with my approval, relieve the Fortified Area Commandant of his duties, and perhaps order the surrender of the fortified area.

Any general could see that such an arrangement was unworkable and quite frankly unreasonable; it stifled all flexibility and meant divisional commanders were answerable to their army group commander not their army or corps commander. This effectively meant the latter had no control over the *feste Plätze* in their area of responsibility.

In April Hitler designated Bobruisk, Mogilev, Orsha and Vitebsk as fortified places to be held to the last. All were to be defended by a division except for Vitebsk, which was to be held by an entire corps. Tying up one-third of 3rd Panzer Army's strength to Vitebsk (four divisions in all, 206th and 246th Infantry and the 4th and 6th Luftwaffe Field Divisions) was a recipe for disaster. It meant that 3rd Panzer Army had no way of stabilizing its front unless these forces were freed up. Again Busch took this lying down like the 'yes-man' he apparently was.

These towns were vital communications hubs, acting as focal points for important regional rail and road links. Stalin needed to take them in order to cut Busch's lines of communication and reinforcement routes. In this respect Hitler was quite right that Busch must hold on to them at all costs.

In theory each *fester Platz* would act as a breakwater once the Soviets had pierced the front-line defences. If Busch had been provided with sufficient mobile reserves then these could have swiftly reinforced these points and counter-attacked the preoccupied Red Army. The reality was that because of Busch's complete paucity of reserves, his lack of tactical flexibility meant the garrisons in the *feste Plätze* were likely to be consigned to lonely and miserable fates once surrounded.

Generalfeldmarschall Erich von Manstein was dismissive of Hitler's obsession with such strongpoints, noting in 1943:

> In practice they required more troops to defend them than was worth devoting to their retention. Since 'strongholds' without proper fortifications or adequate garrisons must inevitably fall to the enemy sooner or later without fulfilling their intended purpose the Army Group in every case but one contrived to get them abandoned before they were hopelessly surrounded. The exception was Tarnopol, where in the end only remnants of the garrison were able to break out. Later in 1944 this method of Hitler's led to considerable losses.

General Hans Jordan, acting commander of 9th Army, disliking this complete lack of flexibility, requested that Busch question the wisdom of the fortified places. Holding Vitebsk and the land bridge between the Dvina and Dnepr was a strategic mistake, he reasoned: why not shorten Army Group Centre's front by 150 miles (240km) with a withdrawal to the Dnepr or Berezina, a move 45 miles (72km) west?

The Dvina–Drut or Berezina lines might have been more manageable. Indeed the Nieman River would have made a better defensive line as it extends almost to the Pripyat marshes, but Hitler would never have countenanced pulling his forces back 45 miles, let alone 150.

Busch saw Hitler on 20 May, just as Stalin was conferring with his generals, and requested a strategic withdrawal. He presented two plans developed by his staff: the 'Small Solution' advocated a withdrawal to the Dnepr, while the 'Large Solution' proposed withdrawing to the Berezina. These were in violation of Führer Order no. 11 and Führer Order no. 7 instructing Army Group Centre to establish contact with Army Group South via Kovel.

Hitler flatly refused, remarking he had not thought Busch to be one of those generals always looking over his shoulder. The accusation was implicit and Busch clearly made a mental note never to question Hitler's orders again. This was unfortunate, for on 15 May Model floated the idea of an offensive operation using Army Group North Ukraine and practically all Busch's armoured formations. He had LVI Panzer Corps reassigned to him on the 29th.

For Busch this was a disaster: while his front shrank by 6 per cent, in one fell swoop he lost up to 15 per cent of his divisions, 88 per cent of his panzers, 23 per cent of his assault guns and 33 per cent of his heavy artillery. Generaloberst Weiss, commanding 2nd Army, warned Busch of Model's intentions, but he did nothing. This poses the question of what kind of general would give up such resources without a fight.

Jordan's 9th Army was thoroughly alarmed at the Soviet build-up, and Busch was only belatedly distracted into getting LVI Panzer Corps back once Model had finished with it. None of the divisions, though, were returned, except for the 20th Panzer Division reassigned in mid-June with just a single battalion of panzers. Reinhardt, commander of 3rd Panzer Army, sensibly suggested pulling back his left flank in order to shorten the front and free up some divisions. Busch, though, was not receptive to this idea and he knew only too well that giving ground up was anathema to Hitler.

The loss of armoured units to northern Ukraine and France meant that Army Group Centre was mainly an infantry force. Critically it only had 553 of the 4,740 tanks and assault guns on the Eastern Front, just 11 per cent of the total, and 480 of these were in fact assault guns. The bulk of the armour, 40 panzers (including 29 Tiger Is) and 246 Sturmgeschütz (StuG) IIIs, was deployed with Tippelskirch's 4th Army defending Orsha.

On top of this Busch had no real reserves except for the 14th Infantry Division, the weak 20th Panzer Division and the remains of Panzergrenadier Division Feldherrnhalle; as a consequence his army group had little strategic depth and lacked punch.

Way to the south, even though it was screened by the Pripyat marshes, Weiss's weak 2nd Army VIII, XX and XXIII Corps were reliant on a few security and training divisions trying to hold the southern shoulder of the 'Byelorussian Balcony', as well as containing the Soviet partisans (see maps pp. 29 and 30). Their operational effectiveness against regular Red Army formations was highly dubious and was simply a matter of expediency in the face of Hitler's growing manpower shortages. These forces were stretched from Kovel and the junction with Army Group North Ukraine's 4th Panzer Army north-eastward through Pinsk to Zhitkovichi and 9th Army.

The 9th Army was holding the Bobruisk area, with LV, XXXXI Panzer and XXXV Corps running roughly south to north. The XXXXI Panzer Corps had no panzer divisions, and the only real armoured unit was that of the 20th Panzer Division heading for Bobruisk. Facing them were the armies of the Soviet 1st Byelorussian Front.

Beyond these forces lay 4th Army with XII Corps south of Mogilev, and XXXIX and XXVII Corps running northward between Mogilev and Orsha. Again the XXXIX Panzer Corps had no armoured divisions, although the other two corps could muster the 19th and 25th Panzergrenadier Divisions. Opposite these troops were the 2nd and 3rd Byelorussian Fronts.

To the north was 3rd Panzer Army with VI, LIII and IX Corps respectively. The LIII Corps defended the Vitebsk bulge, with the 4th and 6th Luftwaffe Field Divisions holding the actual bulge. Despite being a Panzer Army this formation again had no panzer or panzergrenadier divisions and consisted entirely of infantry and Luftwaffe field units. Facing 3rd Panzer Army were elements of the 3rd Byelorussian Front and the 1st Baltic Front.

'No More Doubt'

Army Group Centre's intelligence officers began to assess that a threat was manifesting itself on their front by late May 1944; this assessment was fuelled by the build-up of Soviet artillery and aircraft, though they missed other factors, particularly the tank build-up. The movement of Stalin's artillery, so vital for softening up Busch's defences, was conducted eight to ten days before the start of the operation. This ensured that Busch's intelligence officers failed to spot the main concentrations, and just as importantly the breakthrough sectors.

By 13 June Colonel Gehlen's Foreign Armies East was warning of a major offensive against Army Group Centre, with particular concern for the southeast and east of Bobruisk, the north-east of Orsha and both sides of Vitebsk; the start date was assessed to be between 15 and 20 June. They were on the verge of predicting Bagration. By the 14th Busch's staff were expressing their concerns to the army's high command (Oberkommando des Heeres or OKH) representatives. Reinhardt's 3rd Panzer Army was anxious about a main attack south-east of Vitebsk; the presence of three new divisions, 100 tanks and artillery support also seemed to suggest a supporting attack north-east of the city.

Poor camouflage discipline on the part of Chernyakovsky's 5th Artillery Corps from 13 June meant that Tippelskirch's 4th Army was aware of a concentration north of the Smolensk–Minsk highway through Orsha. While Reinhardt was aware of this, his greatest concern was Vitebsk, which it seemed the Red Army was preparing to envelop. From the 16th, 4th Army detected another build-up opposite Mogilev and accurately predicted an attack on 22 June.

Similarly Jordan's 9th Army was not totally ignorant of what was going on. From the end of May it had watched preparations for an attack toward Bobruisk. It also suspected an attack west of the Berezina and south of Bobruisk, just as Rokossovsky had argued so strongly for. By 12 June, Jordan's intelligence officers were telling him that both locations would be main attacks, with the one west of the Berezina the most threatening. By the 20th they expected an attack within two days, rightly with the intention of seizing Bobruisk, dividing the army and isolating those forces east of the Berezina.

It appeared all three armies had a better appraisal of Stalin's impending offensive than Busch's Army Group HQ in Minsk. Yet all these little warnings did not come together in time to indicate that something simply enormous was about to be unleashed upon them. In the run-up to Bagration on the night of 14 June the Red Air Force attacked Luftwaffe airfields at Brest-Litovsk, Pinsk, Minsk and Orsha. German night fighters and air defences claimed fourteen Soviet aircraft. Despite these attacks Busch was not unduly alarmed, and five days later went home on leave.

Within twenty-four hours of his departure Soviet partisans blew up the Pinsk–Luniniec, Orsha–Borisov, Orsha–Mogilev and Molodechnno–Polotsk railway lines. Colonel Count Kielmannsegg, 1st General Staff Officer OKH, telephoned

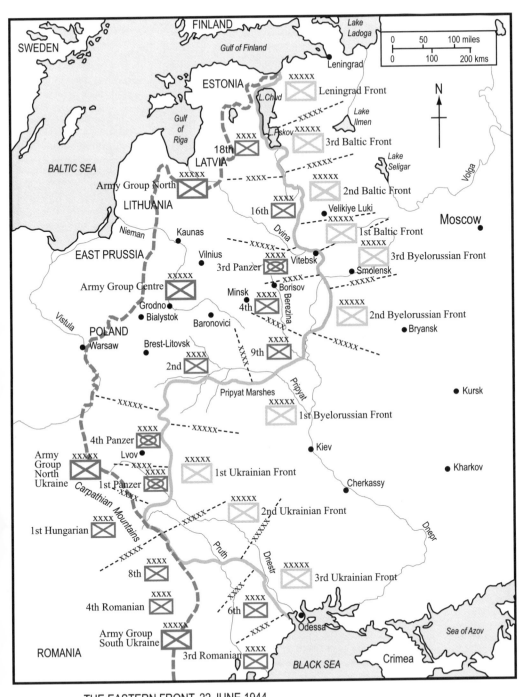

THE EASTERN FRONT, 22 JUNE 1944

THE EASTERN FRONT, 23 AUGUST 1944

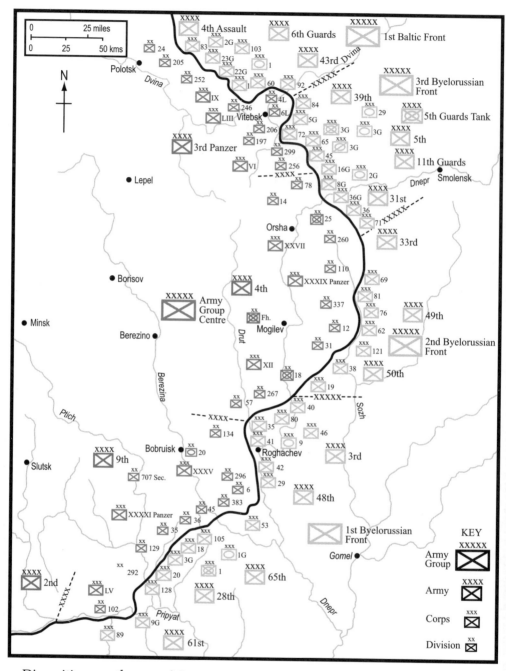

Dispositions on the eve of Operation Bagration, 22 June 1944.

Minsk on the 20th with the warning that the main Soviet effort lay near Polotsk. Army Group Centre's HQ did not believe him.

The men on the front line were better informed than their generals. Armin Scheiderbauer, with the 2nd Battalion, 472nd Grenadier Regiment, 252nd Infantry Division, observed:

> The Soviet Offensive was imminent. We were greeted with that announcement. So for formation and training, for getting to know one's way about, there only remained days, or at the most weeks. On 15 June the Füsilier battalion under Major von Garn deployed in the Main Line of Resistance, had succeeded in shooting down a Soviet reconnaissance aircraft. Its passengers had been general staff officers, who wanted to view from as close as possible the terrain over which their troops would attack...
>
> On 20 June the battalion was moved up to the village of Lovsha along the Vitebsk–Polotsk railway line. Then there was no more doubt that the Soviets would begin their offensive on 22 June, the third anniversary of the beginning of the campaign. On the evening of the 21st the commander, Hauptmann Müller, invited all his officers to celebrate the start of their new posts. For many, it would at the same time be a farewell.

Stalin, Zhukov, Rokossovsky and the others were by no means complacent about the task ahead. Every care had to be taken in the planning and the preparations to ensure success, although in the face of such strong German defences victory was not necessarily assured.

Zhukov was only too well aware of the strength of Army Group Centre's position:

> At the outset of the offensive the front line of the German defences of the Army Group Centre stretched from Polotsk to Vitebsk and further along the line Orsha, Zhlobin, Kapatkevichi, Zhitkovichi and along the Pripyat River. Polotsk, Vitebsk, Orsha and Mogilev were in German hands.
>
> These big towns and the rivers Dnepr, Drut, Berezina and Svisloch, as well as several small, boggy rivers and rivulets, formed the solid basis of a deeply echeloned enemy in defence in the vital Warsaw–Berlin strategic direction. Although the Stavka had concentrated considerable forces against the Army Group Centre, we felt that special care should be given to the preparation of the troops to take part in Operation Bagration so that its success would be ensured.

Communications Cut

As a prelude to Operation Bagration, Soviet partisan forces set about Army Group Centre's rear areas and lines of communication. On the night of 19–20 June 1944 Soviet partisans blew up 40,000 tracks in occupied Byelorussia. The supply lines of 3rd Panzer Army were the main targets, as it was to bear the brunt of the first assault. In just one night 15,000 demolitions were conducted, 10,500 of which were successful.

Army Group Centre found all double track lines blocked for about twenty-four hours and the single track ones out of action for forty-eight hours. Colonel G. Teske, chief of transportation of Army Group Centre, later recorded: 'The lightning operation conducted during the night by partisan detachments halted all railway traffic on individual sections of all the principal communications leading to the breakthrough areas...This operation was carried out brilliantly.'

This was part of the 'Rail War' in which Byelorussian partisans attacked 220 German garrisons and destroyed 132 miles (211km) of railway lines, as well as 295 rail bridges, 2,171 trains, 6 armoured trains and 32 water pumping stations. Army Group Centre was methodically cut off from the outside world.

CHAPTER 4

Stalin and his Warlords

Stalin was ruthless in maintaining his grip on power. As a dress rehearsal of things to come he had conducted a bloodless minor purge in 1929–30, with 4.7 per cent of the military membership expelled from the Communist Party; again in 1933–34 6.7 per cent of the military membership was excluded or demoted. But after his 'Great Terror' was unleashed in the mid-1930s almost the entire Red Army high command were accused of being part of a German military-political conspiracy.

In 1937 approximately 90 per cent of the general officers and 80 per cent of the colonels disappeared; 3 of the 5 marshals of the Soviet Union and 13 out of 15 generals were eliminated, as were 75 of the 80 members of the Supreme Military Council and 11 vice-commissars of defence. Out of 85 corps commanders, 57 were gone within a year; of 406 brigade commanders, 220 were dead by the close of 1938. Some 40,000 senior and medium grade officers were executed, imprisoned or sent to the dreaded Gulag. Ironically the year before the US military attaché had observed that the loyalty of the Red Army to the Soviet government appeared beyond doubt.

In contrast Hitler's purge in early 1938 witnessed the dismissal of just sixteen generals; none were imprisoned or shot, and forty-four others were simply transferred to new jobs. After the disastrous war with Finland, Stalin was forced to release over 4,000 selected officers who had been imprisoned during the Terror, and return them to active service. Among them were future marshals of the Soviet Union – Rokossovsky, Rotmistrov and Tolbukhin. This, though, was not enough to stave off the disaster looming on the horizon. Shmushkevich, the new Air Force commander, was shot in June 1941, the last acknowledged peacetime execution, just two weeks before Hitler's invasion.

To act as Stalin's eyes and ears for Operation Bagration, Georgi Zhukov and Aleksandr Vasilevsky were appointed Stavka special representatives. Vasilevsky was to keep an eye on Bagramyan and Chernyakovsky, who lacked experience. Rokossovsky knew what he was doing, but had a key role serving as the linchpin between the attack on Army Group Centre and the follow-on operation against Army Group North Ukraine. Zakharov as a second choice was a bit more of an unknown quantity. The Stavka also sent General Shtemenko, chief of operations, and a number of other officers to Zakharov's HQ to assist Zhukov.

Zhukov: A Talented Strategist
Seweryn Bialer, chronicler of Stalin's generals, summed Zhukov up thus:

Zhukov's role in the military establishment was unique. A knowledgeable and talented strategist, a man of immense willpower, self-confidence, decisiveness, and toughness toward self and subordinates, he thrived less on staff work in Moscow than on direct supervision of military operations in the field.

Zhukov was already familiar with Byelorussia, as he had briefly served as the deputy commander of the Byelorussian Military District in the 1930s. Prudently he had kept himself away from Soviet politics and had escaped Stalin's purges. Zhukov had been appointed commander of the 3rd Cavalry Corps in 1937, but shortly after was offered the 6th Cossack Corps. He discovered this formation to be in a much better state and found it contained an old command of his, the Don Cossack Division, as well as the 6th Chongar and 29th Cavalry Divisions.

During this time, Zhukov recalled: 'It was clear that the future largely belonged to armour and mechanized units. Hence we gave undivided attention to questions of cavalry–armour cooperation, and the organization of anti-tank defences in combat and in executing manoeuvres.'

At the end of 1938 Zhukov was offered the Byelorussian post commanding the cavalry and tank units, comprising five cavalry divisions and four detached tank brigades. Having said goodbye to the 6th Cossack Corps, Zhukov travelled to Smolensk and during May 1939 conducted exercises near Minsk, little realizing that this would soon be the scene of bitter battles with Army Group Centre's invading panzers.

Zhukov's command was short-lived, for on 2 June 1939 he was summoned to Moscow to see the People's Commissar of Defence, Marshal Klementi E. Voroshilov, who briefed him on the situation in the Far East: 'Japanese troops have made a surprise attack and crossed into friendly Mongolia which the Soviet Government is committed to defend from external aggression by the Treaty of 12 March 1936. Here is a map of the invasion area showing the situation as of 30 May.' Afterwards Zhukov went to see Ivan Smorodinov, acting deputy chief of the general staff, who told him, 'pull no punches'.

Zhukov understood very well that his new appointment could make or break his career. Simply ousting the Japanese from Outer Mongolia would not be enough; the Japanese would have to be dealt such a blow that they would never consider tackling the Red Army again. His successful campaign at Khalkin-Gol severely mauled the Imperial Japanese Army. He claimed 9,284 casualties; however, losses for the Japanese have been put as high as 45,000 killed, and Soviet casualties well over 17,000. Certainly of the 60,000 Japanese troops trapped in Zhukov's cauldron, 50,000 were listed as killed, wounded and missing.

Thanks to Zhukov's actions in June 1940 the Russo-Japanese dispute was settled with a border treaty. This was a strategic disaster for Hitler, as it allowed Stalin to redeploy the bulk of his battle-experienced forces west when Hitler attacked twelve months later. The battle of Khalkin-Gol convinced the Japanese to strike south into south-east Asia against British, French and Dutch interests, and then east against the Americans at Pearl Harbor, thereby saving Stalin from a two-front war.

As a reward Zhukov was promoted and transferred west to the Ukrainian Kiev Military District, and the battle experience gained by his Siberian forces was put to good use at the Battle of Moscow in December 1941. He was then appointed first deputy supreme commander-in-chief of the armed forces in August 1942. He used a very similar tactic to that of Khalkin-Gol during his attack at Stalingrad, and this was reflected in the planning for Bagration.

Zhukov did not tolerate military ineptitude: for example, during the Khalkin-Gol campaign he removed a number of senior commanders for their complete lack of initiative. On 7 June 1944 Zhukov and Rokossovsky unexpectedly visited Lieutenant General P.I. Batov's 65th Army forward command post near the village of Prosvet. They demanded to visit the 69th Rifle Division, part of General I.I. Ivanov's 18th Rifle Corps. Batov was far from happy about this as the 69th's positions were in a swamp, exposed and under German artillery fire. It did not help that Zhukov and Rokossovsky were wearing very distinctive black leather trench coats, which clearly marked them out as senior generals.

Batov noted: 'From the forward trench Zhukov and Rokossovsky looked through their binoculars, appraising the terrain and the tactical depth of enemy defences. A happy thought flashed through my mind: "They are looking for the direction of the main strike. Perhaps our plans coincide!"'

Batov was right, for Zhukov recalled: 'We gave particular attention to a study of the terrain and the enemy defences in the area of the 69th and 44th Guards Rifle Divisions of the 18th Rifle Corps where our main strike was planned.'

Unfortunately Ivanov was late, incurring Zhukov's displeasure before they moved on to the 44th Guards Rifle Division sector. Zhukov did not like what he saw and demanded that Batov remove Ivanov and Colonel P.G. Petrov, the unfortunate commander of the 44th.

Petrov's crime – his nerves got the better of him – was the delivery of a very poor situation brief. Then, not wishing to expose his VIPs, he took them to a secondary observation post, where, according to Batov, Zhukov could see nothing and almost fell out of an ill-prepared tree used as a vantage point: 'Zhukov tried to climb up hastily nailed laths; he reached the middle of the tree and came down, enraged. It was pitiful to watch Petrov. We went to another sector.'

Zhukov's tour of inspection had gone wrong from the very start and he was in a fury, demanding that heads roll. Although he recorded the inspection of the 18th Rifle Corps in his memoirs, he made no mention of this ugly incident. Batov managed to save Ivanov with just a reprimand; Petrov was not so fortunate. Serving as a deputy divisional commander with Gorbatov's 3rd Army, he was involved in forcing the River Drut with the first echelon and was mortally wounded at the bridgehead. He was posthumously awarded the title Hero of the Soviet Union.

For all his brilliance, Zhukov had a very bad temper, as did many senior commanders; this no doubt was in part brought on by stress but also seemed to be part of the accepted culture of the Red Army. Plain talking and a no-nonsense approach seemed very much the order of the day, even if it meant belittling subordinates and failing to recognize their achievements. Zhukov was highly ambitious and prone to rivalry, as his ugly competition with Vasilevsky was later to show.

Zhukov's Rival: Rokossovsky

Of the four front commanders, Rokossovsky stood out as a hardened veteran who had served during the First World War and then fought for the Bolsheviks during the Civil War. In the 1930s, while a cavalry commander, Zhukov had served as one of his regimental officers. Having fallen foul of Stalin, Rokossovsky disappeared into the Gulag prison camp system from 1937 to 1940. Initially he was held in the Kresty Prison in Leningrad.

While held in the Vorkuta camps, some of the largest and harshest, Rokossovsky worked as a warder's servant and managed to avoid the coal mines. However, he was the victim of mock executions and countless beatings inflicted for his refusal to 'confess' to spying for the Polish and Japanese.

Soviet defector Viktor Suvorov catalogued the brutal treatment meted out to Rokossovsky:

> During the investigations he underwent appalling tortures. Nine of his teeth were knocked out, three of his ribs were broken, his toes were hammered flat. He was sentenced to death and spent more than three months in the condemned cell. There is testimony, including his own, that twice, at least, he was subject to mock shootings, being led to the place of execution at night, and made to stand at the edge of a grave as generals on his right and left were shot, while he was 'executed' with a blank cartridge fired at the nape of his neck.

Clearly here was a man who had already seen hell and was not afraid to stand up to Stalin when the time came.

Stalin, desperately short of officers after his purges, rehabilitated Rokossovsky in March 1940 and placed him in command of the new 9th Mechanized Corps in Ukraine. Rokossovsky was told, 'Take command of this mechanised corps, prisoner, and we'll see about your death sentence later.' Once this formation had been swept away by the German invasion Rokossovsky took charge of the Soviet 4th Army during the defence of Smolensk.

It did not take long for Rokossovsky to become critical of Stalin's ability to throw men away for little achievable gain. He was also critical of senior officers who were prepared to pass on such orders, rather than argue with the Soviet leader. In November 1941 he had been forced to abandon his prepared defensive positions south of Moscow to launch two futile attacks by Zhukov. Then lacking reserves and facing being outflanked he wanted to withdraw, but Zhukov refused and threatened to have him shot. Stalin, perhaps deliberately playing the two generals off each other and sensing neither should be allowed to gain the ascendance, phoned Rokossovsky and promised him reinforcements.

The following January Stalin had proposed launching a counter-offensive from Leningrad to the Black Sea. The first blow would fall on Army Group Centre followed by the destruction of Army Group North, as well as the liberation of Ukraine and the Crimea. Zhukov wanted to concentrate on Army Group Centre, but was overruled. Again Rokossovsky was dismayed that Zhukov had acquiesced to Stalin's strategic misjudgement. He sent Zhukov a report opposing the plans, but the latter's response was 'carry out your orders'. Stalin's ambitious plans had been premature.

Rokossovsky briefly commanded the Bryansk Front in 1942 before being assigned to Stalingrad. His performance there ensured that he became one of Stalin's trusted few. At Kursk the Central Front, which subsequently became the 1st Byelorussian Front, was under his able leadership.

Stalin's Front Commanders

Bagramyan, a staff officer by trade, had found himself appointed commander of the Soviet 16th Army in 1942. Its performance at Rzhev that year and Bryansk the following year saw Stalin honour it with the re-designated title of 11th Guards Army. Bagramyan's handling of this formation at Kursk resulted in his promotion to command the 1st Baltic Front. The fact that he was Armenian did not seem to hamper his rise through the Red Army.

Chernyakovsky was a tanker who had led the 28th Tank Division in 1941. This experience ensured that he took a role organizing the new tank corps the following year before taking charge of the Soviet 60th Army, which fought at Kursk, the Desna and Dnepr crossing and Kiev. The Stavka and particularly Stalin saw his potential, appointing him in April 1944 to command the Western Front (subsequently the 3rd Byelorussian Front). He was then earmarked for a key role in the forthcoming Bagration offensive.

Georgi Zakharov also started the war as a staff officer then commanded the Soviet 51st Army and the Soviet 2nd Guards Army in February and July 1943 respectively. In fact General I.E. Petrov, veteran of Odessa and Sevastopol, was intended to command the 2nd Byelorussian Front, but Stalin disliked him. Petrov was removed after only a month and a half, Colonel General L.Z. Mekhlis, a military council member of the front, having accused him of not being up to the job.

Colonel General S.M. Shtemenko, chief of operations, recalled the rather difficult situation:

> Stalin appointed as commander of the 2nd Byelorussian Front Colonel General G.F. Zakharov, an extremely hotheaded man, very eccentric in his actions…It fell to me to make the change of command as painless as possible. I must confess that such a mission was profoundly unpleasant to me. I was afraid that the new commander would start to interpret in his own way the plan of operations already approved by Supreme Headquarters and that serious conflicts might arise first with Mekhlis and then with the Front's Chief of Staff, Lieutenant General A.N. Bogoliubov, an experienced but likewise eccentric and hotheaded man.

Zakharov had commanded the 2nd Guards Army in the Crimea and tried to apply the lessons learned there to the forthcoming Bagration plans, but they were wholly inappropriate for Byelorussia as the geography was completely different. It did not take him long to fall out with Shtemenko and the officers of his new command. He was characterized as having 'serious shortcomings – excessive self-confidence, short temper, harshness and sometimes even rudeness towards subordinates', ironically traits exhibited by many senior Red Army officers.

By 1944 the purges of the 1930s were in the past and, with a war to distract them, Stalin had full confidence in the loyalty of his generals. On the occasions that he had not, Lavrenti Beria's repressive People's Commissariat of Internal Affairs (the dreaded NKVD internal security force and forerunner of the KGB), was just a phone call away. Indeed, Beria recorded the deaths of 114,481 enemies of the state in 1944, and the Gulag system remained very active.

Confident after his early successes, Hitler now wrongly believed that the Soviet Union was on the verge of collapse when in fact the very reverse was actually happening. He felt if the bloodletting continued, the Red Army would eventually sag to its knees. Stalin on the other hand had been shaken by his experiences against the Finns in 1939 and Hitler in 1941–42. He knew that he had potentially sown the seeds of his own undoing with his purges and the subsequent overruling of his generals on strategic matters. By 1944 he was placing more reliance on the advice of the Stavka, and his generals were given a freer hand at the local level, though he was careful to ensure that no general, especially Zhukov, enjoyed pre-eminence.

Even so, Stalin understood only too well that it would be unwise to let Zhukov and Rokossovsky's stars burn too brightly. It is notable that Zhukov and Vasilevsky were constantly toing and froing from Moscow to the front, never having long enough in the capital to plot against their leader. For example, Vasilevsky served as chief of the general staff for thirty-four months, twenty-two of which were spent at the front.

Stalin might be winning the war, but he would have to ensure that his position was unassailable in its aftermath.

CHAPTER 5

Busch: Incompetent or a Safe Pair of Hands?

Adolf Hitler had just over 9 million men under arms by 1944, over half of whom were in the army and Waffen SS, formed into 315 divisions: these comprised 258 infantry, 34 panzer, 17 panzergrenadier and 6 parachute divisions. The lion's share of this massive manpower was deployed on the Eastern Front – 3.1 million men organized into 179 divisions, including 23 panzer and 7 panzergrenadier divisions. Hitler's east European allies supplied another 800,000 men deployed in 49 divisions of variable quality.

The Lion's Share

This meant that 63 per cent of Hitler's divisions and 70 per cent of his manpower were tied up fighting Stalin's Red Army, along with 57 per cent of all his panzers and Sturmgeschütz, 71 per cent of all guns and mortars and 51 per cent of all operational aircraft. The other two active fronts in France and Italy accounted for just 30 to 35 per cent of Hitler's total combat strength.

By the summer instead of the thirteen armies (including four panzer) that had defended the Eastern Front at the end of 1943, there were only ten (of which just two were panzer). Of these one was Hungarian and two were German-Romanian and were of dubious fighting value. There was some expectation of the reorganization of another panzer army with Waffen SS troops and equipment coming from Germany.

Nonetheless, with two armies including the Romanians considered unreliable, and morale of many units shaken by the winter defeats, plus a lack of artillery and transport south of the Pripyat marshes, the defensive strength of Hitler's forces on the Eastern Front was hardly 60 per cent of what it had been six months earlier.

By June Hitler had a total of about 150 combat-worthy divisions deployed on the Eastern Front, compared with 144 divisions in all other theatres of operation including those still in Germany. German and supporting Axis forces ran north to south, with Army Group North formed by the 16th and 18th Armies; Army Group Centre, 2nd, 3rd Panzer, 4th and 9th Armies; Army Group North Ukraine, made up of the 1st and 4th Panzer Armies and the Hungarian 1st Army; and finally Army Group South Ukraine, consisting of the German 6th and 8th Armies and the Romanian 3rd and 4th Armies.

Hitler's strategic vagueness had cost him dearly; in 1941 he cannot have expected that the war would drag on for three long years. After the swift victories in Scandinavia, western Europe and the Balkans, Hitler had assumed that the Red Army would be crushed very quickly. Stalin's purges and the Red Army's subsequent poor performance during the 1939–40 Russo-Finnish War seemed to confirm this. Hitler conveniently forgot about Zhukov's crushing victory over the Imperial Japanese Army at Khalkin-Gol. Ultimately he saw invading Britain and assisting Italian efforts to drive on Suez as an unwanted distraction.

Hitler had presented the invasion of the Soviet Union as a preventative war, but his arguments had failed to convince some senior generals. His aims for the Soviet Union had always been vague other than gaining raw materials and living space or *Lebensraum*. In 1940 he had expressed his aim to defeat the Red Army and occupy as much Soviet soil as necessary to protect Berlin from air attack. His forces were also to drive far enough east for the Luftwaffe to be able to destroy most of the important areas in the Soviet Union (ultimately this meant a barrier against Asiatic Russia on a line from Archangel to the Volga). All this was to be achieved in a rapid campaign.

The desire to destroy Soviet power could not be achieved with the continued existence of the Soviet Union east of the Volga, or indeed east of the Urals, nor were these lines any ultimate safeguard for Germany's security. Plans drafted in the summer of 1940 outlined Moscow, Ukraine, the Donets Basin and Leningrad as the Germans' main goals; however, the destruction of Soviet military power and the occupation of strategic areas immediately relevant to this power formed no part of the main mission. These political and economic goals once achieved, it was hoped, would cripple the Soviet war economy; senior German commanders felt that destruction of the Red Army should take precedence. After Moscow final victory seemed elusive.

In the defensive war of 1942–43 Germany's generals agonized over implementing the strategy of elastic defence in the face of Hitler's intransigence over giving up ground. During 1941–42 many generals agreed that Hitler's policy of holding onto strongpoints creating 'hedgehogs' was the right thing to do. General von Tippelskirch, who was to play a key role in saving 4th Army in the summer of 1944, was among them:

> It was his one great achievement. At that critical moment the troops were remembering what they had heard about Napoleon's retreat from Moscow, and living under the shadow of it. If they had once begun to retreat, it might have turned into a panic flight.

Tippelskirch was to regret these words. Indeed Generalfeldmarschall Gerd von Rundstedt was not so praiseworthy, remarking: 'It was Hitler's decision for rigid resistance that caused the danger in the first place. It would not have arisen if he had permitted a timely withdrawal.'

After the disastrous loss of 6th Army at Stalingrad, the Wehrmacht had bounced back with a quite remarkable recovery at Kharkov in the spring of 1943, but by mid-1944 Hitler was running out of strategic depth in which the Red Army could exhaust itself and men with whom to fend it off.

A Lacklustre Performance

In reality directing Army Group Centre was well beyond Generalfeldmarschall Ernst Busch's capabilities – regardless of the impending Soviet offensive. Some commentators go as far as accusing him of being 'thoroughly incompetent'. Certainly his performance up to June 1944 gave no indication that he would shine when his time came to respond to Operation Bagration. Furthermore his inability to question orders meant that he would not stand up to Hitler's penchant for sacrificing trapped troops.

Busch had served under Wilhelm List during the invasion of Poland in 1939, commanding VIII Corps. Although this had included the 5th Panzer Division he was an infantryman through and through, and he had little understanding of, or interest or faith in, panzer tactics. For the invasion of France he had led the 16th Army, an entirely infantry formation, gaining the Knight's Cross for his efforts.

Busch was subsequently involved in Operation Barbarossa. On 8 September 1941 16th Army, still containing only infantry divisions, took Demyansk before being involved in the siege of Leningrad. Busch's forces held the line from Staraya Russa to Ostashkov in the face of a Red Army counter-attack.

During the Soviet winter offensive of 1941–42 Stalin struck the boundary of Army Group North's 16th and Centre's 9th Armies with the aim of surrounding the latter. In the north in the second week of February the whole of X Corps and part of XI Corps deployed in the Demyansk area south-east of Lake Ilmen, and some six divisions, totalling 100,000 men, were cut off. Another 5,500 were trapped at Kholm.

Busch's vital supply base at Staraya Russa was saved only when he committed his sole reserve, the 18th Motorized Division. Contact was lost with Army Group Centre, and Generalfeldmarschall Georg von Küchler, the newly appointed commander-in-chief of Army Group North, demanded that Busch be relieved. For three whole months Busch's trapped men were sustained by the Luftwaffe; remarkably at Demyansk 15,446 replacements were flown in and 22,093 men evacuated. This success was later to cloud Hitler's judgement at Stalingrad.

Busch was saved when the Soviets attacked into the rear of Army Group Centre and headed for Vitebsk and Smolensk. Subsequently 16th Army was reinforced and the situation retrieved at Kholm and Demyansk. Despite his lacklustre performance Busch was promoted to Generalfeldmarschall on 1 February 1943. Ten months later he found himself in charge of Army Group Centre.

Hitler's Commanders

Many of Army Group Centre's army and corps commanders, though experienced, had taken over their commands only early in 1944. Generaloberst Georg-Hans Reinhardt in contrast was an old hand; he had assumed control of Panzergruppe 3, which subsequently became 3rd Panzer Army on 5 October 1941. It was attached to Army Group Centre and fought around Moscow in late 1941 and early 1942.

General der Artillerie Georg Pfeiffer assumed command of VI Corps on 20 May 1944, replacing General der Infanterie Hans Jordan, who was promoted to take charge of 9th Army. General der Artillerie Rolf Wuthmann had been in command of his IX Corps since December 1943; similarly General der Infanterie Friedrich Gollwitzer had taken charge of LIII Corps on 22 June 1943. Gollwitzer's corps was the strongest in 3rd Panzer Army, with four divisions under his direction.

General der Infanterie Kurt von Tippelskirch had taken command of 4th Army only on 4 June 1944, having previously been in charge of XII Corps since September 1943. Tippelskirch was to be the man of the hour, not Busch. On the Eastern Front during the winter of 1941–42, when he had spent his time as a divisional commander with II Corps in the Valdai Hills, between Leningrad and Moscow, he had watched his command's strength fall by a third. Generalleutnant Vincenz Müller took over XII Corps from von Tippelskirch.

Tippelskirch had flair, as he recounts:

At Mogilev in March, 1944, I was commanding XII Corps – which consisted of three divisions. In the offensive the Russians then launched, they used ten divisions in the assault on the first day, and by the sixth day had used twenty divisions. Yet they only captured the first line, and were brought to a halt before the second. In the lull that followed I prepared a counter strike, delivered it by moonlight, and recovered all the ground that had been lost – with comparatively few casualties.

General der Infanterie Paul Völckers had been in charge of XXVII Corps since June 1943, while General der Artillerie Robert Martinek was only appointed to XXXIX Panzer Corps on 18 April 1944, which had fought at Kholm and in the withdrawal to Smolensk. With four divisions under its command Martinek's corps was the largest within 4th Army.

General der Infanterie Hans Jordan was only appointed to 9th Army on 20 May 1944. Generalleutnant Kurt-Jürgen Freiherr von Lützow was appointed to XXXV Corps on 25 June 1944, replacing General der Infanterie Friedrich Wiese. Lützow's corps, with responsibility for nine divisions, was not only the strongest corps within 9th Army, but within the whole of Army Group Centre.

General der Artillerie Helmuth Weidling commanded XXXXI Panzer Corps from 15 October 1943 until 19 June 1944, when he took two weeks' leave, returning to duty on 1 July. Generalleutnant Edmund Hoffmeister covered in his absence. General der Infanterie Friedrich Herrlein took charge of LV Corps in October 1943.

The XXXXI Panzer Corps had fought at Bely, in the anti-partisan operations at Nikitinka, Yartsevo, Vyazma and Dukhovshchina. It fought at Smolensk, Kromy and Bryansk in March 1943, and Sevsk, Trubchevsk and Ponyri the following month. It then fought at Kursk and resisted the Soviet counter-offensive, withdrawing to East Prussia.

In early February 1943 Generaloberst Walter Weiss took over 2nd Army from Generaloberst Hans von Salmuth. The latter moved to take command of 15th Army, guarding northern Europe in anticipation of an Allied invasion.

Army Group Centre

Army Group Centre had endured three bloody years on the Eastern Front and it was no longer the same formation that had commenced the war. By June, Busch's command was entirely a defensive formation formed largely from infantry divisions; although it included a panzer army and two panzer corps it had no whole panzer divisions. It could muster just three panzergrenadier divisions and their panzer battalions were equipped with assault guns not tanks, while the Panzerjäger battalions of the infantry divisions were armed with self-propelled anti-tank guns, all of which were designed for defence not offensive operations.

The typical panzergrenadier division consisted of two panzergrenadier regiments, a tank battalion with three batteries of StuG or assault guns (essentially turret-less tanks with limited traverse to their guns) and a Panzerjäger battalion with three companies of self-propelled anti-tank guns and a company of self-propelled anti-aircraft or flak guns. A StuG battery numbered up to fourteen vehicles. An artillery regiment with about four batteries of guns provided fire support.

Generalleutnant Karl Zutavern had taken command of the 18th Panzergrenadier Division only at the end of May 1944. This division's principal units consisted of Panzergrenadier Regiments 30 and 51, Panzer Abteilung 118 armed with Sturmgeschütz, Panzerjäger Abteilung 118 equipped with self-propelled anti-tank guns and Artillery Regiment 18.

Similarly Generalleutnant Paul Schürmann had only joined the 25th Panzergrenadier Division in early March 1944. He found his command consisted of Panzer Abteilung 8, Panzerjäger Abteilung 125, Artillery Regiment 25 and Panzergrenadier Regiments 35 and 119.

Panzergrenadier Division Feldherrnhalle had started out as the 60th Motorized Infantry Division; the latter under Generalmajor Hans-Adolf von Arenstorff had been destroyed during Stalingrad. The survivors were regrouped as a panzergrenadier division under Generalleutnant Otto Kohlermann. He was familiar with the 60th, having commanded it during the summer of 1942. Generalmajor Friedrich-Carl von Steinkeller assumed command in early April 1944.

Feldherrnhalle received its honorary title because of the high number of volunteers from the Sturmabteilung (SA) or Brown Shirts. The Feldherrnhalle created in the mid-1930s was the elite unit of the SA and guarded important SA, state and party offices. It was placed under the control of the Wehrmacht in 1938 and the following year most of it was transferred to the Luftwaffe (where it was incorporated into the parachute or Fallschirmjäger units) and the rest became part of the 271st Infantry Regiment.

General Mortimer von Kessel assumed command of the veteran 20th Panzer Division in May 1943, leading it at Kursk. The division had first come into being three years earlier, having been created from the elements of two infantry divisions, and had taken part in Operation Barbarossa. After a brief break in the New Year von Kessel returned to the division in early February 1944. Its fighting strength by the summer comprised a weak panzer regiment, two panzergrenadier regiments, an artillery regiment and a Panzerjäger battalion armed with self-propelled guns.

However, at best his division could muster two Kampfgruppen or battle groups organized around the armoured and infantry formations. As Busch's fighting reserve it was far from adequate and would only be able to respond to a single breakthrough or be fatally weakened by being committed piecemeal to various sectors. Ultimately von Kessel and his immediate superior, Hans Jordan, were given a completely impossible task.

Army Group Centre's armoured forces also included eight independent Sturmgeschütz brigades that had recently been upgraded from battalion strength. These were spread out through the component armies. The 3rd Panzer Army had two assault gun formations, Sturmgeschütz Brigades 28 and 245 assigned to VI and IX Corps respectively. The 4th Army also had two assault gun brigades, the 185 deployed with the XXXIX Panzer Corps and the 190 Light Brigade. Under 2nd Army's direction were Sturmgeschütz Brigades 237 and 904 serving with VIII Corps.

In addition Busch had a powerful assault division, two Luftwaffe field divisions, five security divisions designed for rear area security and a field training division. The remaining twenty-three divisions were all regular infantry units. While all the infantry divisions consisted of infantry or grenadier regiments equipped with towed anti-guns and supported by an artillery regiment, a Panzerjäger or anti-tank battalion could have up to fourteen self-propelled guns; however, not all Panzerjäger or reconnaissance battalions were equipped with armoured vehicles.

Generalfeldmarschall Robert Ritter von Greim, who had been in charge of Luftflotte 6 since early May 1943, had under his command 839 aircraft, mostly fighters, with just 3,800 tonnes of fuel with which to support the operations of Army Group Centre. Operating out of Minsk, Greim had only two fighter groups, which at the end of May 1944 mustered sixty-six aircraft, and by the time of Bagration had only forty Me 109 G/Ks. Ground-attack forces comprised 106 Ju 87 G Stuka tank busters and Fw 190 fighter-bombers. There were also 312 bombers, mainly Heinkel He 111s.

Questionable Loyalty

At the time Hitler was unaware that the loyalty of Army Group Centre was questionable. Personnel from this command were involved in a number of attempts to kill him. The head of German military resistance, Henning von Tresckow, served as Generalfeldmarschall von Kluge's chief of staff of Army Group Centre. In fact Army Group Centre played a key role in the planned assassination of Hitler, as Generalmajor Freiherr Rudolf Christoph von Gersdorff, Army Group Centre's intelligence staff officer, recounts:

> One of the most active cells in the conspiracy was to be found in the staff of Army Group Centre on the Eastern Front, in which I was G2 from 1941 to 1943. It is here that we met von Tresckow, at that time a colonel in the General Staff and G3 of the Army Group. A man of dominating personality,

he handled with great energy both discussion and action…he turned to me in early 1942, as I remember, with his first request to prepare the explosive and fuse for the actual attempt.

Gersdorff was worried about the impact removing Hitler would have:

The conspirators fully realised that the existence and unity of the German Army must not be jeopardised by the planned coup d'état. A Russian breakthrough on the Eastern Front would bring chaos to the heart of Europe; Germany would be overrun by millions of Slavs and Asiatics.

An attempt was made on Hitler's life when he flew from his Wehrwolf, Forward HQ near Vinnitsa, central Ukraine, stopping off at Army Group Centre's HQ at Smolensk en route to Wolfsschanze (*Wolf's Lair*) on 13 March 1943.

'The first assassination attempt was carried out by Tresckow,' says von Gersdorff, 'on the occasion of Hitler's visit to Army Group headquarters in Smolensk. Tresckow personally brought Hitler from the airfield and had planned to place a bomb in the side pocket of the automobile, next to the place Hitler was to occupy.' This failed and the bomb was planted on his plane, that was intended to blow up near Minsk, for which the Red Air Force would be blamed, but it failed to explode.

A second attempt was made by Gersdorff a few days later, when Hitler was visiting an exhibition of captured Soviet weaponry in Berlin's Zeughaus (the old armoury on Unter den Linden). Gersdorff recounts: 'Army Group Centre had prepared in the armoury in Berlin an exhibition of captured Russian arms and equipment, war pictures, models etc, and a few days prior to 15 March 1943 General Schmundt gave out information that Hitler would personally open the exhibition on the occasion of Heroes Memorial Day.'

As an expert on Russian equipment Gersdorff provided the ideal guide. Unfortunately the Führer on 21 March raced through the exhibits, forcing Gersdorff to defuse his bomb once Hitler had gone. This second failure temporarily demoralized the plotters at Army Group Centre, though Gersdorff was not discovered, and he returned to the Eastern Front. In 1944 he transferred to Army Group B, where he served with valour during the battle for Normandy, leading several thousand men to freedom from the Falaise pocket.

Once the Red Army had pushed back into Ukraine, Hitler's Wehrwolf HQ was no longer safe; he last visited it at the end of August 1943. Following his evacuation of Wehrwolf it was taken over by von Manstein's Army Group as its field headquarters and was still in use by it in October 1943. Hitler finally gave orders for it to be destroyed in late December 1943. The location of this HQ had sealed the fate of the local Jewish population, as Hitler ruled it should be a Jew-free zone.

The Nazis murdered 120,000 Jews from the Vinnitsa *oblast* (Bratslav, Tulchin, Shpikov, Ladyzhin and Mogilev-Podolsky) and 50,000 more who were deported to Vinnitsa from other areas during their occupation. The Soviets captured correspondence between the Wehrwolf Guard Service, the *Gebietskommissariat* of

Vinnitsa and the Reich Security Service which showed the level of the atrocities against the civilian population.

Stalin's Traitors

Aside from Army Group Centre in Byelorussia, Stalin also found onerous the presence of Byelorussians fighting for Hitler. Stalin had brought this military collaboration upon himself as a consequence of the Great Terror unleashed in the 1930s, which had fuelled nationalist sentiment within the various Soviet Socialist republics. Collectivization, famine, Gulag and purges had caused the deaths of up to 30 million people, and between 1936 and 1938 up to a million people were executed, with a further 8 million imprisoned. In Byelorussia people were shot in Kurapaty forest, while in Ukraine large numbers were executed outside Chelyabinsk, Kharkov, Kiev and Vinnitsa.

Army Group Centre had within its ranks *Hilfswillige* (auxiliary volunteer) and *Osttruppen* (eastern troops) that were locally recruited. The *Hiwis*, essentially military hangers-on, provided non-combatant support as cooks, drivers and medical orderlies, while the *Osttruppen* were personnel integrated into formed units. By the end of 1941 Army Group Centre had six battalions of *Osttruppen*; three years later the Inspectorate of Eastern or Volunteer Troops under General Kostring had the equivalent of thirty German divisions of volunteers, numbering 427,000 men. The Luftwaffe also had an Inspectorate of *Ostflieger* with some 300,000 auxiliaries.

To combat the growing partisan menace, for rear area security the Germans had to rely on fourteen ill-equipped security divisions, five reserve divisions and seven field training divisions, and fourteen police regiments. Also in German rear areas were locally raised auxiliary police or *Schuma* battalions (*Schutzmannschaft Bataillone*) organized to conduct operations under German officers. In Byelorussia there were eleven of these (45th–49th, 60th, 64th–67th and 69th). They were insufficient, and even with support from Baltic *Schuma* were unable to cope. Also under Army Group Centre was the 2nd Field Railroad Command, which in 1943–44 deployed 112,670 German and Soviet railroad personnel, including communications and security forces.

The Germans knew to their cost they could not rely on such forces. In 1943 Army Group Centre's chief of transportation reported:

> In many instances, the so-called Eastern volunteer units (foreign formations), which were employed to protect the railroad lines, made common cause with the partisans, and took German weapons along with them. In one case, for instance, an entire Russian security detachment of 600 men went over to the partisans. On 17 August 1943 this force attacked the Krulevshchizna railroad station. Using the machine guns, mortars, and anti-tank guns, which they had taken with them at the time of their desertion, the Russians caused considerable damage. German losses in that engagement amounted to 240 dead and 491 wounded.

According to western sources there was also a Self-Defence Corps that in early 1944 was designated the Byelorussian Home Guard (*Belaruskaya krayovaya abarona* – BKA) numbering little more than half a dozen battalions. Similarly the Byelorussian National Guerrillas (*Belaruskaya narodnaya partizanka* – BNP) were fairly ineffective in fighting the Red Army.

The National Archives of Belarus record that the Byelorussian Self Defence Corps was created in June 1942 under Ivan Ermachenko. It was intended to raise three divisions but it consisted of only twenty battalions. They were meant to help the Germans and local police against the partisans; however, the Germans prudently did not arm them and the organization was disbanded in the spring of 1943.

Owing to the escalating partisan problem the Byelorussian Home Guard/ Regional Defence or BKA came into being in early March 1944 under the command of Major F. Kushal. It was formed by the compulsory conscription of all males born between 1908 and 1924. Again according to Belarus sources, by mid-April the BKA numbered 25,000 men, comprising thirty-six infantry battalions and six field engineer battalions – in effect the three divisions originally intended.

Although raised by the collaborationist Byelorussian Central Rada quasi-government to fight partisans, the Red Army and the Polish Home Army, the BKA only saw action against local partisan units. A patriotic view is that it was mainly used as security and labour battalions to help guard buildings and bring in the harvest. There may be some element of truth in this, as Busch is unlikely to have trusted them entirely or to have been keen to have another well-armed and well-organized Byelorussian military formation in his rear.

Governor Kube also established a Byelorussian Youth Organization on the lines of the Hitler Youth, which by April 1944 had 12,633 members. Byelorussian collaboration, though, was nothing like on the scale of the Ukrainians, who volunteered in their tens of thousands.

There was no real Russian Liberation Army until almost the end of the war. On 14 November 1944 Andrei A. Vlasov, a captured Soviet general, inaugurated the Committee for the Liberation of the Peoples of Russia (*Komitet osvobozhdeniya narodov Rossii* – KONR) in Prague. KONR dreamed of a Russian army of twenty-five divisions encompassing the 650,000 Russian troops in German service, but only two were actually formed.

Minsk, like Warsaw, under Nazi occupation had become an appalling place of death. When the city was occupied less than a week after Hitler's invasion, almost a third of the entire population, some 75,000 people, were Jewish. Few were able to flee before the arrival of the German military.

The city's Jews were instructed by the head of the German civil administration, Generalkommissar Wilhelm Kube, to wear a yellow Star of David on their clothing. This was followed by the establishment of a ghetto to which the Germans deported Jews from neighbouring towns, so that its population swelled to some 100,000; soon after the deportations and executions began on a horrifying scale.

The ghetto itself was levelled on 21 October 1943 when the German security forces and auxiliary units rounded up the last 2,000 people in order to kill them. All this culminated on 22 September 1943 in Governor Kube's assassination, orchestrated by the Byelorussian partisans: his Byelorussian mistress killed him by planting a bomb in his bed. By 1944 just 10 per cent of the city's Jews, about 10,000 people, had managed to escape to the neighbouring forests and the local partisans; the rest had been mercilessly exterminated.

Kube's successor, SS-Obergruppenführer General Kurt von Gottberg, hoping to enlist the populace against the partisans, appealed to them by offering limited national autonomy. The SS as head of the new regime selected Radaslau Astrouski, who oversaw the Rada and the BKA, including the 20,000 members of Kushal's Polizei.

Busch had far better things to do than worry about local quisling Astrouski, who as president of the Byelorussian Central Rada in Minsk, ran the administration for the Germans in the occupied territory and the Byelorussian People's Self-Assistance (BPS); though a charitable organization the latter, under Ermachenko and Iu. Sobolevski, had demanded complete autonomy from the occupation authorities and the creation of a Byelorussian government and Byelorussian army. The BPS had come under the Central Rada on 1 March 1944, but the Rada itself was disbanded just as Operation Bagration commenced – no doubt in the full knowledge of what was about to take place. The traitors fled like rats from a sinking ship.

Army Group North

To the north of Army Group Centre lay Generaloberst Georg Lindemann's Army Group North (consisting of Busch's old command, 16th Army, under Hansen and General Herbert Loch's 18th Army), which had by far the fewest armoured formations with just one panzer division and one SS-panzergrenadier division. The rest of its forces comprised twenty-eight infantry divisions, three security divisions, three SS-grenadier divisions, two Luftwaffe field divisions and a field training division. Army Group North's reserve formation was the 12th Panzer. SS-Obergruppenführer Georg Keppler's III SS Panzer Corps consisted of the 11th SS-Panzergrenadier Division Nordland, 20th SS-Grenadier Division and the 285th Security Division. To the south of Busch's command was Army Group North Ukraine and beyond that Army Group South Ukraine.

Army Group North Ukraine

Generalfeldmarschall Walter Model's Army Group North Ukraine at this stage contained two panzer armies and four panzer corps, along with eight panzer divisions, one Hungarian tank division and two panzergrenadier divisions, although it was weaker in armour than Army Group Centre. The rest of the units consisted of twenty-six infantry divisions (including three Jäger and one security division), plus another seven Hungarian infantry divisions.

The Army Group's reserves included the 9th SS and 10th SS Panzer Divisions and the 16th SS Panzergrenadier Division. Generaloberst Erhard Raus's 1st Panzer Army contained the 1st, 7th, 8th and 17th Panzer Divisions, while Generaloberst Josef Harpe's 4th Panzer Army's reserves included the 4th and 5th Panzer Divisions. The XXIV, XXXXVI, XXXXVIII and LVI Panzer Corps component formations were only infantry divisions.

Raus had been involved in the invasion of Russia with the 6th Panzer Division and in early September 1941 took command of the division; following Stalingrad he took charge of the newly formed XI Corps. He was appointed to 1st Panzer Army on 18 May 1944.

The 1st Panzer Army's XXXXVI Panzer Corps had taken part in Operation Barbarossa and fought at Kiev, Putivl, Vyazma and Volokolamsk. It was subsequently involved in the fighting at Rusa-Volokolamsk, Rzhev, Vyazma and Yelnya before fighting at Kursk. The corps withdrew to the Svin area in September 1943 and to Mozyr that December. By the new year it had been transferred to the southern sector and fought at Vinnitsa and later on the Niester. Its XXIV Panzer Corps was formed in June 1942 from XXIV Corps, and up to 1943 had fought on the central sector until switching to the southern sector; by June 1944 it was in southern Poland.

The XXXXVIII Panzer Corps was also involved in Operation Barbarossa and fought at Ostrov, Lutsk, Dubno, Kirovograd, Kremenchug, Lubny, Romny, Lvov and Kursk. It later fought in defensive operations around Kursk and fought south of Stalingrad. During the spring of 1943 it fought at Aksai, Kalinov, Tormosin and Morozovsk. It then took part in Kursk.

The 4th Panzer Army fought at Kursk and later fought on the Don, at Kharkov and at Kiev. It was then attached to Army Group North Ukraine. The LVI Panzer Corps belonging to 4th Panzer Army had spent its time countering Soviet partisans in the Spas-Demensk and Kirov area before withdrawing to Krichev and across the Dnepr. It fought at Zhlobin and Kalinkovichi and withdrew through the Pripyat marshes to Brest-Litovsk in the spring of 1944.

Army Group South Ukraine

Army Group South Ukraine, commanded by Generalfeldmarschall Ferdinand Schörner, numbered some six panzer divisions and one panzergrenadier division, comprising the 3rd and 13th Panzer Divisions and the 10th Panzergrenadier Division with the German 6th Army, and 23rd Panzer Division with the 8th Army, plus the 24th Panzer Division and 3rd SS Panzer Division with the Romanian 4th Army and the 14th Panzer Division with LVII Panzer Corps.

The group also contained about twenty-five German infantry divisions, nineteen Romanian infantry divisions, three Romanian cavalry divisions and one Romanian armoured division.

This army group had been greatly weakened, especially after 6th Army's destruction at Stalingrad and the subsequent liberation of most of Ukraine. It had been reformed two months later and by April that year it was under General der Artillerie Maximilian de Angelis who led it in the summer of 1944.

In its first incarnation the 8th Army had existed for just over a month in 1939, but it was reformed in July 1943 and General der Infanterie Otto Wöhler took charge shortly after. Half the force was made up of two inadequately equipped Romanian armies, which were not capable of withstanding Soviet weaponry. Supporting Hungarian and Italian forces had already been withdrawn after their mauling in the Stalingrad area.

Last-Minute Success

Just as the partisan war was escalating behind Busch's front lines and just as Bagration was commencing, the Luftwaffe enjoyed a last-minute success that showed the American-Soviet relationship in an unsavoury light. Under the designation of Operation Frantic, the 8th and 15th US Army Air Forces were operating shuttle-bombing raids against the Third Reich between the UK, Italy and the Soviet Union.

This was designed to alleviate pressure on the D-Day landings in Normandy by drawing more Luftwaffe fighter units east. The Americans wanted six bases: Stalin granted them three, at Piryatin, Poltava and Mirgorod, where they were allowed to deploy over 1,200 personnel. Frantic Joe, the very first mission, was conducted on 2 June 1944, just three weeks before Bagration commenced.

The Germans were aware of this activity, and General Rudolf Meister, commanding IV Fliegerkorps, ordered Oberstleutnant Wilhelm Antrup to transfer his Heinkel III bomber wing Kampfgeschwader (KG) 55 'Greif' and Oberstleutnant Fritz Pockrandt's KG 53 'Legion Condor' to Minsk from the Brest-Litovsk–Radom area. This brought them into range of the Frantic bases. Two other wings, KG 4 'General Wever' under Major Reinhard Grauber and KG 27 'Boelcke' commanded by Major Rudi Kiel, were also at secret airfields near Minsk, providing a total of 367 bombers.

Hans-Detlef Herhudt von Rohden reported:

> About 1000 hours on the morning of 21 June 1944, the Chief of Staff of IV Fliegerkorps in the Brest-Litovsk area received an emergency telephone call from Luftflotte 6 headquarters [under Generalfeldmarschall Robert Ritter von Greim]. Fifteen minutes later the Commanding General told his staff that a strong unit of US heavy bombers was flying to Russia. Immediately plans are made to attack. At 1500 the Commanding Officer issued the order: 'Tonight you are to attack the airfields of Poltava and Mirgorod. It is important to destroy simultaneously the US bombers.'

His report also made it clear that Meister ordered the attack on the night of the 21st, before the American bombers had even landed. The feeling was that Meister had been tipped off beforehand. The attack was scheduled for 2400 and the Americans were caught napping without any fighter cover. Antrup and his men were expecting a hot reception from Red Air Force Yak and Aircobra fighters, but they did not intervene.

The Luftwaffe caught seventy-three B-17 Bombers at Poltava; those German planes heading for Mirgorod inadvertently ended up there as well. Poltava was bombed and strafed for almost two hours. The Americans lost forty-seven B-17s, with nineteen others damaged but repairable; 200,000 tons of gasoline were destroyed, halting the shuttle raids.

The American aircraft at Mirgorod were evacuated, though on the night of 22–23 June Antrup and the others attacked Mirgorod and stayed over the target for two hours. Again the Red Air Force did not contest the attack. A solitary

B-17 was missed, but hundreds of thousands of gallons of gasoline were again destroyed.

The Red Air Force was nowhere to be seen despite the fact it was massing to support Operation Bagration, while fifty-five American Mustang fighters at Piryatin were not allowed to take off. The conclusion was that Stalin wanted the Americans out of the Soviet Union and had not lifted a finger to help. In some circles there is even speculation that he colluded in some way with the Germans. In total the Frantic missions cost the Americans 1,030 aircraft and were widely viewed as a waste of effort and resources.

CHAPTER 6

Bagration: Stalin's Revenge Unleashed

On 22 June Stalin began to probe Busch's forward units. This was designed to draw the defenders into their positions ready for the massive artillery bombardment the following day. The Soviets also manoeuvred themselves into their off points. The Vitebsk bulge was attacked by Bagramyan's 1st Baltic Front striking from the north, with the 6th Guards Army trying to pierce the defences near Sirotino, while Chernyakovsky's 3rd Byelorussian Front attacked in the Vysochany area south of Vitebsk.

'The Hurricane Broke'

On the northern flank of Reinhardt's 3rd Panzer Army lay the 252nd Infantry Division, nicknamed the *Eichenlaub* or Oak Leaf division, under General der Infanterie Walter Melzer. It occupied the vulnerable junction between Army Group Centre and Army Group North. The 252nd's principal combat units were Grenadier Regiments 7,461 and 472, and Artillery Regiment 252. This division and Korps Abteilung D formed General Wuthmann's IX Corps.

Wuthmann was holding a front north of Vitebsk covering 40 miles (64km). His command lay directly in the path of General Beloborodov's 43rd Army (1st, 60th and 92nd Rifle Corps, 1st Tank Corps and 3rd Air Army), part of Bagramyan's 1st Baltic Front. Beloborodov's seven rifle divisions fell on this sector reinforced by a division from Chistyakov's 6th Guards Army. They were also supported by two of Beloborodov's tank brigades, and it was intended to cut a hole 15 miles (25km) wide in Wuthmann's defences.

Armin Scheiderbauer, serving as the adjutant of II Abteilung, 472nd Grenadier Regiment, having previously served as a platoon and then company commander with the 7th Grenadiers, remembered:

> In the course of the night of 21 June and in the early hours of 22 June, the Soviets pushed up nearer and nearer to our position. At 4am the enemy's heavy barrage began and at 4.20am they attacked on a wide front. Breakthroughs were made in the sector of I Abteilung Grenadier Regiment 7 and the division's Füsilier Abteilung.
>
> As I recall, the hurricane broke at 3.05am, on the dot, just as it had in 1941. The fire was concentrated mainly on the Main Line of Resistance. Only isolated heavy calibre shells dropped in the village. We had long since left our quarters in [the] houses, and were waiting in the cover trenches

beside them. I had been woken by the crash of bursting shells after just an hour's sleep. That action began for me with a thundering within my skull, weakened by schnapps and tiredness. Towards 5am the Abteilung received orders to move to the second line, that is, the trench that was planned for that purpose. It was good news, because as soon as the enemy attacked up front, we could expect the fire to be moved to the rear. Then it would be mostly the firing positions, villages, and roads, the position of which had been long established by enemy reconnaissance, that would be under fire.

The 252nd soon found itself cut in half as the 461st Grenadier Regiment was pushed north-westward and the second line became the main line of resistance. Scheiderbauer joined Hauptmann Müller and an 8.8cm anti-tank gun crew concealed in some woods holding the road to Lovsha. The first two T-34 tanks were knocked out in quick succession.

'The number one gunner of our anti-tank gun watched with a tense expression,' said Scheiderbauer, 'and once again pressed the firing button. Once again the shot scored a direct hit and from the tank the whole turret blew into the air. High flames shot up.'

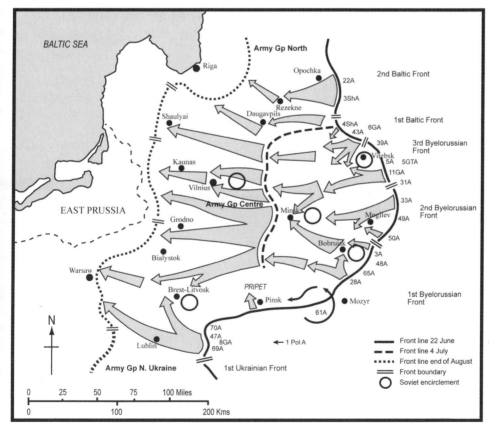

Operation Bagration, June–August 1944.

Busch was immediately advised by telephone of the major attack on the morning of the 22nd, which had overrun the 252nd Infantry, swept aside the 299th Infantry and forced the 256th to withdraw. A counter-attack by the 9th Infantry to seal the Soviets' three deep penetrations achieved nothing. What was particularly worrying was that while the left flank of Army Group Centre was threatening to disintegrate, it had also lost all contact with Army Group North. Busch, cutting short his leave, hurried back to Minsk in the afternoon.

Army Group Centre's combat diary astutely recorded:

> On 22 June – the third anniversary of the beginning of the war with the Soviet Union – the enemy opened their summer offensive with attacks against the front of Army Group Centre. In the 2nd Army area of operations, they had the character of reconnaissance attacks, in the 4th Army area of operations they were assessed as pre-attacks to gain assault departure positions. In the 9th Army area of operations it remained quiet on this day. On the other hand, the enemy began the real attack against the 3rd Panzer Army with the main effort against the VI Army Corps southeast of Vitebsk and, surprisingly, also northwest of the city in the IX Army Corps area of operations between Sirotino and the left boundary of the Army Group... The major attack northwest of Vitebsk came as a complete surprise to the German leadership, because the previous enemy picture did not indicate such an enemy concentration.

During the evening it was proposed committing the 24th Infantry Division and the 909th Assault Gun Brigade to close the gap on the Obol and with Army Group North. This did not really prove possible. Busch was not greatly concerned and flew from Minsk to see Hitler at Obersalzberg in Bavaria.

On the night of 22–23 June the Red Air Force conducted around 1,000 sorties, bombing German positions. Over 1,000 long-range aircraft struck German airfields at Baranovichi, Bialystok, Bobruisk, Brest, Luninets, Minsk and Orsha, as well as the railways. This was nothing compared to what was to come.

The Soviet Barrage

Bagration commenced officially at 0500 on 23 June with a barrage that lasted for over two hours in some sectors, ranging to a depth of nearly 4 miles (6km). The Soviets also used a double rolling barrage for the first time, which consisted of one group rolling back with the second concentrating on the main defence line. The intention was to trap the defenders, and the effect on morale must have been crippling. The defenders would first have to endure the barrage rolling toward them, the shells tearing great chunks out of the ground and up into the air, then over them and behind them, cutting off their retreat.

For the Germans the density of the Soviet barrage was truly shocking. The four Soviet fronts brought to bear 24,000 guns and mortars along the 428 mile (690km) line. Up to 90 per cent of the artillery was deployed on the breakthrough sectors, which only represented 10 to 20 per cent of the overall width of the fronts themselves.

This equated to 35 artillery pieces per kilometre, with 178 per kilometre in the breakthrough sectors. In total about 17,000 weapons were directed in support of the specific breakthrough sectors. To the north on the 1st Baltic Front, the 43rd Army alone had 150 batteries concentrated on the 4 mile (7km) wide breakthrough sector. Way to the south Rokossovsky's 1st Byelorussian Front had massed 69 regiments of artillery, 40 of which had been shipped up to the front by train.

For fifteen minutes the Soviet gunners poured hot metal onto the Germans' positions to a depth of 2 miles (3km); after that there were 90 minutes of fire directed at observed targets, artillery positions and weapons pits. There were also 20 minutes of bombardment dropped onto the Germans' main line of resistance and their rear areas.

The Soviets varied the timing of their traditional rolling barrage; otherwise the German infantry would have withdrawn to their second trench line and simply moved back once the barrage finished. If the Soviets had used a feint barrage the Germans would have withdrawn and had their divisional artillery target their first trench line once the Soviets had occupied it. This tactic, though, had proved so effective that the Soviets soon learned not to risk occupying German positions.

The resulting smoke and early morning fog greatly hampered the supporting air attacks by the Red Air Force. Only Chernyakovsky's 3rd Byelorussian Front enjoyed clear weather, which allowed Pe-2 bombers from General Khryukin's 1st Air Army to carry out 160 sorties. The ground-attack Shturmoviks had to wait until the artillery and rocket launchers had finished their work. Afterwards the Soviet infantry surged forward to seize tactical ground that would provide cover and could be exploited as a springboard for the impending breakthrough.

The German doctrine of elastic defence was designed to beat off enemy attacks with minimum loss rather than holding ground; however, by 1944 Hitler was simply defending too great a front with insufficient forces to conduct this doctrine effectively. Constructing a true picture of how the German divisions reacted to this colossal bombardment is difficult, as few records at divisional and regimental level exist.

Surviving reports for 4th and 9th Armies show that each German division was covering twice the normal prescribed frontage with 15 to 20 miles (about 24–32km): this equated to roughly 80 men per mile, including a handful of artillery pieces and assault guns holding a depth of 3 miles (5km). Trenches, weapons pits, barbed wire and minefields were the order of the day – concrete defences were very few.

This was far too large an area for the divisional artillery to protect. Although the defenders had enough mines, artillery ammunition was a problem, which greatly curtailed the ability to conduct counter-battery fire. Disastrously the 3rd Panzer Army and 9th Army had at most only 3,000 10.5cm howitzer rounds for such operations.

Around midday on the 24th Scheiderbauer and his comrades of the 252nd Infantry withdrew behind the Vitebsk–Polotsk railway line. He and Müller had great difficulty in preventing the men from jumping onto a goods train waiting at Lovsha station about to set off for Polotsk. The train had got no more than 100 metres when it was blasted by Soviet troops.

The 1st Baltic Front, after rapidly breaking through the German defences as early as the 24th, crossed the Western Dvina at Beshenkovichi and established bridgeheads. The 43rd Army's 60th Infantry Corps reached Gnezdilovichi, west of Vitebsk, just 3 to 6 miles (5–10km) from the 3rd Byelorussian Front's 39th Army's 5th Guards Corps pressing from the opposite direction, thereby threatening the two Luftwaffe field divisions exposed in the bulge in the German line west of Vitebsk.

On the first day of the offensive the 3rd Byelorussian Front made short work of the German defences around Bogushevsk, south of Vitebsk. The following day General N.S. Oslikovsky's 3rd Guards Cavalry Corps, overtaking the infantry, pushed west of Bogushevsk. However, in the Orsha area German artillery remained intact and held up the advance, so Rotmistrov's 5th Guards Tank Army was directed toward Bogushevsk.

Fester Platz Vitebsk – 3rd Panzer Army

By mid-afternoon Busch had informed OKH that in the face of the Soviet pincer movement the situation around Vitebsk looked particularly precarious, and Reinhardt's 3rd Panzer did not have the ability to restore the situation. Overall the balance sheet favoured the Soviets, with a three to one advantage in manpower, ten to one in tanks and self-propelled artillery, and eight to one in guns and mortars. The correlation of forces was such that Busch's troops would be overwhelmed if they did not conduct a fighting withdrawal.

OKH, believing that an attack on Army Group North Ukraine was imminent, refused to release any reinforcements. Although 3rd Panzer Army could have been instructed to withdraw behind the Dvina River, Hitler would not abandon Vitebsk.

Vitebsk was not new to war. During the First World War the city served as the headquarters of the regional military district and had a garrison of 40,000 men. It also had a historical link to Prince Bagration – Napoleon had hoped to trap the Imperial Russian Army in the area and bring it to battle; however, Barclay de Tolly, commanding the Russian 1st Army of the West, knew that Bagration's 2nd Army would not reach him in time and, leaving just a rearguard at Vitebsk, withdrew. On 11 July 1812 the 1st Russian Army retreating from Polotsk to Moscow came to Vitebsk, where its 4th Corps, commanded by Count Osterman-Tolstoy, conducted a rearguard action against the French army. For two days, from 13 to 15 July, 9,000 Russians held 20,000 French troops at bay on the western outskirts of the town.

By 1940 Vitebsk was an important industrial centre providing almost a quarter of the republic's industrial output. The population had grown to 180,000, though including the surrounding regions was nearer a quarter of a million people. In 1943 the resistance in Vitebsk numbered 847 underground workers, but during February–October the Germans arrested about 130 of them, putting an end to the activity of many resistance groups. Those arrested were tortured and then shot.

By the end of 23 June overall the Red Army was making good progress and the Germans had still not woken up to the fact that this was Stalin's main assault on the Eastern Front. General Heidkämper, Reinhardt's chief of staff, was dismayed at the rapidity of the Red Army advances, and that day he and Reinhardt were involved in the first of a series of heated meetings with Busch when they demanded the rapid evacuation of Vitebsk. Busch's response was an unequivocal 'no', nor would he permit 3rd Panzer Army's reserves to be deployed until he got permission from the Army's High Command.

By the evening of 23–24 June Malyshev's 4th Assault Army had turned Wuthmann's IX Corps' front line, and in places had pierced the Tiger Line which formed the second belt of defences. The greatest danger though was to the north of Vitebsk, where Chistyakov's 6th Guards Army was on the brink of cutting off Gollwitzer's LIII Corps in the city from Wuthmann's IX Corps.

To the dismay of the defenders of Vitebsk, at 0245 IX Corps was instructed to fight its way back from the Tiger Line to the defences west of the Dvina. By midday the Soviets had reached the river and it was apparent to General Reinhardt that they were intent on cutting Vitebsk off and that there was little to keep the 6th Guards Army and 43rd Army from linking up to the west.

General Kurt Zeitzler, chief of the general staff of the army, arrived at Busch's Minsk HQ early on the morning of 24 June to be briefed on the developing situation. Now was the time for Busch to show his mettle and demand a general withdrawal for Army Group Centre. Instead he opted to request permission to abandon Vitebsk and withdraw 3rd Panzer Army to the south-west.

Afterwards Zeitzler flew to Obersalzberg to report to Hitler. He put the proposal to Hitler that afternoon with predictable results: stay put, and reinforcements would be sent in the shape of just two divisions, 5th Panzer and the 212th Infantry.

That afternoon Zeitzler telephoned Reinhardt, to be told in no uncertain terms that Vitebsk was in imminent danger of being cut off and that this was the last chance to save Gollwitzer's command. Reinhardt must have taken a deep breath when he was informed Hitler was against evacuating Vitebsk because of the loss of equipment this would involve. Reinhardt pointed out that almost five divisions would be lost if they did not immediately withdraw. Zeitzler left his colleague on hold for ten long minutes while he hurried off to confer with Hitler. When he returned to the line he hesitated before announcing: 'The Führer has decided that Vitebsk will be held.'

Minutes later Reinhardt's HQ received a radio message from Gollwitzer: the road west from Vitebsk was under immediate threat from enemy forces. This was relayed to Busch with another plea to withdraw; within the hour Busch was onto Hitler's HQ only to be told that Vitebsk must be held, and if the road was cut it was to be reopened by counter-attack. Busch, knowing full well that they would be too late, plucked up courage and phoned Hitler personally that evening. Whatever argument Busch offered, Hitler was adamant Gollwitzer's corps would remain in Vitebsk.

Busch began planning counter-offensives as if it were the good old days, though Hitler did not make it readily apparent where the forces for such an operation would come from. Pathetically Hitler ordered the other army groups each to send a single division to help Army Group Centre. In the event four divisions were transferred, but even if they had got there in time they would have been unable to affect the impending battle.

'What can I do? What can I do?' lamented Busch to his chief of staff, Lieutenant General Hans Krebs. Clearly he was unable or unwilling to put his career on the line to safeguard his men. But in any case Busch and Hitler had already lost any chance of retrieving the situation and maintaining some level of initiative against the Red Army. Meanwhile the rest of 3rd Panzer Army, IX and VI Corps, were being driven away from *Fester Platz* Vitebsk.

If this had been von Manstein in command he would have simply taken matters into his own hands and found a way of working the situation to his own favour and that of the men under his command. Busch though was a lesser general who could not or would not 'think out of the box'. A general had to be proactive not reactive to stay ahead of his enemy.

General Gollwitzer was determined that his LIII Corps would not become trapped, and sensibly prepared to conduct a fighting withdrawal. He ordered Generalleutnant Robert Pistorius's 4th Luftwaffe Field Division just north of the city to the south-west, ready to spearhead a breakout. While Hitler refused to authorize any retreat, Busch told Gollwitzer to use both his Luftwaffe divisions to prepare two breakouts while Generalleutnant Alfons Hitter's 206th and Generalmajor Claus Müller-Bulow's 246th Infantry Divisions defended Vitebsk.

Reinhardt and Heidkämper paced the room in frustration as situation reports flowed in. Then unexpectedly, two whole hours later at 1830, 3rd Panzer received a radio message from Hitler instructing that LIII Corps should fight its way out to the Tiger Line, but one division should be nominated to hold the fortress. Hitter and his 206th Infantry Division were to stay behind to cover the withdrawal; however, because of all this dithering, Pistorius was now encircled near Ostrovno. Heidkämper was far from happy: what logic was this? If a whole corps could not hold the position what was the point of sacrificing a single division?

Reinhardt sent a message of good luck on the morning of the 25th:

To General Gollwitzer. Best of luck to you and your men in fighting your way out. You must do this soon, but I am convinced you still have a good chance of success. My best wishes to General Hitter and his division, who for the moment must stick to their guns and if needs be, sacrifice themselves for you.

It is doubtful that Reinhardt convinced himself, Gollwitzer or Hitter that his optimism was well founded, but what else could he say? In reality the Red Army's trap was already sprung and nothing would be able to prise it open; Soviet blocking forces were simply too strong.

At 1312 hours on the 25th Gollwitzer signalled: 'Situation has changed. Completely encircled by constantly reinforcing enemy. 4th Luftwaffe Field

Division exists no longer! 246th Infantry Division and 6th Luftwaffe Field Division in heavy combat on several fronts. Various penetrations into the city of Vitebsk.' Ominously at 1500 Gollwitzer's HQ signalled: 'Situation at its climax.'

By early afternoon the 1st Baltic Front's 1st Tank Corps under General Butkov had reached the Dvina and taken a damaged bridge. In the 3rd Byelorussian Front's sector Lyudnikov's 39th Army was also pushing on the river and, supported by some elements of the 43rd, was assigned the task of destroying the German units trapped at Vitebsk. The Germans tried to break through the Soviet cordon, launching twenty-five counter-attacks on the 25th and a similar number the following day, but without success.

Despite the poor flying weather, the Red Air Force's attacks were described as 'murderous', and von Greim, commander of Luftflotte 6, while visiting Reinhardt's 3rd Panzer Army HQ on 25 June, said that 'with his limited resources there was nothing he could do about it'. On the evening of the 25th Lyudnikov finally overwhelmed Pistorius's 4th Luftwaffe Field Division and then turned on Müller-Bulow's 246th Infantry and Generalmajor Rudolf Peschel's 6th Luftwaffe Field Division.

When Busch asked OKH and Hitler for permission to try to save Hitter's 206th Infantry, Hitler ridiculously ordered that a staff officer be dropped into Vitebsk to remind Gollwitzer of his instructions.

Reinhardt was furious and phoned Busch: 'Tell the Führer that if he stands by this order, there is only one officer in the 3rd Panzer Army that can carry it out, and that is the commander. I am ready to execute this order!' All this mattered little as Hitter was trapped and the two other divisions were isolated to the south-west.

Gollwitzer was in a hopeless position by the evening of the 26th and, defying orders, split his forces up with instructions to try to head west. His LIII Corps' last message was sent out at 0345 to Reinhardt requesting air support and the location of the nearest German units. Gollwitzer and his remaining men got a dozen miles before being surrounded again.

South of Vitebsk the 197th and 299th Infantry Divisions were spread too thinly and also under threat. The former withdrew west and the latter was overrun, while the 256th, 3rd Panzer's southernmost division, withdrew to the south-west. The 197th, led by Generalmajor Hans Hahne, from Pfeiffer's VI Corps, was destroyed at Vitebsk, as was Hitter's 206th and Müller-Bulow's 246th from LIII Corps. Sturmgeschütz Brigade 245 was likewise lost near Vitebsk.

The commanders of the ill-fated 4th and 6th Luftwaffe Field Divisions, Robert Pistorius and Rudolf Peschel, were both killed. Gollwitzer and Hitter surrendered on the morning of 27 June. Thus between the second and fourth days of Bagration, Hitler had recklessly thrown away his single strongest position on the whole of the Fatherland Line.

Those men who did escape soon fell prey to bandit country, full of Soviet partisans hell-bent on revenge and with little interest in taking prisoners. The Soviets and the Germans argued over the details, with Gollwitzer claiming his command lost 5,000 killed and 22,000 captured, and the Soviets contesting

20,000 Germans killed and 10,000 captured – no matter the exact figures, the fact remained that Gollwitzer's LIII Corps had been needlessly wiped off the map.

Fester Platz Orsha – 4th Army

To the south Soviet inroads against 4th Army were being made, and they were aiming for the Moscow–Minsk highway that also linked Smolensk with Orsha. During the First World War German troops had occupied Orsha from February 1917 till August 1918. Similarly during the Napoleonic Wars Orsha had been occupied by French troops.

This region was defended by General der Infanterie Paul Völckers' XXVII Corps, consisting of Generalleutnant Paul Schürmann's 25th Panzergrenadier Division, Generalleutnant Hans Traut's 78th Sturm (Assault) Division and Generalmajor Günther Klammt's 260th Infantry Division. The units holding the line north-east of Orsha were the 78th and 256th.

After previous Soviet attempts in this area Traut's command was well prepared and was also the strongest infantry formation in Byelorussia. Known as the Bad-Württ Sturm Division, it was a fairly new unit, having been formed from the 78th Infantry Division in early January 1943 under current corps commander Paul Völckers. The latter unit had been blooded in France and on the Eastern Front. Generalleutnant Hans Traut first commanded the 78th from April to November 1943, before being replaced by Herbert von Larisch; he then reassumed command on 15 February 1944.

Most German divisions' fighting strength was about 3,000 but Traut's unit numbered 5,700 men, fielding three assault regiments, 14,195 and 215, supported by their own dedicated armour units consisting of an assault gun battalion, Sturmgeschütz Abteilung 189, and a tank destroyer battalion, Panzerjäger Abteilung 178. These were equipped with 31 StuG III assault guns and 18 powerful Nashorn 88mm self-propelled anti-tank guns. Artillerie Regiment 178 and Flak Abteilung 293 provided artillery and anti-aircraft support respectively, with 46 light and 55 heavy artillery pieces. For the Soviets this would be a tough nut to crack.

To the south lay the 25th Panzergrenadiers who were also well equipped. Schürmann's division included two panzergrenadier regiments, a panzer battalion (with assault guns), a Panzerjäger battalion, a panzer reconnaissance battalion and an artillery regiment.

Traut's men were used to and expecting Soviet bombardment, but the ferocity of the shelling on the 23rd must have stunned even them. Minefields and barbed-wire belts were obliterated, sandbags were torn asunder and scattered, weapons pits and trenches vanished. Any weapons caught on the surface soon became so many twisted, useless pieces of steel.

General Galitsky's 11th Guards Army, with three divisions striking toward Orsha from the south, had three special assault groups to overcome Traut's defences, which included T-34 tanks fitted with minerollers followed by a heavy tank regiment with twenty-one IS-2 or KV tanks, then assault engineers and a heavy assault gun regiment with twenty-one ISU-152s. Infantry regiments supported by flame-thrower tanks and SU-76 assault guns came behind the armour.

These impressive forces soon came to grief up against Traut's remaining minefields, tank traps and men armed with the Panzerfaust man-portable anti-tank weapon. To the north Galitsky's two other rifle divisions rolled forward without the same level of armoured support, but cleared a wood and Cavalry-Mechanized Group Oslikovsky (3rd Guards Cavalry Corps) was ordered to follow up.

The plan was that Galitsky's 11th Guards would overwhelm the German defences along the Moscow–Minsk highway, which would permit Marshal Pavel Rotmistrov's 5th Guards Tank Army to deploy across the terrain either side. Although the 11th Guards struggled against the determined resistance of Traut's 78th Sturm Division, the 1st Guards Rifle Division pushed between it and the 256th Infantry to the north. Galitsky then pushed Burdeyny's 2nd Guards Tanks Corps through this gap along a railway line.

The Germans counter-attacked south of Lake Orekhi on 24 June and failed. However, the hold-up with the 11th Guards Army meant that Rotmistrov was redirected to Krylov's 5th Army's sector. With Traut's men being slowly overwhelmed General von Tippelskirch knew XXVII Corps must withdraw to the Dnepr. A sense of panic began to fill those in Orsha: defying orders, Tippelskirch allowed some units to fall back, but it was too late. Burdeyny's tanks swept north of the city toward the end of the 26th, and his T-34s rolling to the west caught a German train full of wounded being evacuated from Orsha and blew it from the rails. That night the 11th Guards and 31st Armies overran the city.

The 286th Sicherung or Security Division under Generalleutnant Hans Oschmann was largely destroyed at Orsha. This was 4th Army's only reserve formation, and its remains were eventually used to form the 286th Infantry Division. Also that day Oslikovsky's 3rd Guards Cavalry Corps reached Senno to the south-west of Bogushevsk, while the 5th Guards Tank Army cut the Minsk road near Tolochin south-west of Orsha.

Fester Platz Mogilev – 4th Army

Generalleutnant Rudolf Bamler's 12th Infantry Division, part of 4th Army's XXXIX Panzer Corps, had been defending a 20 mile (32km) sector along the Pronya bend east of Mogilev since March 1944. The city of Mogilev lies on the river Dnepr 125 miles (201km) from Minsk. Under commandant Generalmajor Gottfried von Erdmannsdorf it was an important rail junction, with lines to Orsha, Osipovichi, Zhlobin and Krichev, and roads to Minsk, Gomel, Vitebsk, Bobruisk and other towns.

Mogilev was the site of the first major defection of Soviet troops to Hitler, when on 22 August 1941 Major Ivan Nikitich Kononov and his Soviet 436th Infantry Regiment had crossed over. This unit was allowed to operate independently in Byelorussia with Army Group Centre. Mogilev again had a special historical resonance to Operation Bagration, for it was here while commanding the 2nd

Army of the West that Bagration was defeated before going on to glory at Borodino.

On 12th Infantry's northern flank the I Abteilung or 1st Battalion, Fusilier Regiment 27, under Major Heinz-Georg Lemm, was holding a 2½ mile (4km) front behind the Pronya River. The latter was very wide and provided an effective anti-tank obstacle, while beyond lay Generalleutnant Walter Scheller's 337th Infantry Division. Rather than hold the riverbank the battalion had dug in 300–500 metres away on a series of 30 metre high hills. A second trench line was dug up to 600 metres away on the reverse slopes. In eight weeks the battalion had prudently dug five trench lines.

The 12th and 337th Infantry Divisions lay directly in the path of the 2nd Byelorussian Front's 49th Army under General I.T. Grishin, who had massed ten rifle divisions with which to bulldoze them out of the way. The front also had an artillery density of 181 guns and mortars per mile.

By the evening of the 22nd, 1st Abteilung, Fusilier Regiment 27, had successfully driven the Soviet advance parties back across the Pronya. The battalion then withdrew to its second defensive line, which was fortunate: at 0400 on the 23rd a three-hour Soviet barrage fell on the first line. Secure on the reverse slopes the battalion suffered only forty casualties.

Once the barrage was over the troops bravely reoccupied their first line. The Soviet infantry was stopped 200 metres from these positions, and follow-on attacks of regimental strength were also beaten off. That night the exhausted defenders fell back to their second line once more and in the morning moved back to the first line. Finally on the night of the 24th, under threat of being surrounded, Lemm and his battalion retreated.

Zakharov's 2nd Byelorussian Front offensive opened with Grishin's attack north of Mogilev. Supported by General K.A. Vershinin's 4th Air Army, his men began crossing the Dnepr on the 26th. To the south General I.V. Boldin's 50th Army also thrust toward Mogilev. East of the city the 33rd and 49th Armies hit the 337th Infantry Division and broke through on the Ryasna–Mogilev road. Once the first and second German trench lines were breached, Soviet armour poured into the rear area of Weidling's XXXIX Panzer Corps.

General von Tippelskirch, acting as 4th Army's commander while Heinrici was on sick leave, recommended a withdrawal behind the Dnepr. 'Any voluntary abandonment of parts of the main line [of resistance] still intact is out of the question,' responded Busch, with his characteristic lack of foresight or strategic judgement.

Tippelskirch was dismayed, as was Reinhardt, at Busch and Hitler's complete inflexibility, which was in complete violation of the concept of elastic defence, which had evolved up to 1943:

It would have been much wiser strategy to withdraw the whole front in time. The Russians always needed a long pause for preparation after any German withdrawal, and they always lost disproportionately when attacking. A series of withdrawals by adequately large steps would have worn down the

Russian strength, besides creating opportunities for counterstokes at a time when the German forces were still strong enough to make them effective.

To plug the gap east of Mogilev, Tippelskirch had little choice but to throw in the recently arrived 60th Panzergrenadier Division Feldherrnhalle under Generalmajor Friedrich-Carl von Steinkeller. He was to join the battle in General Robert Martinek's XXXIX Panzer Corps sector. Martinek, who had no panzer units, saw committing the Feldherrnhalle at this stage as folly: what was needed was a new stop line, and Steinkeller's men could provide it.

Martinek asked Steinkeller exactly what he was going to plug. 'We've got nothing but holes here,' said the corps commander. 'Your place is back on the Berezina, so that we should have an interception line there for when we can't hold out on the Dnepr any longer. And that will be pretty soon!'

Once again Busch's complete lack of flexibility was to waste his limited reserves. Predictably the panzergrenadiers were swamped, and just three days later Steinkeller was forced back across the Dnepr with the survivors of his division, only to be taken by the Red Army near the Berezina.

By the 25th Tippelskirch was in a fraught situation: his XXXIX Panzer Corps had been overwhelmed and the armies to the north and south – 3rd Panzer and 9th – were falling apart. Martinek was killed, and was replaced by General Otto Schünemann, who tried to lead the XXXIX Panzer Corps in a westward breakout attempt. He was also killed and the corps disintegrated under the Soviet onslaught.

Two days later Bamler assumed command of Mogilev from Erdmannsdorf just in time to be taken prisoner along with 3,000 troops, all that remained of the 8,000-strong garrison. Lemm's Fusiliers were one of the few units to escape, making it to the Berezina.

Fester Platz Bobruisk – 9th Army

To the south Bobruisk, held by Generalmajor Adolf Hamann, was protected by the Drut River and its marshy flood plain and then the Berezina River. Just as the 3rd Byelorussian Front was pressing on Minsk from the north, Rokossovsky's 1st Byelorussian Front was striking from the south. His front went into action on the 24th in the direction of Bobruisk; Jordan's 9th Army, though suffering heavy casualties, held off his attacks.

Advancing from the Rogachev–Zhlobin sector on the right were General A.V. Gorbatov's 3rd Army, General P.L. Romanenko's 48th Army and General B.S. Bakharov's 9th Tank Corps. On the left were two armies, General P.I. Batov's 65th and General A.A. Luchinsky's 28th pressing south of Parichi, supported by General M.F. Panov's 1st Guards Tank Corps, General I.A. Pliyev's 4th Guards Cavalry Corps and Captain V.V. Grigoryev's Dnepr Combat Flotilla.

The Rogachev assault group made little headway on the first two days because of the swampy ground, bad weather, poor preliminary reconnaissance and the Germans' desperate resistance. The swampy conditions held up Rokossovsky's men, but on the 24th Generalleutnant Ernst Philipp's 134th Infantry Division had its front pierced to a depth of 6 miles (10km) by the Soviet 3rd Army. Philipp had only been appointed at the beginning of June and he had arrived just in time to witness the destruction of his new command.

In contrast the Parichi assault group achieved better results. On the first day the German defences were breached, permitting the 65th Army's mobile group, the 1st Guards Tank Corps, to advance 12 miles (20km); the next day it had pushed to within 6 miles (10km) south-west of Bobruisk. In the meantime the infantry thrust northward towards the city and Glusk. Pliyev's corps also moved to surround the Germans.

General Jordan, commanding 9th Army, sought and received Busch's permission to commit the 20th Panzer Division to try to stem the Soviet tide. The division could muster seventy-one Panzer Mk IVs; its other panzer regiment was busy re-equipping with Panthers. At this moment Batov's 65th Army broke through on the southern approaches to Bobruisk, and Rokossovsky committed the 1st Guards Tank Corps to exploit the breach. Perhaps panicking, Jordan ordered 20th Panzer to retrace its tracks and head south, bumping into the Soviets near Slobodka, south of Bobruisk.

Now not only was Bobruisk under threat but also those German divisions still east of the Berezina. By the 26th, the 20th Panzer had been driven back to the city with the Soviet 9th Tank Corps bearing down on it from the east and the Soviet 1st Guards Tank Corps from the south. The 1st Guards Tank Corps cut the roads from Bobruisk to the north and north-west on the night of 26–27 June.

In the Rogachev sector Gorbatov asked permission to change the line of advance of the 9th Tank Corps to the swampy forest area, where German defences were reported to be weak. Zhukov supported this request and on the 26th the 9th Tank Corps pushed forward to reach east of Bobruisk.

CHAPTER 7

5th and 12th Panzer Strike Back

With the Dnepr and Dvina defences breached, the next obstacle facing the Red Army was the Berezina. Only now, with Rotmistrov's 5th Guards Tank Army (3rd Guards Tank, Cavalry and Mechanized corps) and the 2nd Tank Corps charging south-west toward Minsk, did OKH recognize that this offensive was not diversionary. Once east of Borisov, German resistance held up Rotmistrov for little more than two days.

On 27 June Galitsky's 11th Guards and General V.V. Glagolev's 31st Armies liberated Orsha. The following day, with air cover from the Red Air Force, Soviet motorized units advancing on a 37 mile (60km) front approached the Berezina, with General N.I. Krylov's 5th Army, comprising three rifle corps, reaching the river first.

General von Tippelskirch knew that his first duty was to his men and ordered 4th Army to retire on the Dnepr. Busch countermanded Tippelskirch, who ignored him. Only on the 28th did Busch authorize 4th Army to retreat behind the Berezina, but Tippelskirch was already there, having lost 130,000 of his 165,000 men. In the meantime Rokossovsky's 1st Byelorussian Front smashed through 9th Army's front while Jordan dithered for twenty-four hours over committing his reserve, the 20th Panzer Division.

Borisov – 4th Army

The 5th Panzer Division was moved up from Kovel to defensive positions east of Borisov with a view to covering those troops withdrawing from Mogilev, which had been overrun late on the 27th. Under General der Panzertruppen Karl Decker, 5th Panzer began to arrive in Minsk on 26 June with the all but impossible task of holding the Moscow–Minsk highway. The division was equipped with 70 Panthers and 55 Panzer IVs, supported by Hauptmann von Beschwitz's 29 Tiger Is of Schwere Panzer Abteilung 505. Their first mission was to put a stop line in place north-east of Borisov.

Decker had taken over 5th Panzer in early September 1943 when its key units consisted of Panzer Regiment 31, Panzerjäger Abteilung 53, Panzergrenadier Regiments 13 and 14, and Panzer Artillery Regiment 116. Formed in November 1938 in Oppeln the division subsequently took part in the invasions of Poland and France, before supplying Panzer Regiment 15 to the newly created 11th Panzer Division. It then took part in the Balkans campaign before transferring to the Eastern Front, where it fought on the central sector with Army Group Centre, taking part in the drive against Moscow.

Beschwitz's heavy Tigers soon went into action against the M4A2 Shermans of General I.A. Bobchenko's 3rd Guards Tank Corps near Krupki, on the 28th. At about 0700 the following day Soviet tanks took Krupki station, and their reconnaissance units bumped into Decker's engineers preparing to blow the bridges on the approaches to Borisov.

To the north at Studenka elements of the Soviet 29th Tank Corps tried to force the Berezina, but were driven off by 5th Panzer's reconnaissance battalion. Instead the corps continued through the marshy areas north-west of Borisov.

On the 29th five rifle divisions of 11th Guards Army reached the tanks near the village of Kostritsa and battle followed with one of the 5th Panzer's panzergrenadier regiments. That evening the Germans withdrew into Borisov. However, the Soviet 26th Rifle Division from the 8th Guards Rifle Corps moved to prevent them escaping westward by blocking the Moscow–Minsk highway.

The Soviet 1st and 31st Guards Rifle Divisions, from Vorobyev's 16th Guards Rifle Corps, crossed the Skha River on the 30th, but east of Zembin were stopped from getting over the Berezina by the presence of 5th Panzer. This mattered little as other Soviet units were already over the Berezina both north and south of Borisov.

North of 5th Panzer the 29th Tank Corps was over, as was the 3rd Guards Mechanized Corps after three tanks from the 35th Guards Tank Brigade created an improvised bridge. South of Borisov five German police regiments could do little to prevent two rifle divisions from the 11th Guards forcing the river.

At the town of Berezino, south of Borisov, General Müller, controlling the remains of two infantry divisions, Generalleutnant Otto Drescher's 267th from Müller's own XII Corps and Generalleutnant Wilhelm Ochsner's 31st from Martinek's XXXIX Panzer Corps, was unable to stop the three rifle corps of General V.V. Glagolev's 31st Army from crossing the river.

By the end of 30 June the Berezina had been breached in numerous points north and south of Borisov and the Germans had no reserves with which to counter-attack these developing bridgeheads. The Luftwaffe threw a number of Fw 190 fighter-bombers against the bridges, but to little effect.

For the defenders of Borisov time was rapidly running out as the 5th Guards Rifle Division surrounded the city, while the 3rd Guards Tank Brigade tried to barge its way in via the main Berezina bridge. Dramatically, as a column of tanks under Lieutenant Pavel Rak rumbled across, Decker's engineers blew the bridge. Only Rak's tank and one other got across, and, supported by a few infantrymen, had to hold out while the Soviets assaulted the city from other directions.

During the afternoon bitter street-fighting heralded the end of the occupation, and by the evening the German defenders had withdrawn. The first Battle of Berezina, fought near Borisov in late November 1812 as Napoleon was retreating from Russia, had seen the French fight their way to freedom. There was to be no similar outcome this time.

By 1 July Borisov was liberated, but three or four German divisions from 4th Army were able to cross the Berezina before Borisov fell. Sturmgeschütz Brigade 189, which had only just been formed from a battalion strength unit of the same designation, was destroyed on the Berezina. The survivors were sent to join Panzerjäger Abteilung 178. With Borisov and the Berezina secured, the road lay open to Minsk.

Fester Platz Bobruisk – 9th Army

By the morning of the 27th General B.S. Bakharov's 9th Tank Corps, comprising three tank and one mechanized brigade, had secured the Berezina crossings from the west side. Rokossovsky, sensing the time was right, committed the 1st Guards Tank Corps and 1st Mechanized Corps from Batov's 65th Army, sending them toward Baranovichi south-west of Minsk.

Rokossovsky's 1st Byelorussian Front trapped a sizeable number of German troops east of Bobruisk. Any withdrawal or breakout attempt had now been left far too late. Soviet artillery and the Red Air Force ensured that the eastern banks of the Berezina became a place of wholesale slaughter.

By daybreak on the 27th Bakharov had cut all the roads and seized the ferries to the north-east of Bobruisk. Over six divisions of 9th Army were encircled in the town and to the south-east. Romanenko's 48th and Batov's 65th Armies formed the inner ring, while Gorbatov's 3rd and Luchinsky's 28th Armies created the outer one. The north-western sector of the inner ring, lacking infantry support, was weak, and was held by brigades from the tank corps.

Just three hours after Rokossovsky's order, Rudenko's 16th Air Army launched 526 aircraft, 400 of them bombers, against the trapped Germans, dropping 12,000 bombs in just under an hour, adding to the conflagration created by the Germans who had torched their supply dumps and stores. In desperation the Germans scattered under this air assault: soldiers fled in panic, and panzers and trucks swerved off the roads in a desperate bid to escape the bombs, only to get stuck in the mud. Those men trying to swim the Berezina were gunned down by the Soviets advancing along the western banks.

'The Nazis ran out of the forests, rushed about the clearings, many attempted to swim across the Berezina but even this did not save them,' noted Rokossovsky. 'Soon the bombed area became an enormous cemetery scattered with bodies and equipment destroyed by the bombing.'

Zhukov recalled triumphantly:

Thus on 27 June, two 'pockets' had been made in the Bobruisk area; trapped in them were the German XXXV Corps and XXXXI Panzer Corps, in all nearly 40,000 men.

I was not able to see the liquidation of the enemy in Bobruisk, but witnessed the rout of the Germans southeast of the city. Hundreds of bombers of Rudenko's 16th Air Army, coordinating missions with the 48th Army, struck blow after blow at the enemy group. Scores of lorries, cars and tanks, fuel and lubricants were burning all over the battlefield. More and more bomber echelons took their bearings from the blazing fires, and kept dropping bombs of various weights.

The terror stricken German soldiers scattered in every direction; those who did not surrender were killed.

That same day the defenders began their futile preparations for a breakthrough in the hope of linking up with the German 4th Army. The Soviets were tipped off by radio intercepts and the very visible destruction of local villages and ammunition dumps by German troops preparing to make a run for it.

Attempts by von Lützow's XXXV Corps to break out to the north, spearheaded by 150 panzers and self-propelled guns, were smashed on the evening of the 27th. They ran headlong into General Teremov's 108th Rifle Division, part of General Erastov's 46th Rifle Corps. Teremov witnessed the carnage:

> Not less than two thousand enemy officers and men advanced towards our positions. The guns opened fire against the attackers when they were 700 yards away, machineguns at a distance of 400 yards. The Nazis continued their advance. Shells burst in their midst. Machineguns mowed down their ranks. The Nazis stepped over the bodies of their dead…It was an insane attack. We saw a terrible sight from our observation post.

The Soviets claimed 10,000 Germans were killed and another 6,000 captured, and Bobruisk itself was surrounded. Confusion seemed to reign with XXXXI Panzer Corps: General Edmund Hoffmeister of the 383rd Infantry Division was temporarily in command while Helmuth Weidling was on leave. In fact he had left just three days before Bagration started and was not able to reassert full control until 1 July.

Hoffmeister, losing his head, dithered over the best course of action at Bobruisk. The net result was that contradictory orders were given to the remnants of three divisions still inside the town.

Weidling proved no more able to stop the Soviets than Jordan, and his attempt to use the 20th Panzer Division to hold open the Berezina bridges at Bobruisk was a dismal failure. Hitler agreed to dispatch 12th Panzer from Army Group North to help lift the siege.

Generalmajor Gerhard Müller took command of the 12th Panzer Division at the end of May 1944 (though he would be replaced by Generalleutnant Erpo Freiherr von Bodenhausen in mid-July). By the summer of 1943 its main combat units had consisted of Panzer Regiment 29, Panzergrenadier Regiments 5 and 25, Panzerjäger Abteilung 2, which included a company of self-propelled guns, and Panzer Artillery Regiment 2, which included a battalion of self-propelled guns.

The division had been formed at Stettin in October 1940 from the 2nd Infantry Division. It initially saw action in the invasion of the USSR, fighting first on the central sector and later in the northern sector. In January 1942 it was transferred to Estonia for refitting but soon returned briefly to the northern sector of the front before being sent to the central sector. It had returned to the northern sector in February 1944, but it would not arrive in time.

Hoffmeister's XXXXI Panzer Corps was given permission to make a run for it, although General Hamann, the *fester Platz* commander, drew the short straw, as he and a division were instructed to act as rearguard; also, 3,500 wounded were to be left behind. Some 5,000 men made a dash for it at 2300 on 28 June.

At 0100 hours Hoffmeister's XXXXI Panzer Corps radioed Army Group Centre:

383rd Infantry Division is in combat around Bobruisk. Since darkness, troop units from all the divisions of the XXXV Army Crops have been streaming into Bobruisk, they are disorganised and without heavy weapons. The commander of 134th Infantry Division shot himself. The commander of 36th Motorised Infantry Division declared that he no longer has any control over his division. Artillery and heavy weapons were destroyed. There is no radio contact with XXXV Army Corps, which had ordered the destruction of the guns.

The tanks of 20th Panzer led the breakout north-west along the western bank of the Berezina, with the rearguard instructed to hold until 0200 on the 29th. The panzers and panzergrenadiers soon found themselves under attack by T-34s and by the Red Air Force. Two other groups who set out on the 29th fared even worse. The survivors managed to cut their way through, but they still had to cover 12 miles (20km) to reach the Svisloch river and 12th Panzer.

A panzergrenadier battalion from 12th Panzer, supported by a company of tanks under Major Blanchbois, attempted unsuccessfully to go to the rescue, but could not get over the Svisloch river north-west of Bobruisk, as the Soviets held the only local bridge. However, many German troops made a swim for it, and it has been estimated that Blanchbois managed to save 15,000 to 20,000 'Bobruiskers' before being forced to withdraw.

On the 28th the 48th Army completed the annihilation of German forces south-east of Bobruisk, and those surrounded in the forests laid down their arms. The following day those still in Bobruisk fought on. By nightfall on the 29th Soviet troops advanced over 60 miles (100km) operating north and north-west of Osipovichi, which lay to the north of Bobruisk, and east of Slutsk, way to the east of Bobruisk.

The 6th Infantry Division under Generalleutnant Walter Heyne, part of von Lützow's XXXV Corps, surrendered to the Red Army on 30 June. Lützow's 45th Infantry Division under Generalmajor Joachim Engel was also lost, as was Hoffmeister's 383rd Infantry, comprising the 531, 532 and 533 Infantry Regiments and the 383 Artillery Regiment.

In total some 5,000 German wounded remained in Bobruisk along with General Hamann, who bravely stayed with them. By 2 July the Soviets claimed to have captured 32,000 German troops in and around Bobruisk and killed another 16,000. *Red Star* correspondent Vasily Grossman was with the troops, and witnessed the carnage in Bobruisk itself:

When we entered Bobruisk some of the buildings in it were ablaze and others lay in ruins. To Bobruisk led the road to revenge! With difficulty, our car finds its way amid scorched and distorted German tanks and self-propelled guns. Men are walking over German corpses. Corpses, hundreds and thousands of them, pave the road, lie in ditches, under the pines, in the green barley. In some places, vehicles have to drive over corpses, so densely they lie upon the ground. People are busy all the time burying them, but they are so many that this work cannot be done in just one day. And the day is exhaustingly hot, still, and people walk and drive pressing handkerchiefs to their noses. A cauldron of death was boiling here, where the revenge was carried out – a ruthless, terrible revenge over those who hadn't surrendered their arms and tried to break out to the west.

In 9th Army's area acting XXXV commander Kurt-Jürgen Freiherr von Lützow was captured, as were Hoffmeister and Hamann. Heyne, commander of the 6th Infantry Division, was also captured in the Bobruisk area, along with Generalleutnant Richert, Generalmajor A. Conrady, Generalmajor J. Engel and Generalleutnant A. Kullmer, commanders of the 35th, 36th, 45th and 296th Infantry Divisions respectively.

Generalleutnants Karl Zutavern and Ernst Philipp, the commanders of the 18th Panzergrenadier Division and the 134th Infantry Division respectively, both reportedly committed suicide rather than surrender. However, Zutavern remained in command of the remains of his division until 10 September.

The 35th Infantry Division, led by Richert from Weidling's XXXXI Panzer Corps, was severely mauled. Likewise General Heribert von Larisch's 129th Infantry Division was badly battered, though Heribert to fight another day.

Generalmajor Gustav Gihr's 707th Infantry Division, in reality a security division, had suffered very heavy casualties by the 27th. This was one of Busch's army group reserve formations, but could do nothing to influence events. The 727 and 747 Grenadier Regiments and 658 Artillerie Abteilung were so weakened that the division was beyond saving.

Gihr had only taken command in early May, having previously been in charge of the 35th Infantry Division. The 707th had served largely behind the lines as a reserve unit. However, the longer-serving members of this unit cannot have relished the prospect of capture, as the division had a very disreputable past. It was the only Wehrmacht division to have taken a significant role in the Holocaust in the Soviet Union. In the autumn and winter of 1941–42 it had assisted German security forces in liquidating some 10,000 Byelorussian Jews.

Lützow vented his feelings upon Vasily Grossman, who conducted an interview for his newspaper:

Generalleutnant Lützow does not praise our army particularly highly. The soldiers are devoid of initiative. When they have no leader on the battlefield they do not know what to do. The artillery is strong. The air force drops bombs with no aim whatsoever.

Lützow was complaining about his total lack of freedom of action. For example, he needed permission from army headquarters to leave a position, the army needed permission from the headquarters of the army group, and the army group needed that of the general staff headquarters. Lützow received permission to retreat with XXXV Army Corps only when the ring of encirclement had already been closed.

In total some 15,000 German troops escaped the Soviet net though had little immediate combat value. Rokossovsky's 1st Byelorussian Front had all but smashed Jordan's 9th Army. Once the Red Army had liberated Bobruisk it spread out behind 9th Army, and of 100,000 men only 30,000 escaped. Rokossovsky now swung toward Minsk and the 3rd Byelorussian Front trapping 4th Army and the survivors of the 9th. In under a week Rokossovsky's troops had killed 50,000 Germans, taken 20,000 PoWs and captured or destroyed 366 armoured vehicles and 2,664 artillery pieces.

Heads Roll

Inevitably heads had to roll for the destruction of Army Group Centre. General Jordan's 9th Army front was in tatters, and Busch flew to Obersalzberg late on the 26th to try to persuade Hitler to rescind his hold-fast orders. Jordan, who accompanied Busch, found himself relieved on the 27th. Jordan's chief of staff, Generalmajor Helmut Staedke, lasted until mid-July, only to return in mid-August.

Busch suffered the same fate as Jordan the following day. Generalfeldmarschall Walter Model, commander of Army Group North Ukraine, was appointed to replace Busch and instructed to fly to Minsk to try to retrieve the situation immediately. The 9th Army's staff, who had no faith in Busch's abilities, greeted the news with a sense of relief.

General Heinz Guderian recalled:

In view of these shattering events Hitler moved his headquarters in mid-July from Obersalzberg to East Prussia. All units that could be scraped together were rushed to the disintegrating front. In place of Generalfeldmarschall Busch, Generalfeldmarschall Model, who already commanded Army Group A [Army Group North Ukraine], was also given command of Army Group Centre – or to be more precise of the gap where that army group had been… He was the best possible man to perform the fantastically difficult task of reconstructing a line in the centre of the Eastern Front.

General Harpe took charge in Model's absence and General Guderian was confident in his abilities, noting: 'Harpe was a former panzer officer of Westphalian origin, calm, reliable, brave and determined. A man of cool understanding and with a clear brain. He too was the right man for the job he had now been given.'

Jordan was succeeded by General der Panzertruppen Nikolaus von Vormann, and two corps commanders from 3rd Panzer Army were replaced, Pfeiffer (by General der Infanterie Horst Grossmann) and Gollwitzer. Reinhardt himself was safe and in fact was soon to find himself stepping into Model's shoes.

Tippelskirch lost command of 4th Army and was replaced on 30 June by Generalleutnant Vincenz Müller, though he briefly reassumed command during 7–18 July until General der Infanterie Friedrich Hossbach took charge. Martinek also went, replaced by Generalleutnant Otto Schünemann, who lasted a single day, then General der Panzertruppen Dietrich von Saucken. Völckers was removed in early July (and eventually succeeded by General der Infanterie Hellmuth Priess).

Remarkably Weiss was to remain with 2nd Army until 12 February 1945, when he was replaced by von Saucken. Likewise his three corps commanders remained in place.

Hitler's usual crisis musical chairs also extended to Army Group North. Lindemann, consulting Zeitzler, gained his support for a limited withdrawal in the face of the powerful wedge driven between his army group and Army Group Centre by Bagramyan's 1st Baltic Front. Zeitzler even suggested evacuating Estonia, which, coupled with Lindemann pulling back his southern flank, would have permitted the creation of a small reserve with which to launch local counter-attacks.

Hitler did his usual trick of demanding that Lindemann not only hold his ground, but also launch a counter-attack to the south-east in support of Army Group Centre. Lindemann was simply not in a position to comply, and found himself replaced by Generalfeldmarschall Friessner.

General der Panzertruppen Walther Nehring took command of Army Group North Ukraine's 4th Panzer Army on 28 June. Harpe's successor was a highly experienced individual. During the invasion of Poland, Nehring served under Heinz Guderian; he later took command of the Afrika Korps in May 1942 and took part in the Battle of Alam Halfa (31 August–7 September 1942), during which he was wounded in an air raid. Between November and December 1942 he commanded the German contingent in Tunisia. After North Africa, Nehring was posted to the Eastern Front, where he commanded the XXIV Panzer Corps from early February 1943.

Effectively the fall of the defensive line Vitebsk, Orsha, Mogilev and Bobruisk meant that it was all over for Army Group Centre. The entire defensive system in the central zone had collapsed. The trail of destruction was truly appalling, and Model must have looked on in despair as the reports on the devastation came in.

By 30 June the first phase of the battle for Byelorussia was over. According to the Soviets they had killed 132,000 Germans and taken another 66,000 prisoner, as well as capturing or destroying 941 tanks, over 5,000 guns and about 30,000 motor vehicles. The German 9th Army had only three to four divisions left, the 4th was facing complete annihilation, and 3rd Panzer Army had lost most of its infantry.

These figures were recorded by Captain Allen and Paul Muratoff in 1946, according to whom the tally breaks down as follows. Bagramyan's 1st Baltic Front accounted for 20,000 killed and 5,000 captured; 300 tanks and self-propelled guns; 626 guns and 2,450 motor vehicles. Chernyakovsky's 3rd Byelorussian Front claimed 32,000 killed; 20,000 prisoners; 195 tanks and self-propelled guns; 1,448 guns and 5,140 motor vehicles. Zakharov's 2nd Byelorussian Front accounted for 30,000 killed; 3,000 prisoners; 80 tanks and self-propelled guns; 410 guns and 6,150 motor vehicles. Rokossovsky's 1st Byelorussian Front claimed the top score for death and destruction inflicted on Army Group Centre: killed, 50,000; captured, 24,000; tanks and self-propelled guns, 366; guns, 2,664; and motor vehicles, 15,920. While the fatalities and equipment totals balance, Allen and Muratoff claim a total of 66,000 PoWs were taken: however, the fronts only account for 52,000, and unfortunately they make no attempt to reconcile the missing 14,000 men.

Nonetheless this catalogue of losses was appalling. It was also clear that the dazed survivors and those fortunate to escape the fortresses of Vitebsk, Orsha, Zhlobin and Bobruisk had left all their weapons and stores behind.

Over the following days Model and his staff must have looked aghast at the reports flowing in from the various army HQs. The messages streaming in from divisional and corps level via field radio, field telephone and those unsevered landlines all said the same thing: can't hold, must evacuate casualties – need reinforcements.

To make matters worse at least nine divisions were to be removed from Army Group Centre to recoup or because they were needed elsewhere: these consisted of the 6th, 12th, 31st, 45th, and 78th Infantry Divisions, as well as the 18th, 25th and 60th Panzergrenadier and 20th Panzer Divisions. All Army Group North could spare were elements of just two infantry divisions to help defend Minsk, while a jäger and panzer division from Army Group North Ukraine were to be rushed to Baranovichi.

Once the situation reports were assessed weak reconstituted units from the mauled infantry divisions largely of battalion strength were dispatched to help: 2nd Army was sent troops from the 35th, 129th (to help 4th Panzer Division) and 232nd Infantry, while the 7th infantry were strengthened by the 102nd; 3rd Panzer Army was provided with men from the 95th, 197th and 246th Infantry; it was intended that 4th Army would get the remnants of the 110th, 267th and 299th Infantry and lastly 9th Army was to be bolstered with the remains of the 134th, 296th and 383rd Infantry. All this though took precious time.

In the coming days a series of battlegroups were hastily thrown together under Anhalt, Flörke, von Gottberg, Harteneck, Lindig, Rothkirch, von Saucken, Tolsdorf and Weidling amongst others to cover the ongoing retreat. The 170th Infantry Division grudgingly dispatched by Army Group North was instructed to reinforce the remains of the 14th and 299th Infantry Divisions as well as the 221st Security Division, which included units from Kampfgruppe Lendle. Along with elements of the 18th Flak Division and the 31st Police Battalion this force was melded into Kampfgruppe Metz to help 5th Panzer north of Minsk. In the meantime Model had a desperate battle to fight before the Byelorrusian capital.

CHAPTER 8

Minsk Freed from the Nazi Yoke

Although by the end of June Hitler and his cronies had grasped that Stalin's offensive in Byelorussia was clearly not a localized operation or a diversionary offensive, concern that the Red Army would strike in Ukraine and the distraction of the fighting in Normandy ensured only limited reinforcements for Army Group Centre. Owing to Hitler's steadfast refusal to allow an orderly fighting withdrawal, all those men fleeing the advancing Red Army were now a demoralized and disorganized shambles.

Closing the Trap on Minsk

On 28–29 June the Stavka clarified the tasks of the four Soviet fronts. The 1st and 3rd Byelorussian Fronts' primary role was the liberation of Minsk; the 2nd Byelorussian Front and 1st Baltic Front were tasked with pursuing the Germans to prevent them catching their breath and either putting together a credible defence or launching a counter-attack.

The presence of 5th Panzer on the Moscow–Minsk highway forced Chernyakovsky to redirect his armoured forces, 29th Tank Corps and 3rd Mechanized Corps, north of the city. In the meantime the rest of Rotmistrov's 5th Tank Army, largely Bobchenko's 3rd Guards Tank Corps supported by Galitsky's 11th Guards Army, forced its way down the highway. At the same time Burdeyny's 2nd Guards Tank Corps, having reached the west bank of the Berezina near Murovo, began driving on Minsk from the south.

On the Berezina near the villages of Brod and Sinichino, the Zheleznyak Partisan brigade held a 10 mile (17km) wide bridgehead and helped General A.A. Aslanov's 35th Guards Tank Brigade from Obukov's 3rd Mechanized Corps build bridges in order to cross the river.

The remains of the 12th Infantry Division under Generalleutnant Rudolf Bamler, part of Martinek's so-called XXXIX Panzer Corps, surrendered to the Red Army east of Minsk on 27 June. Generalleutnant Wilhelm Ochsner's 31st Infantry Division was also lost around this time.

The second phase of the battle for Byelorussia commenced only three days later with the crossing of the Berezina and the opening of the attack on Polotsk, and Rokossovsky's moves to outflank Minsk from the south-west.

Army Group Centre's combat diary noted with an air of optimism on the 30th:

Today, for the first time in the nine day battle of Byelorussia, there was some relief from the tension. The enemy did indeed occupy Sluzk after a see-saw battle, however, they were tied down there by the tenacious resistance offered by the weak German forces committed there, which allowed us to make use of the time to unload operational reserves, which had arrived in the Baranovichi area. Also, the enemy mobile formations, which were attacking through Borisov toward Minsk, ran into strong resistance on the Berezina; one of the enemy groups advancing through Bogoml was thrown back.

Also on the 30th, with the collapse of Army Group Centre seemingly halted, Model issued his orders: 4th Army's divisions to move immediately behind the Berezina, 9th Army to stop the enemy in front of Minsk, 2nd Army to hold the Slutsk–Baranovichi area, and 4th Panzer Army (Army Group North Ukraine) to take over the defence of the Brest-Litovsk area. To the north-west of Minsk 5th Panzer and the Tiger tanks of the Heavy Tank Battalion 505 during 1–2 July did all they could to hold off Rotmistrov's encroaching 5th Guards.

Oslikovsky's forces from the 3rd Cavalry Corps (5th, 6th and 32nd Cavalry Divisions) by 2 July had raced 75 miles (120km) to reach the area of Vileika and Molodechno, north of Minsk. Notably Molodechno sat astride the strategic Minsk–Vilnius railway, and on the same date one of the two cavalry corps from the 1st Byelorussian Front cut the line from Minsk south-west to Baranovichi. Rapidly the Byelorussian capital was being cut off from the outside world. German resistance to the east and south-east of Minsk had also collapsed by the 2nd.

On this occasion Model was unable to work his usual miracles and had to face up to the fact that he did not have the wherewithal to cling on to Minsk or indeed save many of the trapped troops of 4th and 9th Armies. Even juggling units from Army Group North Ukraine, which he now had the luxury of doing as he commanded both army groups, Model still did not have sufficient manpower to bring Stalin to a halt in Byelorussia. To make matters worse the Lithuanian capital, Vilnius, was now under threat, and Model sided with Zeitzler vainly trying to persuade Hitler to allow Friessner and Army Group North to withdraw west of Riga.

Model knew there was little chance of getting the remains of 4th Army to Minsk: the latter was being threatened from both north and south, and the Berezina had been breached west of Lepel. Unlike Hitler, Model cared little about the defence of the Byelorussian capital – what was more important was to keep open the escape routes to the north-west and south-west.

Army Group Centre had little in the way of manpower reserves that it could draw on in the Minsk area. Rear echelon security forces used for anti-partisan operations were little better than brutal thugs, who would not stand up to the Red Army. Kampfgruppe von Gottberg provided some reinforcements, drawing on the Dirlewanger and Kaminski Brigades, though these were little better than lightly armed anti-partisan militias. The 132nd and 170th Infantry Divisions, provided by Army Group North, were instructed by Army Group Centre to assist in the defence of Minsk. The 170th had already arrived in the area with the 221st to support 5th Panzer.

Kaminski's forces also included Byelorussian police of dubious loyalty. Kaminski himself was a Red Army deserter who had governed Lokot province behind Army Group Centre lines from 1942 to 1944, keeping it free from partisans. His hated brigade contributed to the deaths of 7,000 people in 1944 during a series of brutal operations.

Gottberg's command also seems to have ended up with responsibility for the Anhalt and Flörke battle groups. In addition to these ad hoc formations was Kampfgruppe Lindig, incorporating elements of 12th Panzer and the 390th Field Training Division. To the south the crossing points on the Berezina were guarded by Kampfgruppe Anhalt, consisting of a number of police and security detachments, and elements of Müller's XII Corps, which had fallen back on the town of Berezino.

The main elements of Kampfgruppe von Saucken sought to screen Minsk from the north-west, where the 5th Guards Tank Army was threatening to cut the railway lines. The fighting was bitter, and within a week the Tigers claimed 128 Soviet armoured vehicles and 5th Panzer another 167. This success came at a price: by the 8th all the Tigers had been lost, and 5th Panzer had just 18 tanks left. Having done all they could, von Saucken and the 5th Panzer were ordered to fall back towards Molodechno to the north-west of Minsk.

Gottberg, after reporting that the defences of Minsk were crumbling, withdrew his Kampfgruppe toward Lida, east of Minsk, from where he would retreat yet again without orders. On 4 July Kampfgruppe von Gottberg found itself in the path of the advancing Red Army, in particular the 26th and 83rd Guards Rifle Divisions, east of Minsk along a line Smilovichi–Smolevichi–Logoysk.

Model desperately put together a defensive line west of Minsk between Baranovichi and Molodechno: notably the 5th Panzer Division was on the Vilnius rail line north of Minsk and 12th Panzer was to the south-west, while the 4th Panzer and 28th Jäger Divisions were before Baranovichi, and the 170th Infantry had dug in around Molodechno. The idea was that this line would be held until those forces trapped at Minsk could fight their way out.

Fester Platz Minsk

Panov's 1st Guards Tank Corps from the 1st Byelorussian Front followed the armour of the 3rd Byelorussian Front to Minsk from the south-east. The German 4th Army now found itself being squeezed by seven tank, motorized and cavalry corps around Minsk. In the meantime other troops of the 1st Byelorussian Front were chasing the Germans toward Pukhovichi–Minsk and Slutsk–Baranovichi.

On the first route the Germans resisted fiercely, particularly along the Svisloch River, where the 12th Panzer Division was deployed. Resistance was also encountered in the Slutsk area, although by nightfall on the 4th Soviet troops were well beyond Baranovichi. The fleeing Germans, fearful of taking to the partisan-infested forests, clung to the roads, much to the satisfaction of the Soviet 4th and 16th Air Armies, which set about destroying the exposed columns.

Fester Platz Minsk was held by a mixture of units, including elements of 5th Panzer. The defenders' priority, regardless of Hitler's grand designs, was to get the wounded and administrative staff out and to hold the railway open for as long as possible. The situation in the city was grim, especially as it was full of non-combatant rear echelon staff and demoralized stragglers.

The garrison, just 1,800 strong, had the unenviable task of protecting 12,000 support staff, 8,000 wounded and 15,000 unarmed stragglers. Everyone had one thing on their minds – boarding a train westward. In total 53 trains were available in Minsk, and on 1 and 2 July many of the wounded and support staff were shipped out. They were the lucky ones; apart from the threat of air attack they were relatively safe.

The process of blowing up key installations commenced on the 1st, and Hitler belatedly gave permission to start the evacuation the following evening. The garrison began to systematically demolish Minsk in anticipation of being thrown out by the Red Army. Zhukov and the others realized quick action was needed:

The Byelorussian partisans operating in the Minsk area informed us that the Government House, the buildings of the republican Party Central Committee and the Officers' House were being hastily mined for demolition before retreat. To save the city's biggest buildings we decided to accelerate the advance of our armoured troops and send along engineers for de-mining. Their task was to fight their way into the city – avoiding engagement with the enemy on the approaches – and seize the government buildings.

Once past 5th Panzer the Soviet 2nd Guards Tank Corps broke into the southern outskirts at 0200 on 3 July. The corps' 4th Guards Tank Brigade, loaded with tank riders, burst through the remaining defences. They were followed by the 1st Byelorussian Front's 1st Guards Tank Corps, which attacked from the south-east. At the same time Rotmistrov's 5th Tank Army appeared north of Minsk and moved north-easterly to cut the road from Minsk to the north-west. Reinforcements also arrived from the 11th Guards Army and 31st Army.

Minsk was cleared by the evening of the 3rd, and the people danced in the streets of rubble, tears in their eyes as they welcomed the Red Army with flowers. The destruction was terrible, as Zhukov lamented:

The capital of Byelorussia was barely recognisable. I had commanded a regiment there for seven years and knew well every street, and all the main buildings, bridges, parks, stadiums and theatres. Now everything was in ruins; where whole apartment buildings had stood, there was nothing but heaps of rubble.

The people of Minsk were a pitiful sight, exhausted and haggard, many of them in tears.

The liberation of Minsk, the first real objective of Operation Bagration, had been achieved. There were still numerous German units east of Minsk, and just as the city was being cleared they were attempting to pull back across the Berezina.

Conference of the Damned

Trapped in the Minsk pockets were men from the 4th and 9th Armies' XII, XXVII and XXXV Army and XXXIX and XXXXI Panzer Corps. According to Zhukov, 100,000 men were encircled east of Minsk. The two main groups, to the east and the other to the south-east, had little choice but to break out. The Luftwaffe flew a final airdrop on the 5th before the Smilovichi airfield was lost.

Notably Müller's XII and Völckers's XXVII Corps were among those caught, and the two generals found themselves together. To the east of Minsk and south of Smolevichi a German pocket had formed near Pekalin. Three relatively intact divisions defended this, namely the 31st, 57th and 267th, along with units from the 78th, 260th and 25th Panzergrenadiers. While the latter had mustered thirty-two assault and twenty self-propelled guns, they were down to just five to ten rounds of ammunition per gun. Some of XXVII Corps was also present, as were all six divisional commanders and Müller and Völckers.

On 5 July what was essentially a conference of the damned was held. It took place against a backdrop of Soviet artillery fire and air attacks. Either in person or over the radio all the commanders were consulted. From the situation reports and their maps it was now apparent that the Soviets had penetrated over 62 miles (100km) to the west: Müller and Völckers knew that pushing their men, who were short of fuel and ammunition and without air cover, over such a distance was an impossible task. However, there was little alternative.

Deep down Müller really had no stomach for anything but surrender, while Völckers was all for standing where they were and making a fight of it. The fear was if they attempted to escape they would lose all cohesion and be cut to pieces. General Adolf Trowitz, commander of the 57th and a veteran of the bloody Korsun pocket, and General Günther Klammt, commander of the 260th, were prepared to try for a breakout. Traut, though a hardened soldier, was worried about the wounded, numbering up to 5,000, who would have to be left behind.

In the event and after much debate it was decided that the two corps would each make separate attempts to break free, with XII Corps heading north-west and XXVII Corps pushing westward. It seemed better than awaiting the inevitable. Those units of XXXIX Panzer Corps that were available were divided between the two breakout groups. General Otto Drescher's 267th Infantry would continue acting as rearguard for XII Corps, while the 25th Panzergrenadiers would spearhead the breakout efforts.

A Foiled Breakout

The operation began at 2359 hours on 5 July, attacking west toward Dzerzhinsk, south-west of Minsk. Their wounded were left behind with a doctor and a letter appealing for clemency. Having used up all the ammunition for their armoured fighting vehicles the panzergrenadiers resorted to bayonet charges to break the

Soviet cordon. General Paul Schürmann, leading about 1,000 men, one of three groups, stormed a Soviet artillery battery and escaped with just 100 troops. He eventually reached German lines between Molodechno and Vilnius with only thirty men from his division.

Panzergrenadiers of the Feldherrnhalle joined forces with Trowitz's 57th Infantry from XII Corps, in an attempt to slip the clutches of the Red Army, but like the other breakout efforts they were eventually dispersed in the face of heavy Soviet resistance. Initially the 57th, some 12,000 to 15,000 men, bravely stuck together, joining the Feldherrnhalle at daybreak on the 6th. At nightfall together they set about the Soviet troops holding the Cherven–Minsk road. In the fighting that followed the panzergrenadiers were scattered, killed or captured. The infantry then split up, with the divisional commander and two vehicles carrying the wounded being the last to get over the road. Over the next two days the Red Army rounded up Trowitz and most of his men.

Traut's 78th, which had borne the brunt of Bagration when it commenced, managed to escape only to have the Soviets catch up with them, with predictable results. General Müller's attempts to escape with the 18th Panzergrenadiers were likewise thwarted. Once in Soviet hands he issued an order for all trapped troops to lay down their arms: the Soviets broadcast this over a mobile speaker system and dropped the order printed on leaflets. Most chose to ignore his instructions.

Part of the 14th Infantry Division under its commander, General Flörke, succeeded in reaching remnants of Martinek's 12th and 31st Infantry Divisions; his Kampfgruppe Flörke, discovering Minsk abandoned and torched, was eventually able to escape the pocket and reach the 12th Panzer Division's positions. The 14th had started life as an infantry division and become a motorized infantry division and then a panzergrenadier division, but by 1943 it had reverted to being a regular infantry formation.

Drescher's 267th Infantry made a break for it in three columns heading for the Orsha–Minsk railway followed by the highway. The group on the left got over both but then ran into Soviet tanks and was forced to surrender. The right-hand group, fleeing through forest, came under partisan attack, and many also surrendered. Those left pushed on, heading north-west, but encountered Soviet infantry and mortars: armed with just rifles and a handful of rounds per man, they faced an inevitable outcome.

General Drescher, with the central column, had better luck crossing the railway and highway and headed for Molodechno, but he then split his group up. Few eluded the Red Army or the partisans.

Cat and Mouse

The Soviets were now faced with a major mopping-up operation. In the following week whole German divisions tried to cut their way clear of the Red Army. Responsibility for rounding up the German stragglers after the fall of Minsk initially fell to Rokossovsky's troops, then Zakharov took over. His men scoured the ground between the Velma, Usha and Plissa rivers.

Authors Captain W.E.D. Allen and Paul Muratoff, chronicling the Russian 1944–45 campaigns just after the war ended, recorded:

> In this region (thirty miles north to south and more than forty west to east) not only small parties of enemy stragglers but whole units with artillery and even a few tanks found refuge. Some of them fought well, others only made a show of fighting before surrendering; many capitulated as soon as they were discovered.

For several days the survivors from these shattered divisions fled from the pursuing Soviets through the forests and swamps in a desperate bid to escape. The Red Army hunted them down with great efficiency, and the main units were annihilated or captured by 7–8 July. By the second week, as ammunition and food began to completely run out, the fighting abated and the German formations broke down into ever smaller and smaller units trying to infiltrate westward.

By the 9th the largest remaining German forces had been rounded up or killed; however, a deadly game of cat and mouse continued with the isolated and scattered stragglers. Special Soviet units were assigned the task of combing the surrounding countryside.

The Soviets recorded their successes during 5–11 July: in the first three days they claimed to have killed 28,000 Germans and captured another 15,000; in total the number captured rose to 27,000. The loss of 55,000 men meant the total destruction of at least eight of 4th Army's divisions belonging to XII, XXVII and XXXIX Corps. The prisoners included twelve generals: three corps and nine divisional commanders. Müller and Völckers, who was also acting as commander of 4th Army, were among the captured, along with the divisional commanders of the 57th, 60th, 78th and 260th Divisions.

The few survivors from Traut's 78th Sturm Division, also briefly commanded by Siegfried Rasp, found themselves merged with the 543rd Grenadier Division and designated the 78th Grenadier Division under Generalleutnant Karl Löwrick, before Rasp reassumed command. Klammt's 260th Infantry was also lost at Minsk. Just before Bagration its order of battle consisted of Grenadier Regiments 460, 470 and 480; Füsilier Bataillon, Feldersatz Bataillon and Nachrichten, all designated 260; and Pionier Bataillon 653.

General Alexander Conrady's 36th Infantry Division, from Martinek's XXXIX Panzer Corps, was lost, along with Generalleutnant Eberhard von Kurowski's 110th Infantry Division. Scheller's 337th Infantry Division was so badly battered that it was largely beyond redemption, and was used to form the battalion-strength Korps Abteilung G.

Generalleutnant Alfred Jacobi's 201st Security Division, part of General Weiss's 2nd Army, sustained major losses near Minsk. Before being transferred to Army Group Centre it had served in Army Group North's rear areas until September 1942. It had spent a year conducting rear area security operations for Busch until deployed to the front lines, a role that it was clearly ill-equipped for,

In the summer of 1944 Stalin wanted not only to liberate Byelorussia but also to smash Hitler's Army Group Centre, which formed the very heart of the Wehrmacht on the Eastern Front. (Scott Pick collection)

Generalfeldmarschall Busch (centre) in happier days with Generalfeldmarschall von Rundstedt (left). He was appointed to command Army Group Centre in October 1943. (Author's collection)

Despite the smiles for the camera, Hitler's occupation of both Byelorussia and Ukraine was brutal. By the time the former had been liberated up to 3 million of its population were dead. (Scott Pick collection)

Throughout the winter of 1943-44 the German army was pushed back on the Eastern Front. Come the summer the question was whether Stalin's main blow would fall first in Byelorussia or Ukraine. (Scott Pick collection)

A German flak unit guarding one of the vital crossings over the Dnepr or Berezina, which provided natural defensive lines, though Hitler chose to ignore them. (Scott Pick collection)

A dusty German motorized column in the midst of Byelorussia. Defending Army Group Centre's extended lines of communication from constant partisan attack proved a major problem during 1943-44. (Scott Pick collection)

Generalfeldmarschall Busch's command was entirely a defensive formation by June 1944; although it included a panzer army and two panzer corps it had no actual panzer divisions apart from 20th Panzer.
(Scott Pick collection)

Army Group Centre's panzergrenadier divisions were equipped with the Sturmgeschütz III assault gun rather than panzers.
(Author's collection)

A Luftwaffe infantryman keeps watch. The 4th and 6th Luftwaffe Field Divisions played a key role in the defence of Vitebsk.
(Scott Pick collection)

Once it had become evident that the Stuka Ju 87 dive-bomber (seen here) was too slow to survive combat conditions, units were re-equipped with the Focke-Wulfe 190 – though this did not start until the spring of 1944. (Scott Pick collection)

Freshly dug German trenches: such defences were enhanced by barbed wire, mines, anti-tank ditches, and anti-tank and anti-aircraft gun positions. The weapon in the foreground is a tripod-mounted MG34 machine gun. (Scott Pick collection)

By 1944, despite its massive losses in killed, wounded and captured during the previous three years, Stalin's Red Army was at the height of its combat power. (Scott Pick collection)

The T-34/76 medium tank (this particular one was knocked out in the forests of Byelorussia) was supplemented by the up-gunned T-34/85 just in time for Operation Bagration. (Scott Pick collection)

A column of T-34/85s waiting to go into action. During the spring of 1944 Soviet Guards armoured brigades were issued with this new tank for the first time. (via Nick Cornish)

Soviet 'tank riders' such as Evgeni Bessonov, because of the Red Army's lack of transport, had to hitch a ride on the tanks, where they were dangerously exposed to enemy fire. (via author)

By far the Red Air Force's best ground-attack aircraft was the famous Ilyushin 'Flying Tank' or Il-2 Shturmovik. Pilots employed the 'circle of death' for attacking panzers. (Scott Pick collection)

The reconnaissance companies of the Red Army's rifle divisions were equipped with rubber rafts and rubber swimming suits for tackling river crossings and securing bridges. (via author)

Soviet partisans played a key role in disrupting Army Group Centre's lines of communication both prior to and during Bagration. (via author)

A Red Army mortar crew soften up the enemy's defences. The density of the opening Soviet barrage in support of Bagration was truly shocking, involving 24,000 guns and mortars. (via author)

Entrenched German troops watch an advancing Soviet barrage: some 17,000 guns and mortars were concentrated on Stalin's breakthrough points on 23 June 1944. (Scott Pick collection)

Apprehensive-looking German troops watch the opening of a Soviet attack; they had little means of stemming the flow of angry steel unleashed upon them. (Scott Pick collection)

Soviet assault troops hurry past a knocked-out StuG III. There was little the panzergrenadiers' armour could do to stop Stalin's Red tide. (via Nick Cornish)

Soviet infantry liberating a Russian village in a clearly staged propaganda photo. Outlying German positions were swiftly overrun just prior to Bagration. (via author)

An MG34 machine-gun crew laying down fire on attacking Soviet troops: this weapon could manage up to 900 rounds per minute and was one of the Germans' key infantry-support weapons. (Scott Pick collection)

Cumbersome German heavy artillery engaged in counter-battery fire with Soviet guns: the Red Army swiftly overran such weapons.
(Scott Pick collection)

This exposed German 105mm field gun is providing covering fire for the front lines that were rapidly abandoned in the face of Soviet bombardment and heavy assault.
(Scott Pick collection)

German officers planning what would be a futile counter-attack. Army Group Centre's lack of reserves and Hitler's refusal to yield ground left them with no strategic flexibility.
(Scott Pick collection)

Another model T-34/76 that came to grief in the swamps of Byelorussia. In the opening stages of Bagration the Soviets threw 4,000 tanks and assault guns against Busch's 550 assault guns. (Scott Pick collection)

A grim-faced Generalfeldmarschall Busch (far left) receives bad news; within just a week of Bagration commencing Hitler replaced him with Walter Model. (Scott Pick collection)

Soviet infantrymen attack across a railway line. Once the line had been cut north and south of Minsk on 2 July 1944 the city was swiftly liberated.
(via author)

A German column withdrawing through a burnt-out Russian city; the Byelorussian capital Minsk was cleared by the Red Army on 3 July 1944.
(Scott Pick collection)

Army Group Centre lost 55,000 men killed and wounded in the Minsk area alone during 5–11 July 1944.
(Scott Pick collection)

Abandoned German motor vehicles: in the first eight days of Bagration the Red Army claimed to have destroyed or captured almost 26,000 vehicles. (Author's collection)

In the wake of Bagration Generaloberst Lindemann (centre left), commander of Army Group North, was replaced by Friessner for failing to close the gap with Model's Army Group Centre. (Author's collection)

Death of a Soviet soldier shot through the head. Such casualties did not hinder Stalin's quest for revenge on Hitler. (Scott Pick collection)

During June and July 1944 the Wehrmacht suffered over 670,000 casualties, half of whom were lost by Army Group Centre. (Scott Pick collection)

Grim-faced retreating German troops: the loss of so much equipment in Byelorussia was a major disaster for the Wehrmacht, which was already reliant on horse-drawn transport. (Scott Pick collection)

Triumphant-looking Soviet troops pass a knocked-out Panzer Mk IV – the summer of 1944 was an unimaginable success for Stalin and his warlords. (via Nick Cornish)

German PoWs await an uncertain fate; most would die in Stalin's brutal Gulag. Hitler's forces suffered well over half a million killed and wounded – another 120,000 men were captured. (Scott Pick collection)

Bagration cost the Red Army 178,000 casualties, and during the Lvov–Sandomierz offensive it suffered a further 198,000 casualties. Stalin viewed this as a small price to pay for the annihilation of Army Group Centre and the mauling of Army Groups North and North Ukraine. (Scott Pick collection)

consisting of a single grenadier regiment, a security regiment and a company of artillery. The survivors found themselves sent back to Army Group North.

Similarly Weiss's 221st Security Division, under Generalleutnant Bogislav von Schwerin, was mauled in the Minsk area, and Albrecht Baron Digeon von Monteton's 391st Security Division suffered the same fate. The latter's command had only come into being in late March, having been formed from the 391st Field Training Division; it was clearly yet another unit totally ill-suited to front-line operations. Hans Bergen's 390th Field Training Division had converted to security division status just days before the Soviet offensive.

Clearing Baranovichi

In the meantime, throughout 6 July the Dirlewanger Brigade was entrenched south-east of Lida, where it launched a flank attack against the leading units of 26th Tank Corps to prevent the Kampfgruppe being overrun. On the 8th the Soviets counter-attacked and the 3rd Guards Cavalry Corps captured Lida, despite the arrival of Kampfgruppe Flörke and Kampfgruppe Weidling to strengthen the SS defence.

Having handed the town over to the 31st Army, the 3rd Guards Cavalry shifted south. Kampfgruppe Weidling withdrew on the 9th, while Kampfgruppe Flörke resisted the 2nd Guards Tank Corps for another day before retreating westward to Lithuania.

For the defence of Baranovichi south-west of Minsk, Model had brought up reinforcements from Army Group North Ukraine; these included a panzer division and a division of Hungarian cavalry. On 3 July, the very day that the Soviets entered Minsk, the Germans had launched a local counter-attack, recapturing Nesvizh and Stolbtsy, south-west of Minsk – both points reached by Pliyev's cavalry. Some 25 miles (40km) west of Slutsk the Germans also prepared a rearguard on a position Semezhevo–Timkovichi to protect the Bobruisk–Baranovichi highway.

Although still occupied with those forces trapped east of Minsk, Rokossovsky began his operations against Baranovichi on 4 July. In just three days a column pushed down the Minsk–Baranovichi railway and cleared the Germans from the region near the source of the Niemen; Stolbtsy and Nesvizh were also recaptured. On the road from Slutsk the Germans were thrown back and took up positions just a few miles east and north-east of Baranovichi.

General Batov says:

Slutsk [between Baranovichi and Bobruisk] was liberated. Nesvezh was captured. While the 48th Army was cutting off the communication lines of the Minsk enemy grouping and was blocking its retreat in the direction of Baranovichi, our Army was to capture this major railroad junction and thus make our contribution to the encirclement of the German 4th Army.

When Zhukov caught Batov and military council member Radetsky shaving and washing, he flew into a rage, kicking over a stool and slamming a door, because Baranovichi had not yet been taken. Batov was shaken by Zhukov's outburst, but Radetsky put his finger on the problem – rivalry: 'Vasilevsky is nearing Vilnius. And here is Zhukov competing to be the first to report to Supreme Headquarters.'

The following day, when Batov informed Zhukov that Radetsky was now in Baranovichi, all he wanted to know about was Vilnius. On 7 July the defenders held off the Soviet attacks, but their centre was broken, and the Red Army streamed into Baranovichi, which was cleared by the following day.

Battles for Polotsk and Vilnius

To the north-east of Minsk Bagramyan's 1st Baltic Front was advancing north-westward towards Polotsk and westward in the direction of Glubokoye. To prevent him entering south-eastern Latvia, the Germans had to hold Polotsk. The town, on an important junction and crossroads, is protected by the Dvina to the south, while to the north and east is shielded by small lakes, streams, marshy ground and forests. The local garrison had fortified all this, and every avenue of advance had been turned into a killing ground. The southern suburbs beyond the Dvina were protected by a defensive line anchored on the Ushacha river and along a chain of small lakes that ran to the Ulla river.

While the defence of Minsk was a largely disorganized and half-hearted affair, the battle for Polotsk was a completely different matter. To hold Polotsk two panzer and two infantry divisions were concentrated to the south of the Dvina, while the town itself on the north side had a garrison of two divisions. Although this enabled Polotsk to be held for a few days longer, it opened up a dangerous gap between the Dvina and Vilnius.

By 28 June, with Bagramyan across the Ulla, the Red Army had been able to penetrate Polotsk's outer defences, and the next day he cut the railway to Molodechno. Then advanced units reached Disna on the Dvina, just 30 miles (48km) west of Polotsk, on 1 July. Infantry and tanks of General Chistyakov's 6th Guards Army launched the decisive attack from the south. Here of course lay the Germans' main strength.

On the 2nd heavy fighting broke out on the small river Turovlya, just 10 miles (16km) from the town; the Germans were driven back, and the following day the Soviets entered the suburbs near the Dvina bridge. Panzers fled over the bridge with Soviet tanks in hot pursuit, but only three got over before the defenders blew the bridge into the river. Undeterred the Soviet infantry improvised and were fighting in the streets by nightfall.

On the 4th Bagramyan's forces also stormed Polotsk from the east, though the garrison still had an escape route to the north in the direction of Osveya or Sebezh. The gap in the Germans' defences between Drissa and Molodechno was 120 miles (194km) wide. Bagramyan and Chernyakovsky moved into this, and during 3 and 4 July occupied Sharkovschina, Glubokoye and Dokshitsy way to the west. The approaches to Lithuania were also reached, driving a wedge between Army Group Centre and Army Group North.

With the liberation of Minsk the Red Army set its sights on Kaunas, Grodno, Bialystok and Brest-Litovsk. Model desperately tried to hold a line from Vilnius to Baranovichi, but it was an impossible task once Baranovichi had fallen. Hitler exhibited his usual obsession with strongpoints and declared Vilnius a *fester Platz*, demanding it be held to the last. Rotmistrov's 5th Guards Tank Army quickly surrounded 3rd Panzer Army, and permission to try to escape was not granted until 11 July. The following night 6th Panzer cut a rescue corridor, but few of the 15,000 troops trapped in Vilnius managed to get out.

It took Chernyakovsky's 3rd Byelorussian Front from 5 to 13 July to overcome German opposition at Vilnius. Generalleutnant Stahel, an air defence officer, was the fortress commandant and could muster just two grenadier, one SS police and an airborne regiment, supported by an artillery regiment and a single anti-tank and air defence battalion. By 9 July his men had suffered 1,000 killed and wounded. One German division in the area fought to the last, losing 8,000 killed and 5,000 captured. A breakout was authorized, and on the night of 13–14 July only 2,000–5,000 men made it to German lines and the safety of 6th Panzer.

On 7 July the Polish Home Army rose up against the Germans in Vilnius. Battling for a week about 12,500 fighters attacked the garrison and seized the city centre. Despite cooperating with the 3rd Byelorussian Front, once the Soviets had entered the city on the 15th the Polish insurgents found themselves being rounded up by the NKVD.

Some 5,000 men were interned and invited to join General Berling's Soviet-backed Polish 1st Army. Another 6,000 men, plus 12,000 local volunteers, sought shelter in the nearby forests, but were surrounded and forced to surrender. The NKVD continued to round up Polish stragglers well into late August, many of whom ended up in the Gulag.

The loss of Vilnius was followed by Pinsk and Grodno, and German hopes of holding the Nieman river were now dashed. West of Minsk Chernyakovsky broke into Grodno on the Niemen on the 16th, and a bridgehead was established to the north at Olita (Alytus), shattering any dreams Hitler may have harboured of Army Group Centre stabilizing the situation on a 'Niemen Line'. As 4th Army was dying the Red Army covered up to 15 miles (25km) a day, sweeping to the East Prussian border and further into southern Poland. Operation Bagration had been completed.

While the Niemen Line might be breached there were East Prussian defences behind it; to the south the dense Augustov forests and the marshy boundaries of the Bóbr and Narev rivers would also serve to slow the Soviets. The line of the Narev, lower Western Bug and Vistula was likewise a natural defensive line further south.

The German soil of East Prussia was now under direct threat: while 9th Army was beyond repair the remains of the 4th Army were instructed to go to the defence of Prussia. Its remaining divisions were concentrated at Bialystok, and reinforcements were sent from Denmark and Norway.

The German 252nd Infantry's divisional history reported:

On 26 July the enemy crossed the Ulla in several places and there rolled up the weakly manned positions from the rear, mostly from two sides. The combat weary troops – they had been in combat without a break since 22 June – had had no sleep and only a little food. They were trying, after their ammunition had run out, to make a fighting withdrawal over the rushing Ulla. Without bridges, without boats, under fire from the enemy the few survivors were trying to reach the opposite bank. Men who could not swim were hanging like grapes on men who could and dragging them down into the depths. Swimmers were pulling wounded men across the river and trying that several times until their strength was exhausted. Watery death reaped a rich but cruel harvest. On the morning of the next day on the road there appeared individual naked men, who were carrying nothing but a weapon. Everything was done to get these men fresh clothes, if only they could join the fighting again.

Through July/August the division fled before the advancing Red Army, covering 310 miles (500km) from Vitebsk, all the time leaving gaps of up to 40 miles (65km) between Army Groups Centre and North. On 3 August the 252nd Infantry made a stand at Raseinen, driving out Soviet tanks. Six days later, despite the support of the 7th Panzer Division, the town was lost again. On the 15th a counter-attack by the two divisions drove the Red Army away once more.

In the meantime Rokossovsky's forces manoeuvred themselves into position ready for Konev's 1st Ukrainian Front's assault on Army Group North Ukraine and their supporting Lublin–Brest offensive. It was vital to secure Kovel, which formed the shoulder of the two fronts, and it was stormed on the 5th; the Germans withdrew behind the protection of the Pripyat marshes and the headwaters of the river.

Also way to the north Zakharov's 2nd Byelorussian Front took Volkovysk, west of Baranovichi, on 14 July after heavy fighting with the remnants of one of 9th Army's last remaining divisions in the field, the 45th Infantry under Generalmajor Joachim Engel from XXXV Corps.

Before Bagration commenced there were under the command of Busch and Model some seventy-five German divisions on a front stretching from Vitebsk to the Carpathians, a distance of some 600 miles (968km). Now there were fifty, with another ten on their way, holding about 500 miles (806km) running from the Dvina to the Carpathians. Some Red Army units were 300 miles (484km) from their starting point and at the very limits of their supply routes.

Army Group North

After commanding Army Group Centre for just twelve gruelling days, Model and Friessner, who had been in charge in the north for just five days, piled onto an aircraft on 9 July and flew to see Hitler to try to prevail upon him again to evacuate Estonia before General Eremenko's 2nd Baltic Front, supported by the 15th Air Army, attacked on Bagramyan's right. They got the usual answer.

Eremenko launched his forces against Friessner on the night of 11–12 July along a 100 mile front (160km). The area of attack was the extension of the 'Panther Line' south of Opochka, which had a strong double bastion between Idritsa and Sebezh.

Although the German defences were extensive the Soviet artillery did its work as usual. The German 16th Army put up a stout fight, but after two days of resisting was driven from Idritsa. On the 15th Opochka on the Velikaya, a key point in the 'Panther Line', fell. This meant that Ostrov in the north and Sebezh in the south could be outflanked, and Sebezh fell two days later.

The inability of Army Groups Centre and North to effectively help each other soon manifested itself in open friction between Model and Friessner. On 18 July the pair visited Hitler again. Model pleaded for the closing of the Lithuanian gap between their two commands, arguing that as he had insufficient troops to achieve this that it should fall to his colleague.

Friessner saw this as preposterous: Army Group North was in danger of being cut off if the Red Army broke through to the Gulf of Riga, and any push south would simply be putting his command further into the noose. If he were to prevent Army Group North being driven into the Baltic he would need every soldier he could muster.

Model must have glowered at Friessner with indignation: when Friessner had taken charge with energy and enthusiasm he had made it clear that he would follow Hitler's orders and support Model with a swift counter-offensive to the south-east. Now that his staff had briefed him and the full realities of the situation in the Baltic States had sunk in, Friessner knew that such an offensive was never going to take place.

Stalin Gloats

Incredibly the bulk of Army Group Centre had been destroyed in just twelve days and a breach 250 miles (403km) wide ripped open in the Eastern Front. Between twenty-five and twenty-eight German divisions were destroyed, and ten generals killed and twenty-one captured.

The near-total annihilation of Army Group Centre in the space of just under two weeks cost Hitler 300,000 dead, 250,000 wounded and about 120,000 captured – overall casualties of 670,000. In addition he lost 2,000 panzers and 57,000 other vehicles. Stalin's losses were 60,000 killed, 110,000 wounded and about 8,000 missing, 2,957 tanks, 2,447 artillery pieces and 822 aircraft.

Only about 20,000 troops from Army Group Centre escaped the debacle unscathed. If Tippelskirch had not acted 4th Army would have vanished completely: both his command and 9th Army were reduced to shells, while 3rd Panzer Army had been reduced to just three understrength divisions with seventy guns. In total 8 scattered divisions remained to hold a front of 200 miles (323km) in the face of 116 infantry divisions, 6 cavalry divisions, 16 mechanized infantry brigades and 42 armoured brigades.

Thanks to 20th Panzer's appropriation of some new tanks it was able to block Soviet attacks, allowing the exposed left flank of the German 8th Army to withdraw beyond the Carpathian Mountains to fight another day.

Stalin wanted the Western Allies to be made fully aware that he had torn the beating heart out of the Wehrmacht on the Eastern Front. In the Soviet capital, General Burrows, the head of the British Military Mission in Moscow, was summoned on 6 July to be conducted on a three-day tour of Chernyakovsky's 3rd Byelorussian Front.

Burrows found his host, Chief of Staff Vasilevsky, who had coordinated the northern pincer, unusually open and talkative. He informed Burrows that Soviet troops had noted deterioration in the combat value of the German forces, and that their success was due to the massed artillery and the Red Air Force. The Soviet general also observed that the Germans had 'a blockhouse mentality': little did they know that they had Hitler to thank for that.

The German order of battle for Army Group Centre by mid-July included the remnants of 9th Army incorporated in 2nd Army; 3rd Panzer Army reduced to Korps Abteilung G and fragments of IX and XXVII Corps; and 4th Army consisting of the battered 5th Panzer and 50th Infantry Divisions, along with Kampfgruppe Flörke, some remnants of the security divisions and part of the *Totenkopf* under Helmuth Weidling, previously 9th Army Corps commander, at Bobruisk, plus 7th Panzer.

The remnants of the 95th, 197th and 256th Infantry Divisions were used to create battalion-strength Korps Abteilung H at the end of July, and this was later re-designated the 95th Infantry Division in September. The 299th Infantry Division, commanded by General Hans Junck from Pfeiffer's VI Corps, was destroyed in July.

Stalin paraded 57,000 bedraggled German prisoners through the streets of Moscow on 17 July. Some might question the wisdom and security of marching so many men through the Soviet capital, but Stalin, as well as wishing to gloat, on a more practical level wanted to disprove German claims of a 'planned withdrawal from Byelorussia'.

Alexander Werth recalled that it was a memorable sight:

Particularly striking was the attitude of the Russian crowds lining the streets. Youngsters booed and whistled, and even threw things at the Germans, only to be immediately restrained by the adults; men looked on grimly and in silence; but many women, especially elderly women, were full of commiseration (some even had tears in their eyes) as they looked at these bedraggled 'fritzes.' I remember one old woman murmuring, 'just like our poor boys...*tozhe pognali na voinu* (also driven into war).'

Although three armies of Army Group Centre had been routed (and according to Soviet figures thirty entire divisions wiped out), the remaining divisions were bolstered by reinforcements from Model and Lindemann's army groups as quickly as possible. By the end of July these reinforcements numbered at least fifteen divisions, and only then did the front begin to stabilize.

CHAPTER 9

Lvov–Sandomierz: The Second Blow

Generaloberst Josef Harpe had assumed command of Army Group North Ukraine on 28 June. Throughout the summer this army group had been able to match the 1st Ukrainian Front, but the drain of units caused by Bagration now ensured that the balance was in the Soviets' favour. In the desperate and fruitless attempt to save Army Group Centre Hitler had stripped it of six divisions including three panzer from the western regions of Ukraine. Only now did the long-anticipated assault on Army Group North Ukraine take place.

General von Mellenthin, in appraising the situation, quoted Guderian:

By 13 July the Russians had taken Vilnius and Pinsk, and had reached the outskirts of Kovno and Grodno. They were within a hundred miles of the German frontier, and there was 'a very real danger' of their 'breaking through into East Prussia as a result of their victory and our absence of reserves.' This was the moment chosen by Marshal Konev to launch a new offensive in Galicia.

Strong Defences

According to Soviet intelligence, Army Group North Ukraine consisted of thirty-four infantry divisions, one motorized and five panzer divisions and two infantry brigades. This totalled 600,000 men, plus another 300,000 in logistical units, with 900 panzers and assault guns and 6,300 field guns and mortars. Harpe's other asset was the 700 aircraft of Luftflotte 4, in particular the veteran VIII Fliegerkorps, although he did not have direct control of them. The Soviets assessed that at the approaches to the Vistula and Carpathians German defences had been constructed to a depth of almost 31 miles (50km).

Lvov (also spelt Lwów/Lviv) was a key communications hub, acting as an important road and rail junction. Indeed after the Germans were driven from much of Ukraine during the first half of 1944, Lvov was of great importance to Hitler as a nodal point between his forces in Poland and those in Romania. It also provided the shortest route to the upper Vistula, particularly the Silesian industrial region, and it protected the Polish oilfields in the region of Berislaw and Drohobycz.

The Lvov region was ideal for defence, being shielded by the tributaries of the Dniester; the surrounding geography of high ground divided by parallel

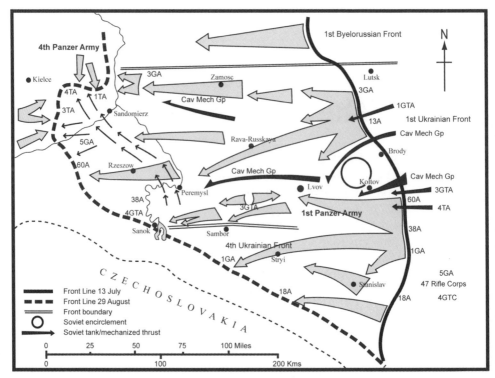

The Lvov–Sandomierz offensive, July–August 1944.

valleys was ideal for defensive positions. However, the key tributaries were not considerable obstacles: the Zlata Lipa and Gnila Lipa could be outflanked to the north by advancing along the Dubno–Brody–Busk–Lvov highway. The region between Brody and Zolochev has a series of heights that the Germans had fortified with a system of trenches, pillboxes and minefields.

History has a way of repeating itself, and in 1914 the fate of Lvov had been settled with two battles, one on the Zlata Lipa and the other on the Gnila Lipa. The Russian left wing had played the decisive role against the Austro-Hungarian Army; the Russian right, though, had not extended itself far enough, and the opportunity to trap the 3rd and 4th Austro-Hungarian Armies was lost. This meant that the Austro-Hungarians, though defeated to the east of Lvov, were able to give battle again to the west. No doubt Konev took this valuable lesson on board.

German defences in the region in 1944 were vastly stronger than the Austro-Hungarian fieldworks in 1914. German troops were entrenched east of the Western Bug and everywhere between Brody and Vladimir Volynsk. Konev planned to cut his way through the German lines in the region of Zolochev, which would provide the tactical breach, while the strategic line of attack would be to the north toward Kamenka (or Mosty Velikie) and Rava Russkaya.

However, Harpe's command had created three main defensive belts that were 19 miles (30km) deep. In addition Vladimir Volynsk, Brody, Zolochev,

Rava Russkaya and Stanislav had been turned into strongpoints. The III Panzer Corps was deployed from Lvov to Brody to the north-east, which was expected to be the main Soviet line of attack. The area east of Lvov, the sector where the main attack thrust was expected, was mined with 160,000 anti-personnel and 200,000 anti-tank mines.

Freedom Fighters or Traitors

The Jews of Lvov had suffered at the hands of the Nazis and Ukrainian nationalists, who felt the region should belong to Ukraine not Poland. The Soviet Union occupied Lvov in September 1939, in accordance with the secret provisions of the Nazi-Soviet Pact. After the German invasion it was discovered that Stalin's secret police had massacred thousands of prisoners, many of them Ukrainian nationalists. The Germans claimed the city's Jewish population had helped, and in the pogroms that followed Ukrainian partisans supported by the German authorities killed about 4,000 Jews.

The scale of Byelorussian collaboration was nothing like that of the Ukrainians'. Ukraine hoped it would gain independence by helping Hitler's war machine, and about 180,000 volunteers served the Wehrmacht. Some 70,000 were recruited into the German Schuma (police), with 35,000 serving in 71 battalions, which included some Cossack forces, conducting anti-partisan duties.

The Ukrainian Insurgent Army (*Ukrains'ka povstans'ka armiia* – UPA) created in 1944 fought both the Russians and the Germans. The Ukrainian Liberation Army (*Ukrainske vyzvolne viysko* – UVV) was little more than a German propaganda tool, and two Ukrainian divisions numbering 40,000 men designated the Ukrainian National Army (UNA) in 1945 were never really effective as such.

The Ukrainians also provided recruits to create a Waffen SS division, though these were largely Galician Ukrainians, as Reichsführer Heinrich Himmler stipulated they must come from western Ukraine (Galicia) and be Greek Catholic rather than Russian Orthodox, thereby barring Russian Ukrainians. The idea was that anti-Communist volunteers would be drawn from the part of Poland that had once been incorporated in the Austro-Hungarian Empire and therefore loyal servants of the Habsburg Emperor.

Recruitment commenced in April 1943 and there were 100,000 applicants for 30,000 places (typically a Waffen SS division numbered about 15,000 fighting men and 5,000 support troops). Many of the surplus were not turned away and were used to form five Galician police regiments. Training finished in May 1944 and the 14th SS-Freiwilligen Division Galizien was shipped to the Eastern Front the following month in time to face Konev's Lvov–Sandomierz offensive.

Konev's Unusual Operation

Zhukov was instructed to coordinate Konev's 1st Ukrainian Front, but advocated strengthening Vasilevsky's group of fronts with an aim of cutting off Army Group North and occupying East Prussia.

'Are you in cahoots with Vasilevsky?' asked Stalin. 'Because he also asks for his fronts to be reinforced.'

Zhukov replied that he was not, but said that Vasilevsky was correct.

'The Germans will fight for East Prussia till the very end,' warned Stalin, 'and we may get stuck there. We should first of all liberate the Lvov Region and the eastern part of Poland.'

Zhukov later noted: 'I thought it expedient to allot some of the forces of the 1st Ukrainian Front to strike at East Prussia. For some reason, however, the Supreme Commander was against it.'

Zhukov was highly dismissive of the intelligence effort for the offensive toward Lvov, perhaps still smarting that Stalin had thrown away the chance to secure East Prussia, observing:

When the preparations were being made for the operation on the Lvov sector, the intelligence agencies of the 1st Ukrainian Front failed to disclose the enemy's entire defence system and to locate the operational reserves of the German High Command, first of all its armoured troops. The result was that the Front Command could not foresee the possible counter manoeuvre by the enemy when his defence was penetrated. Artillery preparation and air support was poorly planned due to inadequate study of the enemy fire layout.

Zhukov also felt that the area bombardment rather than concentrating on specific targets failed to yield results.

Lvov–Sandomierz was an unusual operation in that it was the only time during the war that a single front was tasked with destroying a whole German army group largely unassisted. Nonetheless, Konev's forces were significantly reinforced: he mustered 7 tank corps, 3 mechanized corps, 6 cavalry divisions and 72 rifle divisions, numbering over a million men, equipped with 1,600–2,200 tanks and assault guns, 14,000 guns and mortars, and 2,806 combat aircraft from General S.A Krasovsky's 2nd Air Army.

North of Lvov the 3rd Guards and 13th Armies, 1st Guards Tank Army and General V.K. Baranov's mechanized cavalry corps were to strike in the direction of Rava Russkaya and 4th Panzer Army. In the south the 60th and 38th Armies, plus the 3rd Guards and 4th Tank Armies and General S.V. Sokolov's mechanized cavalry group were to push on the city of Lvov, cutting their way through 1st Panzer Army. Even further south the 1st Guards and 18th Armies, with the 5th Guards Army following up, were to attack the Hungarian 1st Army guarding the approaches to Stanislav. Further north beyond Konev's front lay the elements of Rokossovsky's 1st Byelorussian Front, which had not been committed to Bagration and would attack LVI Panzer Corps.

Evgeni Bessonov recalled:

In early July our battalion along with the other battalions of the 49th Kamenets-Podolsk Mechanised Brigade, marched on foot towards the front line, to the concentration area, from which we were supposed to go over to the offensive. Intensive fighting was ahead of us.

We only marched in darkness and till dawn; in daytime we stayed in forests and groves, taking camouflage measures. By night the road to the front turned into a mighty stream of troops of all branches of service: infantry, artillery of all calibres, armoured personnel carriers. Tanks drove on other roads in order to confuse the enemy. Camouflage and concealment requirements were strictly followed; all soldiers understood its necessity – otherwise we would have been bombed.

The Soviets tried to convince Harpe the main attack would fall way to the south of the city rather than on it; indeed Harpe's intelligence did not notice the Soviet 1st Guards Tank Army moving north. Konev's deception plans made it appear he had a major strike group on his left flank poised to thrust toward Stanislav rather than toward Lvov and Rava Russkaya. Opposite Stanislav he simulated the concentration of a tank army and a tank corps behind the 1st Guards Army, and a tank army behind the 18th Army. These efforts included 453 mock-up tanks and 568 mock-up guns, 30 fake field kitchens and 6 dummy fuel points.

While German intelligence spotted the dummy assembly areas behind the 1st Guards Army and 18th Army, they did not detect the regrouping of some army-size units from the left flank. Generalleutnant F.W. von Mellenthin, chief of staff for the XXXXVIII Panzer Corps lying before Lvov, noted: 'Wireless intercept and interrogation of prisoners produced most contradictory reports… Only second rate Russian formations were identified in the front line.' The XXXXVIII Panzer Corps did not detect the 38th Army's shift north opposite its sector in front of Lvov as the 1st Ukrainian Front's first echelon until two days before the attack.

Nevertheless, the Germans, predicting an offensive and the preceding metal deluge, began to withdraw their troops out of harm's way. In response Konev decided to go without a full preliminary barrage and attacked on 13 July with the 3rd Guards Army and 13th Army north of Lvov against XIII Corps. He had massed a devastating 240 guns and mortars per kilometre. Unlike Bagration this time the German defenders received air and artillery support.

'The Great Onslaught Began'

Konev's offensive opened with General V.N. Gordov's 3rd Guards Army and General N.P. Pukhov's 13th Army launching their attacks toward Soka, Radekhov, Rava Russkaya and Lublin respectively. The main assault with 38th and 60th Armies toward Lvov via Zolochev commenced the following day.

Bessonov was with the 1st Motor Rifle battalion riding with the 56th Tank Regiment:

At dawn on 14 July 1944, after an extensive artillery barrage and numerous air strikes, the infantry's offensive operation began; the goal was to break through the strongly fortified German defences. On 17 July, after breaking through the German positions, our 4th Tank Army entered the gap with the mission to penetrate deep into the enemy's rear in the direction of Lvov.

Soviet resources staggered von Mellenthin, who recorded:

At 0820 on 14 July the great onslaught began. The Red Army employed masses of material on a scale never known before; in particular they flung in thousands of aircraft and for the first time in the war enjoyed unquestioned command of the air. The preliminary bombardment lasted an hour but was very violent; it was followed by concentrated attacks in two sectors. By 0930 it was clear that two of our infantry divisions had been hit very heavily and would be incapable of mastering the situation on their own, so we asked for the 1st and 8th Panzer Divisions to counterattack.

Zhukov, ever at the forefront, ensured that he was not far from the action: 'I set up my command post in the area of Lutsk so that I could be closer to the Kovel grouping of the 1st Byelorussian Front and to the troops of the 1st Ukrainian Front.'

The defence by the 1st and 4th Panzer Armies was much better than that conducted by Army Group Centre's armies. Konev threw his tanks in a two-pronged attack; the right forced its way across the Bug and headed north for Rokossovsky's planned push on Lublin and the Vistula, but panzer and SS divisions initially held up his left as it fought its way south toward Lvov.

The northern attack ran into the prepared positions of the weak 291st and 340th Infantry Divisions, but these were easily penetrated. To the north-west into the gap either side of Radekhov Konev poured Cavalry-Mechanized Group Baranov and the 1st Guards Tank Army. It took 13th Army two days of tough fighting to surround Brody.

To the south the Soviets hit the 349th and 357th Infantry Divisions. The former disintegrated, and it was only through the action of the latter and Korps Abteilung C that the Soviet breakthrough was restricted. But this did not prevent a wedge being driven between XIII Corps and XXXXVIII Panzer Corps.

Zolochev

With the German defence east of Lvov holding, Harpe decided to commit his tactical reserves, the 1st and 8th Panzer Divisions, in an attempt to stifle the Soviet offensive on 14 and 15 July. Although Konev had been ordered by the Stavka to hold back the 3rd Guards and 4th Guards Tank Armies until a deep penetration had been made, he knew he must act quickly to exploit the situation.

After some fierce fighting 1st Panzer Army's 1st Panzer successfully brought the Soviets to a halt at Oleyev on the 15th. The Germans also counter-attacked 38th Army south of Zolochev, which lay east of Lvov. But, instead of striking eastward along a previously arranged route, 8th Panzer swung south on the Zlochuv–Jezierna road. General Balck had forbidden troop movements along this route for fear of the Red Air Force. His fears were realized when fighter-bombers swooped and reduced the 8th Panzer columns to blazing wrecks.

Zheleznov, serving with 4th Tank Army, took part in the Lvov–Sandomierz offensive. He recalled:

The next operation in which I participated was the Lvov-Sandomierz offensive. I fought in a T-34/85 there. There were still only a few of them at that time – my platoon had just one. Our corps was sent to exploit the breakthrough. We marched towards Lvov, not encountering any resistance. When we liberated the town of Zolochev [south-west of Brody], the corps commander replaced the 61st Brigade, marching in the vanguard, with our 63rd Brigade. The brigade commander assembled us and said: 'Lieutenant Kriukov's platoon will form the forward detachment, Lieutenant Poligenki's platoon will be on the right flank, and Zheleznov's on my left.'

Konev had trouble bringing his tank armies to bear in the Lvov attack because the 15th Infantry Corps from 60th Army had only managed to hack a corridor only 2½ to 4 miles (4–6km) wide to a depth of 11 miles (18km). General P.S. Rybalko, commander of the 3rd Guards Tank Army, took the decision to shove his men along this corridor on the 16th and was followed up by General D.D. Lelyushenko's 4th Tank Army.

This was the only time during the war that two tank armies were committed to combat on such a narrow front and while the flanks were being counter-attacked by the Germans. While German artillery bombarded the 'Koltiv Corridor' the 1st and 8th Panzer Divisions prepared to counter-attack, supported by the 14th SS-Grenadier Division Galizien.

Once Rybalko's men were in the corridor, General Arthur Hauffe's XIII Corps knew it must withdraw immediately, and fell back to the Prinz Eugen *Stellung*. By the 17th the Soviets had captured parts of this strongpoint, which the 14th SS attempted to recapture until the appearance of the powerful Soviet IS-2 tank. Rybalko's gamble paid off, and on the evening of 18 July the 1st Ukrainian Front cut through the German defences to a width of 124 miles (200km), advanced 30–50 miles (50–80km) and surrounded 45,000 men near Brody. Despite pleas to General Hauffe from his subordinates, there was little he could do to help the four divisions in the Brody salient escape.

The battle was soon joined at a village 7½ miles (12km) from Zolochev. Zheleznov deployed his armour defensively along the edge of a forest 400 metres from the village to meet an oncoming German column. Taking up the story, he recounts:

There were motorcycles and three Panthers in the forward detachment of the column. I said on the radio: 'The first one's mine. Kozlov, yours is the second one. Tikhonov, take the third one.' After letting them close to about 600 metres, we fired on my command. The tanks burst into flames and our infantry and artillery eliminated the motorcyclists. Then the German column deployed, and it turned out that it had no less than twenty tanks! They pulled back to the village and started shooting at us and I ordered a retreat. I said to my driver, Petukhov: 'Kolia, let's go right.' He turned, and then an armour piercing round slammed into the gearbox. It got jammed, and our fuel tank broke open. The tank started burning. I managed to yell: 'Guys, bail out!' Thank god, everyone got out.

When his brigade entered Lvov, Zheleznov lost his replacement tank and again narrowly missed being burned. East of Lvov the vital Zolochev bastion fell on the 17th, and despite a counter-attack by the panzer divisions from 1st Panzer Army the Germans were unable to capture it. The German divisions at Brody to the north were unable to retake Zolochev or hold Brody.

The Soviet 4th Tank Army's advance did not go uncontested. 'We were hit hard during the march to Lvov,' said Bessonov, 'especially by the Luftwaffe, which never stopped strafing our column, trying to slow down our advance.' These attacks normally consisted of twenty to twenty-five German bombers supported by fighters. Bessonov adds: 'First they all dropped their bombs, aiming for the tanks, and simultaneously fired the large calibre machine guns, trying to set them on fire. The planes attacked twice or three times.' Often he and his men had to flee their tanks, seeking shelter in the roadside ditches.

The infantry pressed on while the tanks took shelter, catching up at night. There was bitter fighting on the 18th around Bobrka, south of Lvov, which was defended by German Panther tanks. Bessonov's column lost its lead tank and suffered heavy casualties, and the men were given a choice – advance or be executed. Fortunately the Germans fled, abandoning a Panther that had run out of fuel. Bessonov regretted that he had forced his men to attack, but what else could he have done? He was relieved that they did not hold it against him.

The Brody Pocket

By nightfall of the 15th the Rava Russkaya attack had managed about 9 miles (15km) in the face of heavy fighting. It was soon developed, with Baronov's mechanized cavalry corps and General M.Y. Katukov's 1st Guards Tank Army pouring into the breach on the 16th and 17th, both toward Jaroslav and behind Brody.

On 16 July, with the Red Army slicing through between Brody and Zolochev, the Germans expected the Soviets to push south toward the Zlata Lipa. Instead the following day they struck north along the banks of the Styr, pushing through Gorokhov and Radziechow, while Soviet tanks drove on Busk and cavalry reached Kamenka, crossing the Western Bug north of Lvov.

Konev's troops took not only Busk, to the north–east of Lvov, on the 18th, but also the junction at Krasnoe, some 30 miles (48km) south-west of Brody and the same distance east of Lvov. On the 19th the panzer divisions escaped to the south-west via Gologory to Peremyshlyany; the infantry were not so lucky. Four infantry divisions and one security division were trapped east of Brody between the town and the headwaters of the Styr. Also, the Soviets crossed the Western Bug and entered Poland.

The following day 4th Panzer Army committed the 16th Panzer Division and the 20th Motorized and 168th Infantry Divisions in the vicinity of Zholkov to block the advance toward Lvov of the 1st Guards Tank Army. But meeting no serious resistance the latter continued west and did not turn south, where the Germans were waiting. By the end of the day, its forward detachment had advanced to a depth of 19–25 miles (30–40km) and was approaching Rava Russkaya.

The XXXXVIII and XXIV Panzer Corps attempted to reach XIII Corps but to no avail. On the 18th von Mellenthin, taking command of 8th Panzer, tried to cut his way through to the trapped men of XIII Corps at Brody. The Soviets were waiting for him with minefields and concentrated artillery and tank fire. Mellenthin remembers:

Two days later the bulk of XIII Corps, led by Generals Lasch and Lange, succeeded in fighting their way through to our lines. Thousands of men formed up in the night in a solid mass and to the accompaniment of thunderous 'hurrahs' threw themselves at the enemy. The impact of a great block of desperate men, determined to do or die, smashed through the Russian line, and thus a great many of the troops were saved. But all guns and heavy weapons had to be abandoned, and a huge gap was opened in the front. Marshal Konev's tanks poured through and the whole German position in southern Galicia became untenable.

Those forces remaining in the Brody pocket resisted for four days until it was cut in half and they were finally wiped out on the 22nd. The Germans suffered 30,000 killed and 15,000 captured, as well as losing 68 panzers, 500 guns and 3,500 lorries.

Some 14,000 men of the 14th SS Grenadier Division were caught in the Brody area and only 2,000–3,000 managed to escape. Those caught could expect little leniency from their captors. The survivors were sent to Slovakia to refit, and the division was rebuilt using Soviet Ukrainians, which was reflected in its re-designation to 14th Waffen Grenadier Division of the SS (*ukrainische* no. 1).

Five days after the offensive started, Konev's forces had cut a breach in the Germans' defences 155 miles (250km) wide by 62–87 miles (100–140km) deep, and had routed 4th Panzer Army and 17th Army. The 13th Army, 1st Guards Tank Army and General Baranov's mechanized cavalry group reached the San river on 29 July and secured bridgeheads on its western banks near Jaroslav.

Hitler Distracted

Hitler was distracted from the Eastern and Western Fronts by an attempt on his life carried out at Wolfsschanze, his Führer headquarters near Rastenburg (Kętrzyn, Poland) in East Prussia. 'On the evening of 22 July,' recalled Scheiderbauer of the 252nd Infantry Division, 'it was announced that an assassination attempt had been made on the Führer on 20 July. Among us there was more surprise than fury. We had no time to comment on the event and scarcely had any time to reflect upon it.'

Although four people were killed and five injured as a result of the Wolfsschanze bombing, Hitler survived the blast with only minor injuries. He spent the following weeks devoting his energies and those of the Gestapo to tracking down the plotters: in total some 5,000 people were arrested and 200 executed. This was at a critical time for both the Eastern and Western Fronts, as the Allies were making considerable progress against his forces. Understandably Hitler's trust in the German army waned even further; Generalfeldmarschalls von Kluge and Rommel took their own lives to avoid public disgrace over their complicity.

Although neither had been active supporters of the plotters, von Kluge knew about von Tresckow's plan to shoot Hitler during a visit to Army Group Centre, having been informed by his former subordinate, Georg von Boeselager, now serving under von Tresckow. Boeselager was dispatched by Tresckow in mid-1944 to urge his old commander to change his strategy and to join the conspiracy against Hitler.

Gersdorff concludes rather haughtily:

It must be said that the conspiracy of 20 July was the only active effort to overthrow the National Socialist [Nazi] government and to remove the chief criminals. It should be emphasised that this only attempt was planned and executed by members of the officer corps and that the dominant role was played by the General Staff, the nobility, and the large landowners.

The following day, in a fine example of understatement, Guderian recalled: 'When I was compelled to assume the duties of Chief of the General Staff, on 21 July 1944, the situation on the Eastern Front was far from satisfactory.' Only Army Group South Ukraine was in a reasonable situation, while Army Groups Centre and North Ukraine were in complete disarray. As a result of the disaster that had engulfed Army Group Centre, Army Group North had withdrawn to a line Mitau–Dünaburg–Paleskau.

In agreement with General Wenck, Army Group South Ukraine's chief of staff, Guderian proposed to Hitler that all those divisions that could be spared from Romania be sent north to plug the gap between army groups Centre and North. Hitler agreed and also made Friessner, commander of Army Group North, exchange places with Schörner, commander of South Ukraine.

Battle for Lvov

In the meantime at Lvov the Germans put on a show of strength in an attempt to thwart the 3rd Guards and 4th Tank Armies' ambitions on 19–20 July. The 3rd Guards swung north and in three days covered 75 miles (120km) and were in the Yavorov area, and then moved in two directions, toward Lvov and south-west toward Przemyśl.

After the capture of Rava Russkaya on the 23rd, Konev moved to sweep north of Lvov. He had hoped to quickly seize the city and press on, but Rybalko's 3rd Tank Army became bogged down; Harpe had also reinforced the city with several infantry divisions. Konev's main concern now was that Harpe must not be given breathing space in which to further prepare his defences along the San river. At this crucial moment the 3rd and 4th Guards were freed up by the arrival of rifle divisions following the liberation of Brody on 22 July.

While the bulk of the Germans withdrew from Lvov on 17 July, the presence of large numbers of German troops still in the area made the Polish Home Army postpone its rising in the city. Only when the Soviet 29th Tank Brigade of the 4th

Tank Army reached the city's limits on 23 July did the Polish Home Army rise up as part of Operation Tempest, the national Polish insurrection.

Bessonov was ordered to gain a foothold in Lvov with just two platoons:

> We approached Lvov from the south, not from the east; the enemy did not expect us there and there were almost no German troops in the area. To be honest, I was afraid to enter the city without armour support. I did not like to assault or advance without tanks. Tanks always meant additional courage for us and additional fear for the enemy. We supported each other in battle, especially in built up areas and forests.

Bessonov and his men infiltrated the outskirts of the city, supported by a 45mm gun with just five rounds, and dug in. It was not until late on the 25th or 26th that they were reinforced by the 10th Guards Tank Corps. The Polish Home Army had quickly overwhelmed the token German forces and secured the city; in the city centre the partisans were aided by the arrival of Soviet tanks. However, the NKVD quickly moved into the city and the Poles were disarmed and forcibly conscripted into the Red Army or sent to the Gulag.

The remaining Lvov garrison had no intention of being trapped, and on the night of the 26th successfully broke out. It took the Soviets the following day to clear out the German rearguard, and bitter street-fighting raged for seventy-two hours before Lvov was finally liberated on 27 July. About half of the 40,000 German troops in and around Lvov were killed or captured.

Przemyśl also fell that day to the 3rd Guards and the Red Army's seemingly unstoppable streamroller took Stanislav in the Carpathian foothills, Bialystok in northern Poland, Dvinsk in Latvia and the Siauliai (also spelt Shaulyai) rail junction between Riga and East Prussia. The 4th Panzer Army fell back on the Vistula and the 1st Panzer Army retreated south-west to the Carpathians.

On 25 July Moscow issued figures for German losses during the first month of the Soviet offensive operations: 381,000 dead, 158,000 captured, 2,735 tanks and assault guns, 8,702 guns and 57,000 motor vehicles. This showed the incredible tempo of the Red Army's summer offensives, which easily outstripped its winter operations.

A plea was also issued by sixteen former German generals, captured from Army Group Centre, that their comrades be made aware that thirty divisions had been annihilated and that the old Army Group Centre had ceased to exist. They blamed Hitler for this disaster and called on their comrades to disobey him.

CHAPTER 10

Rokossovsky: Defeat at the Gates of Warsaw

It seemed appropriate to Stalin that eastern Poland be liberated as part of Byelorussia, as that is how Hitler had treated it. For administrative purposes parts of German-occupied Poland had been lumped in with western Byelorussia. When Hitler divided prostrate Poland with Stalin in 1939, he also annexed the region south-west of East Prussia (Wartheland) to the Reich, while the Reichskommissariat of 'Ostland' (an area incorporating Minsk and the Baltic States) and 'Ukraine' governed parts of eastern Poland, with the rump in the middle run as the 'Generalgouvernement'.

Rokossovsky's Lublin–Brest Offensive was conducted from 18 July to 2 August as a follow-up to Bagration and to support Konev's Lvov–Sandomierz offensive by tying down German forces in central-eastern Poland. It culminated in the Battle of Radzymin. To the north of Konev's 1st Ukrainian Front, Rokossovsky's 8th Guards, 47th and 69th Armies, supported by the 2nd Tank Army and the Polish 1st Army, struck from the Kovel area towards Lublin and Warsaw, thereby making Army Group North Ukraine's position untenable.

Poland's Fate Preordained

The Polish 1st Army was instructed to cross the Vistula at Puławy on the 31st on a wide front in order to support other elements of the Soviet 69th and 8th Guards Armies crossing near Magnuszew. The Polish 1st and 2nd Infantry Divisions gained the west bank on 1 and 2 August, but by the 4th had suffered 1,000 casualties and were ordered to withdraw. They were then assigned to protect the northern part of the Magnuszew bridgehead.

General Zygmunt Berling's Soviet-trained and equipped Polish 1st Army had reinforced Rokossovsky's front during the spring of 1944. This in fact was the second Polish army to be formed in the Soviet Union and was the military wing of the so-called Union of Polish Patriots, which had come into being with Stalin's approval in 1943. The earlier Army of General Władysław Anders had managed to slip Stalin's grasp in 1942, getting itself redeployed to fight with the British in the Middle East and Italy.

By 29 April, when Berling joined Rokossovsky he had 104,000 men under arms, comprising five infantry divisions, a tank brigade, four artillery brigades and an air wing. Many recruits who were former PoWs from 1939 were looking for a way to return home, though Stalin kept them on a tight political leash.

When Poland was cynically partitioned between Stalin and Hitler under the non-aggression pact of 1939, 130,000 Polish officers and men immediately fell into the hands of the Red Army. In total some 250,000 Polish officers and men were eventually moved into the Soviet Union as PoWs. Stalin had a long memory and a score to settle with the Poles, who in 1920 had defeated the Red Army; also he wanted to destroy the basis for any future opposition to the Soviet occupation of eastern Poland, which would act as a buffer against post-war Germany.

Stalin acted swiftly. He had every Polish officer in his part of pre-war Poland (now western Ukraine and western Byelorussia) rounded up, and in early 1940 Beria ruthlessly organized the slaughter. In April–May 1940 15,000 Polish officers and policemen were evacuated from camps at Kozielski, Starobielsk and Ostashkov and turned over to the NKVD in the Smolensk, Kharkov and Kalinin regions.

With the German invasion of the USSR the Polish government in exile signed an agreement with Moscow; the provisions included raising a Polish Army in the Soviet Union. However, of the 15,000 Polish officers held by the Soviets, only 350–400 reported for duty. Like the kulaks and Red Army officers before them, the Polish officer class had been ruthlessly liquidated.

Stalin's duplicity in his treatment of Poland and the Polish army knew no bounds. In December 1941 generals Władysław Sikorski and Anders and the Polish ambassador met Stalin to discuss the whereabouts of approximately 4,000 named Polish officers who had been deported to Soviet prisons and labour camps. Stalin initially claimed rather disingenuously they had escaped to Manchuria. He then changed tack, suggesting they had been released, adding: 'I want you to know that the Soviet Government has not the slightest reason to retain even one Pole.' What he meant was even one living Pole.

Hitler announced he had found the mass grave of 3,000–4,000 Polish officers in the forest of Katyn, near Smolensk, in April 1943. The Germans continued to dig, unearthing an estimated 10,000 bodies, and Hitler set up a committee of inquiry which 'proved' the Poles had been shot in 1940 by the NKVD. The Soviets dismissed the claim as propaganda, calling it 'revolting and slanderous fabrications'.

The German discovery had strained even further Soviet-Polish relations, allowing Stalin to undermine the validity of the Polish government in exile in London as a prelude to establishing a Communist government in Warsaw. On retaking Smolensk the Soviets set up their own commission, which stated categorically that the men had been killed in 1941 while road building for the Germans. As far as Stalin was concerned, Poland lay within his sphere of influence and he had every intention of it remaining so.

Berling, like Rokossovsky, was a career soldier who had served with the Austrian and Polish armies. The fact that Stalin had spared him and that he had not stayed with Anders made him appear a turncoat to many of his countrymen. Berling was also given the onerous task of endorsing the Soviet lie that the Germans had perpetrated the massacre of Polish officers in Katyn Forest.

Model's Gathering Riposte

In five weeks of fighting Rokossovsky had covered 450 miles (725km) and was within reach of Warsaw. The Polish capital now looked a tempting prize as a culmination of Bagration's remarkable success, but Stalin's summer offensive was beginning to lose momentum. Rokossovsky's 1st Byelorussian Front was at the very limit of its supply lines; ammunition and rations were exhausted, as were his men.

In many ways the defence of Warsaw echoed that of Minsk – the eastern approaches of the Polish capital were protected by a 50 mile (80km) ring of strongpoints. The only difference was that this time Model had sufficient mobile reserves with which to parry Rokossovsky's thrusts.

By this stage the German defences were coalescing around five weak panzer divisions deploying around 450 tanks and self-propelled guns. Over the next week things would start to go badly wrong for Rokossovsky, and his front would experience its first major setback.

North of Warsaw Model turned to SS-Reichsführer Heinrich Himmler's Waffen SS for assistance in stabilizing the front. The remnants of the 1st SS and 2nd SS Panzer Divisions had been shipped west after their mauling in the Kamenets-Podolsk Pocket to re-equip and prepare for the anticipated Anglo-American landings in France. However, the 3rd SS and 5th SS Panzer Divisions remained in Romania and Poland to rearm.

The 3rd SS was notified to move north as early as 25 June, but the disruption to the rail networks and roads meant that it took two weeks to get to north-eastern Poland. Arriving on 7 July it found the Red Army was already striking toward the Polish city of Grodno, threatening the southern flank of Army Group Centre's 4th Army and the northern flank of 2nd Army.

Deployed to Grodno the 3rd SS was assigned the task of creating a defensive line for 4th Army to retire behind. Spectacularly the division held off 400 Soviet tanks for eleven days before withdrawing south-west toward Warsaw. Joined by the Hermann Göring Panzer Division at Siedlce, 50 miles (80km) east of the Polish capital, it held the Soviets for almost a week from 24 July, keeping open an escape corridor for 2nd Army as it fled toward the Vistula. Three days later the Soviets threw almost 500 tanks to the south and by the 29th were at the suburbs of Warsaw.

The 5th SS arrived in western Warsaw on 27 July and trundled through the city to take up positions to the east. The next day Stalin ordered Rokossovsky to occupy Praga, Warsaw's suburbs on the eastern bank of the Vistula, during 5–8 August, and to establish a number of bridgeheads over the river to the south of the city.

Rokossovsky at this stage enjoyed a three to one superiority in infantry and five to one in armour and artillery. His front had at its disposal nine armies: one tank army, two tank corps, three cavalry corps, one motorized corps and two air armies. Against this Model's 2nd Army could muster four understrength panzer divisions and one infantry division, while 9th Army had just two divisions and two brigades of infantry.

As instructed the Soviet 2nd Tank Army and 8th Tank Corps attacked westward along the Warsaw–Lublin road toward Praga. About 40 miles (64km) south-east of Warsaw in the Garwolin area 2nd Tank was opposed by two advanced battalions of Generalleutnant Dr Fritz Franek's 10,800-strong German 73rd Infantry Division. Holding the north bank of the Swidra river, they were backed up by the Hermann Göring Panzer Division 12 miles (19km) east of Praga.

In addition four panzer divisions, the 3rd SS, 5th SS, 4th and 19th, poised to counter-attack, now defended the approaches to the Polish capital. The men of 19th Panzer were veterans of the Eastern Front having fought on the central and southern sectors from June 1941 to June 1944, before being shipped to the Netherlands for a refit.

Hasso Krappe, an officer with 19th Panzer, recalled the fighting around Warsaw:

After the defeat of Army Group Centre in the middle of July, my division (the Lower Saxon 19th Panzer Division) was sent by train from southern Holland to a base in the Karvitse region near Elk. Before all the units were gathered, we were ordered to march in a south-westerly direction to set up a bridgehead to the east of Praga. Yet after the arrival of the last transports from Holland my regiment [73rd Hanoverian] was once again despatched by rail…to Warsaw's Danzig Station. This was on 1 August…

It was an entirely different story for the remainder of our division, which on 3 August was supposed to reach the Varka from the other side of the Vistula, via Praga…They suffered heavy losses. As the armoured column of the third company passed the main station in Warsaw, it came under such intense fire that it could not continue, and its commander decided to reverse and seize the station instead. He and his soldiers remained there for close on two months. His column only rejoined the [division] on 2 October.

Over the next two weeks the battles centred on the region north of Warsaw [between the Bug, Narev and Vistula], and on the Varka, which has gone down in military history as the 'Magnushev Bridgehead'.

The 73rd Infantry had endured a rough time during its career, having taken part in the invasions of Poland, the Low Countries, France and Greece before entering the Soviet Union via Romania. It fought at Nikolayev, Kherson, Sevastopol and the Kuban bridgehead. Having suffered heavy losses near Melitopol the division was withdrawn, only to be trapped by the Red Army in Sevastopol in May 1944 and reformed in June in Hungary under Franek.

This division and the Hermann Göring bore the brunt of the attacks launched by the Soviet 3rd and 8th Tank Corps on the 27th. Garwolin was partially captured during the night of 27–28 July, and the 73rd fell back to the strong Siennica–Kołbiel–Latowicze line. Despite the presence of elements of 19th Panzer and the Hermann Göring, by noon on the 29th the Soviet 8th Tank Corps had secured Kołbiel and Siennica.

Brest-Litovsk fell to Rokossovsky on 28 July, and, with his troops at Garwolin, three German divisions tried to escape toward Siedlce, south-east of Warsaw.

They were surrounded between Biała and the river and crushed on the 29th and 30th, with 15,000 killed and just 2,000 captured. In Moscow Stalin and his Stavka were very pleased with Rokossovsky's efforts, and on 29 July he was nominated a marshal of the Soviet Union.

By early on the 30th the Germans held a line consisting of Zielonka, Cechowa, Mińsk Mazowiecki and Otwock. About 26 miles (41km) from Warsaw at Mińsk Mazowiecki, Lieutenant-General N.D. Vedeneev's 3rd Tank Corps broke the Germans' defences, and at Zielonka General Franek and some of his staff were captured.

Documents in their possession revealed German dispositions, showing that the 5th SS reconnaissance unit was deployed near Mińsk Mazowiecki; units of Hermann Göring and the 73rd Infantry were holding the Cechowa and Otwock sector of Warsaw's outer defences; 19th Panzer was defending the approaches to Praga; and the 3rd SS was in the Okuniew and Pustelnik suburban areas. Such information could be highly damaging to the Germans' ability to hold the Polish capital.

Defeat before Warsaw

When the 2nd Tank Army's 16th Tank Corps struck toward Otwock along the Lublin road, 19th Panzer counter-attacked with forty panzers and an infantry regiment, but was unable to hold Otwock, and by the evening the Soviets were a mere 15 miles (24km) from Warsaw, having taken the villages near Miłosna Stara. They were now poised to assault the key defences of Okuniew. The 8th Tank Corps opened the attack only to be stalled by determined German air and artillery attack.

In the meantime Vedeneev's 3rd Corps, bypassing German positions in the Zielonka district, drove them from Wołomin (also spelt Volomin) and Radzymin, just 12 and 16 miles (19 and 25km) north-east of Warsaw, where they took up defensive positions along the Długa river. Having outstretched his supply lines and outrun the rest of the Soviet 2nd Tank Army, Vedeneev was in a dangerously exposed position. The XXXIX Panzer Corps was in the area, and five German panzer divisions were coming together in the direction of Radzymin–Wołomin.

Rokossovsky's forces were quick to react to this threat, and attempted to alleviate the pressure on Vedeneev's 3rd Tank Corps with a diversionary attack. At dawn on the 31st, followed by heavy air and artillery bombardment, the Soviet 8th Tank Corps threw itself at the Germans, who fell back toward Okuniew. The 5th SS counter-attacked in a westerly direction with fifty panzers from Stanisławów in an effort to link up with the Hermann Göring and 19th Panzer, which were fighting a tank battle with the Soviets at Okuniew and Ossow.

The 5th SS was repulsed and on the evening of the 31st the Soviets took Okuniew, but could not budge the Germans from their strongpoint at Ossow. North of the Soviet 8th Tank Corps, the 3rd Tank remained unsupported, and like the 16th Corps had endured a day of heavy attacks from German armour, artillery and infantry. The commander of the Soviet 2nd Army was in an impossible position: his units were enduring heavy casualties, he was short of supplies and his rear was under threat.

Rokossovsky simply could not fulfil his orders to break through the German defences and enter Praga by 8 August. On the 1st at 1610 hours he ordered the attack to be broken off just as Model launched his major counter-attack.

On the 2nd all Soviet forces that were assaulting Warsaw were redirected. The 28th, 47th and 65th Armies were instructed northwards to seize the undefended town of Wyszków and the Liwiec river line. Crucially this left 2nd Tank Army without infantry support. This situation was compounded when 69th Army was ordered to halt while the 8th Guards Army under Vasily Chuikov ceased the assault to await a German attack from the direction of Garwolin.

Model began to probe the weak spot in Rokossovsky's line between Praga and Siedlce. His intention was to hit the Soviets in the flank and the rear, and soon to the north-east of Warsaw the XXXIX Panzer Corps was counter-attacking the 3rd Tank Corps and driving it back to Wołomin.

The 3rd SS, Hermann Göring, and 4th and 19th Panzer Divisions struck south into the unsupported Soviet columns. The Hermann Göring's 1st Armoured Paratroop Regiment launched the counter-attack from Praga toward Wołomin on the 31st, heralding a much larger effort to halt the Red Army before Warsaw, while from the south-west along the Warsaw–Wyszków road attacking toward Radzymin came the 19th Panzer. From Wyszków 4th Panzer acted in support.

The next day from Węgrów pushing toward Wołomin came the 5th SS. At the same time the 3rd SS was launched into the fray from Siedlce towards Stanisławów with the intention of trapping those Soviet forces on the north-eastern bank of the Długa.

General Nikolaus von Vormann, appointed by Guderian to command 9th Army, bringing up reinforcements from 2nd Army's reserves, also launched a counter-attack. Using units of the 5th SS and 3rd SS attacking from the forests to the east of Michałów, he drove the Soviet 8th Tank Corps from Okuniew at 2100 hours on 1 August, and linked up with XXXIX Panzer Corps from the west.

By 2 August, 19th and 4th Panzer were in Radzymin and the Soviet 3rd Tank Corps was thrown back towards Wołomin. The following day the Hermann Göring Panzer Division rolled into Wołomin. Pressed into the area of Wołomin, Vedeneev's 3rd Tank Corps was trapped. Attempts by the 8th Guards Tank Corps and the 16th Tank Corps to reach it failed, with the 8th Guards suffering serious casualties in the attempt.

After a week of heavy fighting the Soviet 3rd Tank Corps was surrounded by 4th and 19th Panzer; 3,000 Soviet troops were killed and another 6,000 captured. The Soviets also lost 425 of the 808 tanks and self-propelled guns they had begun the battle with on 18 July. By noon on the 5th the Germans had ceased their counter-attack and the battle for the Praga approaches had come to an end. Two German divisions had to be transferred south to deal with the Soviet threat there.

The 3rd Tank Corps was destroyed and the 8th Guards Tank Corps and the 16th Tank Corps had taken major losses. The exhausted Soviet 2nd Tank Army handed over its positions to the 47th and 70th Armies and withdrew to lick its wounds. Post-war Communist propagandists cited the Battle of Radzymin as evidence that the German counter-attack prevented the Red Army from helping the Warsaw Uprising.

Stalin clearly did not hold Lieutenant-General N.D. Vedeneev responsible for the encirclement and destruction of his command. He remained in charge, and the 3rd Tank Corps was honoured by being designated the 9th Guards Tank Corps in November 1944.

It was not until 25 August that Rokossovsky would inform Stalin that he was ready to have another go at Warsaw. After such heavy fighting north-east of the Polish capital it is easy to see why Stalin saw the Polish Home Army's Warsaw rising of little consequence to the overall strategic scheme of things.

Sacrifice of Warsaw

Just 12½ miles (20km) south of Warsaw Chuikov's 8th Guards Army crossed the Vistula on 1 August at Magnuszew. He held onto his tiny bridgehead despite determined counter-attacks by 9th Panzer, Hermann Göring and 45th Grenadier Divisions. By the 8th the bridgehead contained the Soviet 4th, 28th and 29th Guards Rifle Corps. Holding the northern shoulder of the bridgehead, preventing the Soviets from expanding it, were the 1132nd Volksgrenadier Brigade and the Panzer Abteilung 902, while to the south was the 17th Infantry Division.

General Tadeusz Bór-Komorowski, commander of the underground Polish Home Army, ordered his men to rise up against the German occupation of Warsaw on 1 August. In stark contrast Rokossovsky, ordered to go over to the defensive, watched the Germans systemically crush the Poles for two whole months. Likewise the Red Air Force, which was just 100 miles (160km) away, did very little.

On the morning of the 2nd Rokossovsky went to view the Polish capital and got a good indication of the Polish Home Army's efforts, as he recalled:

> Together with a group of officers I was visiting the 2nd Tank Army, which was fighting on that sector of the front. From our observation point, which had been set up at the top of a tall factory chimney, we could see Warsaw. The city was covered in clouds of smoke. Here and there houses were burning. Bombs and shells were exploding. Everything indicated that a battle was in progress.

Why did Rokossovsky not try for a bridgehead at Warsaw if the Red Army had established footholds at Magnuszew, Puławy and on the upper Vistula near Sandomierz? To have done so would have been far tougher than in the Radom region way to the south. Sandomierz had cost them dearly, and the Soviets saw Warsaw as anchoring the Germans' line on the Narev and Bóbr and in turn East Prussia, and knew they would fight bitterly to defend this. Without the Baltic States secured Hitler could strike from East Prussia against the flank and rear of the Red Army once it was advancing beyond the Vistula.

Also by now Rokossovsky was facing twenty-two enemy divisions, including four security divisions in the Warsaw suburbs, three Hungarian divisions on the Vistula south of Warsaw, and the remains of six or seven divisions which had escaped from the chaos of Bialystok and Brest-Litovsk, that could be deployed between the Narev and the Western Bug. At least eight divisions were identified fighting to the north of Siedlce, among them two panzer and three SS panzer or panzergrenadier divisions. In reality Stalin was waiting in the wings with his own Polish government and armed forces.

Zhukov blamed Bór-Komorowski for a lack of cooperation with the Red Army:

> As was established later, neither the command of the Front [Rokossovsky] nor that of Poland's 1st Army [Berling] had been informed in advance by Bor-Komorowski, the leader of the uprising, about forthcoming events in Warsaw. Nor did he make any attempt to coordinate the insurgents' actions with those of the 1st Byelorussian Front. The Soviet Command learned about the uprising after the event from local residents who had crossed the Vistula. The Stavka had not been informed in advance either.
>
> On instructions by the Supreme Commander, two paratroop officers were sent to Bor-Komorowski for liaison and coordination of actions. However, Bor-Komorowski refused to receive the officers…
>
> I have ascertained that our troops did everything they possibly could to help the insurgents, although the uprising had not been in any way coordinated with the Soviet command.

In light of Rokossovsky's efforts to the north-east and south-east of Warsaw in the face of the tough Waffen SS, this is largely true.

At Kraków, the capital of the 'Generalgouvernement', the Wehrmacht garrison was 30,000 strong, twice that of Warsaw, which had a much bigger population. In addition there were some 10,000 armed German administrators in the city. As a result there was no secondary Home Army rising in Kraków.

In Warsaw General Reiner Stahel's 12,000-strong garrison included 5,000 regular troops, 4,000 Luftwaffe personnel (over a quarter of whom were manning the air defences) and the 2,000-strong Warsaw security regiment. Wehrmacht forces in the immediate area numbered up to 16,000 men, with another 90,000 further afield.

With the Wehrmacht fully tied up fending off Soviet attacks, it was left to the hated SS to stamp out the Polish rising. Police and SS units totalled 5,710 men under SS-Standartenführer Paul Geibel, supported by 3,500 factory and rail guards. Geibel also managed to scrounge four Tiger tanks, a Panther tank, four medium tanks and an assault gun off the 5th SS to strengthen his forces.

A motley battle group of 12,000 troops under SS-Gruppenführer Heinz Reinefarth, supported by thirty-seven assault guns and a company of heavy tanks, was assembled to crush the Polish Home Army in Warsaw. SS reinforcements included SS-Brigadeführer Bratislav Kaminski's hated Russian National Liberation Army

(*Russkaya osvoboditelnaya narodnaya armiya* – RONA) Brigade, numbering 1,585 Cossacks and Ukrainians.

Kaminski supported SS-Oberführer Oskar Dirlewanger's anti-partisan brigade, some 3,381 strong. This consisted of two battalions of 865 released criminals, three battalions of former Soviet PoWs, two companies of gendarmes, a police platoon and an artillery battery. Additionally Colonel Wilhelm Schmidt supplied 2,000 men drawn from his 603rd Regiment and a grenadier and police battalion.

Army Group Centre was to have a limited role in fighting the Warsaw rising. General Vormann, commanding 9th Army, sent 1,000 East Prussian grenadiers to Praga to help hold the Poniatowski Bridge; an additional three battalions were also sent to help the Hermann Göring regiment clear a way through the city to the Kierbedz Bridge.

All the forces in Warsaw were placed under SS-Obergruppenführer Erich von dem Bach-Zelewski, who had been overseeing the construction of defences on the Vistula near Gdansk. He was the nemesis of partisan forces in the east. Bach-Zelewski was soon to find both Kaminski and Dirlewanger's formations were of poor fighting value, prone to drinking and lax discipline.

Their conduct in Warsaw was to horrify the battle-hardened SS, and von dem Bach-Zelewski thought they were the lowest of the low, remarking: 'The fighting value of these Cossacks was, as usual in such a collection of people without a fatherland, very poor. They had a great liking for alcohol and other excesses and had no interest in military discipline.'

The people of Warsaw had experienced this type of Nazi campaign before. In fact the Polish intelligentsia and Poland's Jews had faced persecution from the moment of the German invasion in 1939. Three years later 310,332 Polish Jews had been deported from the Warsaw Ghetto, with most being sent to the Treblinka death camp. In 1943 Himmler had ordered the rest be sent to the labour camps or executed.

SS-Brigadeführer General Jürgen Stroop, with 2,096 security police, including two SS training battalions, supported by some Wehrmacht units, set about forcibly removing the 56,000 surviving Jews. The ghetto's inhabitants resisted, but by the end of April 1943 Stroop by his own estimate had seized or killed 37,359 people.

On 5 August 1944 Dirlewanger and Kaminski's troops were thrown into the counter-attack against the brave Polish Home Army. An appalling massacre took place in Elektoralna Street, carried out by Kaminski and Dirlewanger's men. At the Marie Curie Radium Institute, drunken Cossacks perpetrated terrible atrocities against the civilian staff and patients. For two days they ran amok in Wola, the western part of the city centre, and Ochota. After the war German officers involved disingenuously laid the blame firmly on Kaminski and Dirlewanger.

On the 19th the Polish Home Army's efforts to fight its way through to those forces trapped in the Old Town came to nothing, and it was clear they would have to be evacuated to the city centre and Żoliborz district. About 2,500 fighters withdrew via the sewers, leaving behind their badly wounded. It was now only a matter of time before the SS crushed resistance in the city centre and cleared resistance between the Poniatowski and Kierbedz bridges.

To ward off a wider encircling movement by the Red Army to the north, Model deployed the IV SS Panzer Corps with the 3rd SS and 5th SS moved into blocking positions. From 14 August the Soviets attacked for a week but the SS successfully held off fifteen rifle divisions and two tank corps.

In mid-August Generalfeldmarschall Walter Model relinquished his command of Army Group Centre and hastened to France to take charge from Günther von Kluge, in a vain attempt to avert the unfolding German defeat in Normandy. Reinhardt of 3rd Panzer Army now found himself leading Army Group Centre; Generaloberst Erhard Raus took over his old command, which withdrew through Lithuania and Courland.

Rokossovsky's Poles

The great offensive that commenced in Byelorussia on 23 June had all but ended by 29 August. By the 26th the 3rd SS had been forced back to Praga, but a counter-attack by it on 11 September thwarted another attempt to link up with the Polish Home Army. It was the 3rd SS and 5th SS that achieved the dubious distinction, along with Stalin, of consigning Warsaw to two months of bloody agony.

From 13 September the Red Air Force spent two weeks conducting 2,000 supply sorties to the insurgents. The supplies were modest 505 anti-tank rifles, nearly 1,500 submachine guns and 130 tons of food, medicine and explosives. By the time Berling's Polish 1st Army was committed to the battle for Praga time was running out, with Żoliborz under attack by elements of the 25th Panzer Division and just 400 insurgents left holding a narrow strip of the river.

Berling recklessly and of his own volition threw his men over the river at Czerniaków, but tragically could make no headway. He landed three groups on the banks of the Czerniaków and Powiśle areas and made contact with Home Army forces on the night of 14–15 September. His men on the eastern shore attempted several more landings over the next four days, but during the 15th to 23rd those that had got over suffered heavy casualties and lost their boats and river-crossing equipment.

On 22 September Berling's men were ordered back across the Vistula for a second time. There was hardly any Red Army support, and of the 3,000 men that made it across just 900 got back to the eastern shores, two-thirds of whom were seriously wounded. In total Berling's Polish 1st Army losses amounted to 5,660 killed, missing or wounded trying to aid the Warsaw Uprising.

After sixty-two days, having lost 15,000 dead and 25,000 wounded, the Polish Home Army surrendered in Warsaw on 2 October. Up to 200,000 civilians had also been killed in the needless orgy of destruction. After the surrender 15,000 members of the Home Army were disarmed and sent to PoW camps in Germany, while up to 6,000 fighters slipped back into the population with the intention of continuing the fight. The vengeful Himmler, though, expelled the rest of the civilian population and ordered the city be flattened.

Crushing the Poles had been a pointless exercise which cost Hitler 10,000 dead, 9,000 wounded and 7,000 missing. It was clear from the fatalities outnumbering the wounded that no quarter had been given. However, the Germans' morale was given a much-needed boost by the belief that they rather than Stalin had halted Rokossovsky at the very gates of Warsaw.

Hasso Krappe recalled:

When General [Bor] met my divisional commander, Lieutenant General Källner, after the capitulation, both stood proudly to attention. As cavalrymen, they knew each other from prewar fencing competitions. [Bor] said to Källner, 'If I'd known, sir, that you were on the other side I'd have surrendered a lot sooner.' He didn't know that 19th Panzer had only spent five days fighting in the city.

Rokossovsky would not occupy Warsaw for another six weeks.

CHAPTER 11

Konev: To the Vistula and Beyond

The infantry corps spearheading Konev's 69th Army fought its way through to the eastern bank of the Vistula on 28 July near Puławy east of Radom. The following day Soviet troops crossed north of Kazimierz and in the face of German resistance secured a bridgehead near the Janowiec area. Although other bridgeheads were secured under pressure, the 69th Army went over to the defensive while Rokossovsky struggled before Warsaw.

In the south the priority now became to smash Army Group North Ukraine's reserves and force the Vistula. To achieve this Konev's 1st Ukrainian Front transferred its main effort to the right, deploying the 1st and 3rd Guards Tank Armies for a drive on Sandomierz.

The renewed Soviet offensive got under way with the advanced units of the 3rd Guards and 13th Armies as well as the 1st and 3rd Guards Tank Armies reaching the Vistula. Their spearheads quickly established a strong bridgehead near Baranów, south-east of Sandomierz and north-east of Kraków, on the 29th.

Sandomierz Bridgehead

In the Baranów area Pukhov's 13th Army and the lead elements of Katukov's 1st Guards Tank Army swiftly secured their foothold. Using boats and rafts Pukhov got two divisions over, and by the evening of the 29th the 305th Rifle Division had forced a bridgehead some 8 miles wide by 5 (13 by 8km) deep.

The Luftwaffe did what it could, but by 1 August the 6th Bridging Brigade and 20th Bridging Battalion had constructed pontoons and heavy bridging equipment. Over these flowed the men and equipment of two corps, plus 182 tanks and 55 guns, eventually creating the Sandomierz bridgehead.

The Germans attempted to nip off this breakthrough by counter-attacking from Mielec to the south and from Tarnobrzeg to the north toward Baranów. The arrival of General A.S. Zhadov's 5th Guards Army on 4 August ensured that this did not happen. Once it had crushed the German forces on the east bank it moved to reinforce the Sandomierz bridgehead. This was also reinforced with the 4th Tank Army, several infantry corps, and artillery and engineer units.

Inside the lodgement the Soviet 1st Guards, 3rd Guards Tank and 13th Armies were squeezed by General Hermann Breith's depleted III Panzer Corps and General Herman Balck's XXXXVIII Panzer Corps. Walther Nehring replaced the latter on the 4th. The Soviet 3rd Guards and 5th Guards Armies held the flanks to the north and south respectively.

While the two panzer corps counter-attacked at Baranów, alleviating the pressure on XXXXII Corps, just to the north LVI Corps attacked the bridgehead at Kozienice held by three Soviet divisions. Only six German battalions were available, but the supporting firepower was simply overwhelming, consisting of 120 assault guns, XXXXII Corps' artillery and the artillery of three panzer divisions. Not surprisingly, despite the promise of reinforcements, Soviet resistance collapsed.

The Germans took a heavy toll on the Soviet armour, as Zheleznov recounts:

When we reached the Vistula and crossed to the Sandomierz bridgehead, only five tanks remained in the battalion. The first company had three tanks, and the second two. And we, the officers of the battalion, were all in these five tanks. Where else would we go? We had no reserves. So, willy-nilly, you became an extra crewmember. With these forces and the 6th Mechanised Corps, which had also suffered losses, we were defending ten kilometres of the front.

While we were deployed at the Sandomierz bridgehead, I destroyed a Panzer IV…I was an excellent shot with a tank gun. I even participated in the best gunner competition that Leliushenko, the 4th Tank Army Commander, organised during a lull in the fighting. So, one time the battalion commander said to me: 'Look over there, there's a German tank.' I said: 'I see it.' The German tank was crawling along parallel to our defences minding its own business, about 1,200–1,300 metres distant. 'You can shoot well. Go ahead, kill it.' I got into a tank, looked through the sight, aimed, and fired. The round went to the left and above the German tank's turret. I fired again – the same thing happened. The German had already turned towards us – he'd noticed we were shooting at him, and was trying to find out where we were. I got out of the tank – why would I want to get burned in it?

Zheleznov, convinced that his tank's gun sight was damaged, commandeered a second tank and blew the panzer up with his first shot. His reward was the Order of the Red Star and 500 roubles.

In the fighting against the Soviets' Baranów bridgehead, the massive Tiger II went into combat for the first time on the Eastern Front on 12 August, with Schwere Panzer Abteilung 501. In this action under Guards Lieutenant Os'kin a single Soviet T-34/85, from the 53rd Guards Tank Brigade, knocked out three Tiger IIs by hitting their side armour from an ambush position. In addition eleven IS-2 heavy tanks of the Soviet 71st Heavy Tank Regiment took on fourteen Tiger IIs, knocking out four and damaging another seven, for the loss of three IS-2s.

Those Tiger IIs captured near Sandomierz were soon tested by the Soviets at Kubinka. The range trials revealed that they were less of a threat than the much lighter and cheaper Tiger I, and the Soviets were puzzled at the German decision to produce it. Tests showed that the transmission and suspension broke down regularly and the engine was likely to overheat.

The Soviets also discovered surprising deficiencies in the Tiger II's armour: not only was the metal poor quality, so was the welding. As a result, even when shells did not penetrate the armour, there was a large amount of spalling, and when struck by heavier shells the armour plating cracked at the welds. However, the IS-2's armour was also shown to be faulty because of bad casting.

The Soviets broke into Sandomierz from two directions, from the Koprzywnica and from downstream of the Vistula, on 16 August; it took two days of heavy street-fighting to clear the town. The survivors from elements of three divisions which had constituted the garrison were surrounded in the Opatowka valley and cut to pieces on the 20th.

On Konev's left flank the 1st Guards, 38th and 4th Tank Armies surged forward; the 1st Panzer Army managed to hold the latter at Drohobycz. By the evening of the 30th Rybalko had gained three small bridgeheads north and south of Annopol, but there was no opportunity to enlarge them.

In the north the Germans managed to keep the Red Army in check and in the centre they gained a much-needed respite. By mid-August the Germans had contained and stabilized the Soviets' Vistula bridgeheads, although on the 17th the hammer and sickle was hoisted for the first time on German soil when Soviet infantryman Aleksandr Afanasevich Tretyak crossed the East Prussian border.

The 4th Panzer Army did not have the strength to eliminate the Sandomierz bridgehead, and to the south the German 17th Army, having been driven westward from the San, was not in a position to help. Throughout August 4th Panzer Army's two panzer corps did all they could to eliminate the bridgehead, but toward the end of the month it was enlarged to a depth of 31 miles (50km) and a width of 46 miles (75km).

The Red Army Rests on Its Laurels

Konev's 1st Ukrainian Front killed 140,000 Germans and captured 32,000, along with 1,900 panzers and assault guns, 3,600 guns and 12,000 motor vehicles. The scale of the defeat of Army Group North Ukraine was not quite on the same level as Army Group Centre's.

Even so, eight divisions had been completely wiped out and another thirty-two had lost 50 to 70 per cent of their manpower. Although Model's 1st Panzer and 2nd Armies had been severely defeated in the battles for Lvov and Lublin, at least twenty divisions could still be mustered to create a new defensive barrier.

The Red Army had now inflicted crippling defeats on two of the four German army groups on the Eastern Front. According to Soviet figures, in total eighty-two German divisions lost 60 to 70 per cent of their effectives, and twenty-six divisions were completely destroyed. German forces had been encircled near Bobruisk, Brest, Brody, Minsk, Vilnius and Vitebsk. The strategic situation in the east had changed beyond recognition: in Byelorussia the front line had been pushed 310–372 miles (500–600km) westwards, and in Ukraine in the direction of Lvov and Sandomierz it had shifted about 186 miles (300km).

By the close of August the Red Army could rest on its laurels: it had liberated Byelorussia and over three-quarters of Lithuania, driven Hitler completely out of Ukraine and begun liberating Poland. It had restored the Soviet frontier over almost 590 miles (950km) from Kaunas to the west of Sambor. As a result of the offensive in Byelorussia and western Ukraine, the position of Army Group South Ukraine defending Moldavia and Romania had sharply deteriorated, and would be attacked before the month was out.

The Soviet 3rd and 2nd Baltic Fronts in July and August took the opportunity to improve their positions, advancing 70 miles (113km) and 137 miles (220km) respectively, sweeping into Estonia and Latvia. Army Group North, with just a 25 mile (40km) corridor between Jelgava, south-west of Riga, and the Gulf of Riga was under threat of being cut off.

Hitler announced on 1 September that the Soviet summer offensive had been 'held' along a continuous line from the Carpathians to the Gulf of Finland, preposterous nonsense that gave no indication of the disaster that had preceded this 'achievement'. The reality was that Rokossovsky, Zakharov and Chernyakovsky had reached their natural stop points, namely the Vistula, Narev and Niemen.

By October the momentum of Bagration was completely expended, the 1st Byelorussian Front still had to take Warsaw, and the 2nd and 3rd Byelorussian Fronts had yet to crush the East Prussian citadel of Koenigsberg. Stalin, though, had unfinished business in the south with Bulgaria, Hungary and Romania.

Beyond the Vistula

At the end of November Konev was summoned to Moscow to see Stalin and set out his plans:

> We were to advance from the Vistula to the Oder, where the enemy had thrown up beforehand seven defence zones to a depth of up to 500km. Most of these zones ran along the banks of the rivers Nida, Pilica, Warta, and Oder, which themselves presented additional obstacles. Three of the zones were manned by enemy troops. Behind them was Berlin, and they had no choice. To retreat was to sign their own death warrant.

Events in the west required that this attack be brought forward, Konev recalls:

> On 9 January I had a call from General A.I. Antonov, Acting Chief of the General Staff, who informed me that in view of the grave situation which had taken shape in the Ardennes on the Western Front, the Allies had asked us to start our offensive as soon as possible. Antonov said that, following the Allied request, Supreme Headquarters had reviewed the offensive. The 1st Ukrainian Front was to start its offensive on 12 January instead of the 20th.

At the start of the operation the German divisions in the area, especially those deployed against the Sandomierz bridgehead, had been brought up to strength and numbered about 12,000 men each (equivalent to two Soviet rifle divisions). The Soviets also assessed that there were still 100,000 German troops in Silesia.

In addition they noticed a rise in German morale: despite the defeat in the Ardennes German hopes had been raised by the prospect of a victory there, which would allow reinforcements to be sent east.

The Soviet Vistula–Oder Offensive was conducted from 12 January to 2 February 1945 and carried the Soviet troops from the Vistula in Poland to the Oder deep inside Germany. The German divisions that had participated in the Ardennes offensive could not be transferred fast enough from the Western to the Eastern Front, and Hitler ridiculously forbade the evacuation of Army Group North, stuck in the Courland peninsula.

The offensive was launched from the large bridgehead near Sandomierz. Stalin threw over 2 million men supported by 4,529 tanks and 2,513 assault guns at Army Group A. Containing the survivors from Army Group Centre, this consisted of 9th Army deployed around Warsaw, the 4th Panzer Army opposite the salient and the 16th Army to its south, totalling 400,000 troops with 1,150 tanks and 4,100 artillery pieces. Those units resisting the bridgehead included 16th and 17th Panzer.

Evgeni Bessonov was involved in the Vistula–Oder operation:

Finally, the big day, 12 January 1945, came. After a long artillery preparation and air force strikes, infantry units of the front went over to the offensive and in a dashing assault captured the first and the second lines of the enemy. Artillery preparation and air force strikes lasted at least one and a half hours, if I am not mistaken. Guns, including 76mm to 152mm, 82mm, 120mm and 160mm mortars as well as Katyushas firing on the enemy defences. Bombers and Il-2 Shturmoviks raided the defences as well. It was a permanent rumble.

Reminiscent of Bagration, after twenty-three days of the Vistula–Oder operation troops of the 1st Byelorussian and 1st Ukrainian Fronts, supported by the 2nd Byelorussian and 4th Ukrainian Fronts, tore open a breakthrough 625 miles (1,000km) wide by 375 miles (605km) deep and swept across the Oder. The 1st Byelorussian Front secured a bridgehead at Kuestrin just 35 miles (56km) from Berlin. Hitler had been driven from southern Poland and those forces that had been in Silesia were reduced to about 25,000 men.

The Red Army easily overran the industrialized area of Silesia, the loss of which was a heavy blow for Germany's weapons industry and meant that Hitler's cause was now completely hopeless. By 31 January the Red Army had secured bridgeheads over the frozen Oder, 310 miles (500km) west of its starting point.

Owing to logistics problems aggravated by the spring thaw, the Soviets decided to stop. At that time Berlin was undefended, and Stalin lost a golden opportunity as the Battle of the Seelow Heights (16–19 April) and the Battle of Berlin (April until early May) were to be bloodbaths, but that's another story.

Chernyakovsky's 3rd Byelorussian Front finally opened the East Prussia Offensive on 13 January 1945, which ran until the end of April. The 3rd Panzer Army and 4th Army from Army Group Centre under Reinhardt put up stiff resistance. Chernyakovsky was killed in action and replaced by Vasilevsky. Rokossovsky also supported the attack on the left flank (until early February when his forces were committed to the East Pomeranian Offensive to the west, along with the 1st Byelorussian Front). The 1st Baltic Front also struck on Chernyakovsky's right. Stalin's prediction about East Prussia came true as the battle cost the Red Army an appalling 585,000 casualties.

Betrayed to Stalin
In the west things had gone just as badly for Hitler following the Allies' liberation of France. By the end of August 1944 the Germans had lost forty-three divisions (thirty-five infantry and eight panzer divisions) on the Western Front, sustaining a total loss of 450,000 men as well as most of their equipment, consisting of 1,500 tanks, 3,500 pieces of artillery and 20,000 vehicles.

Only in Italy were the German armed forces keeping the Allies at bay, following the landings there in 1943, although this secondary theatre of operations was a constant drain on their resources. The loss of Rome in June 1944 had cost them about 30,000 troops alone.

The continuing success of the Red Army and events in France meant that Hitler's eastern allies were increasingly disillusioned. As a follow-up to the Bagration, Lublin–Brest and Lvov–Sandomierz offensives, Stalin now launched his Jassy–Kishinev operation into southern Europe. In Romania in late August King Mihai (Michael), sick of the war, had Marshal Antonescu arrested and his entire government dismissed, and within a few weeks an armistice was signed with Stalin. The German instructors manning the Romanian 4th Armoured Regiment seized the panzers supplied by Hitler and used them to help cover the German withdrawal.

Just before the fall of Antonescu, once loyal Romanian troops blocked the Danube bridges to Hitler's forces. Generaloberst Johannes Friessner's Army Group South (formerly South Ukraine), comprising the German 6th and 8th Armies and the Romanian 3rd and 4th Armies, was attacked by the 2nd and 3rd Ukrainian Fronts' Jassy–Kishinev offensive on 20 August.

The Romanians laid down their arms and secured the crossings over the Danube, Prut and Siret for use by the Red Army. Within two days the German 6th Army was trapped in the Kishinev area and the Romanian 3rd Army along the Black Sea coast.

Almost all of the German 6th Army and part of the 8th, some sixteen divisions from a force of twenty-four, were forced to surrender to the Soviets. The rest fled over the Carpathians to fight on in Hungary. Bucharest lay open, as did the rear of Hitler's Balkan front. Hitler lost 60,000 killed and 106,000 men captured, including 2 corps commanders, 12 divisional commanders and 13 other generals. He also lost 830 tanks and self-propelled guns, 5,500 guns, 33,000 trucks and 338 aircraft. While the 6th Army was swept away the German 8th withdrew into the Carpathians.

Writer Mihail Sebastian recorded on 29 August: 'How shall I begin? Where shall I begin? The Russians are in Bucharest.' Two days later he noted:

A parade of Soviet heavy tanks on Bulevardul Carol, beneath the windows of the house where we have taken refuge. It is an imposing sight. Those tired, dusty, rather badly dressed men are conquering the world. They're not much to look at – but they are conquering the world.

Afterwards a long column of trucks full of Romanian soldiers: former prisoners of war in Russia, now armed and equipped and fighting in the Red Army. They are young and happy, with excellent equipment. You can see they are not coming from battle. They are a parade unit, probably kept in waiting for the entry into Bucharest.

Inspired by Romania the Slovaks were premature in trying to throw off the Nazi yoke on 23 August. Despite being once loyal allies, the Slovaks under defence minister General Catlos and part of the Slovak Army under General Golian rose up against Premier Tiso and the Germans at Neusohl in the Carpathians. For Hitler this was a potential disaster as it not only threatened the vital tank plants in neighbouring Bohemia and Moravia, but also impeded the retreat of the defeated German 8th Army.

Hitler had no troops available and an improvised armoured regiment had to be raised from the various SS training schools in Bohemia and Moravia. The Slovaks had no tanks with which to resist the panzers, as their remaining armour had been lost on the Eastern Front.

Hitler moved quickly to disarm the Slovak Army's two regular infantry divisions, and many Slovak soldiers fled to central Slovakia to join the partisans. Czechoslovak airborne forces flown in by Stalin also joined them. However, Neusohl could not be held without heavy weapons and fell by the end of the month to the German armour. The arrival of elements of two SS divisions sealed the fate of the remaining rebels. The Slovaks would have to wait until the spring for the arrival of the Red Army before they would taste freedom.

When Romania swapped sides Bulgaria was also secretly negotiating with Stalin. In addition to its commitments in Greece and Yugoslavia the Bulgarian Army found itself countering a growing partisan movement at home. Hitler switched further shipments of panzers en route to German troops in Yugoslavia, as Bulgarian loyalty was now suspect, and he secretly planned to disable their existing panzers and assault guns.

Crucially Romania's defection exposed Hungary's southern frontier and, desperately trying to stem the Soviet and Romanian forces pushing from the east, the Hungarians succeeded in briefly giving the Soviets a bloody nose at Arad on the River Lipova. Admiral Horthy's government began to wobble, and remaining units were transferred to the battered Hungarian 3rd Army south of Lake Balaton or to the German 6th and 8th Armies now in northern Hungary.

In the meantime Stalin declared war on Bulgaria on 5 September and commenced hostilities three days later. In turn the Bulgarians sought to save themselves by declaring war on Hitler. Pushing through Romania the Red Army thrust into Bulgaria north of Varna and veered west; the Soviet motorized columns, outstripping their infantry, met no resistance and arrived in Sofia on the 15th.

Hitler acted quickly to deal with his turncoat allies deployed in Serbia and Macedonia, ordering the disarming of the Bulgarian 1st Army; only the 5th Army offered short-lived resistance. German instructors from the combat school at Niš in Serbia were put on alert to move to the German training camp at Plovdiv in Bulgaria, from where they would act against the Bulgarian panzers.

Instead a column consisting of sixty-two panzers and other armoured fighting vehicles from the Bulgarian 1st Armoured Brigade moved to block the Sofia–Niš road outside Sofia, and local German forces were arrested. Bulgarian troops were then withdrawn from Greece ready for an inevitable Soviet attack on Hitler's forces in Yugoslavia. At the end of November the Bulgarian panzers were in Pristina and Kosovska Mitrovica, marking the end of operations in Yugoslavia. Elements of the brigade subsequently fought with the Bulgarian 1st Army and the Red Army in Hungary.

In Hungary it was very clear Horthy was intent on abandoning Hitler. The latter temporarily stabilized the situation with Operation Panzerfaust, dramatically installing a puppet government and placing Horthy under house arrest in Bavaria. The Hungarian response was predictable: General B. Dalnoki Miklos, commander of the Hungarian 1st Army, after telling his countrymen to treat the Germans as foes defected to the Soviets; Colonel General L. Verres, commander of the Hungarian 2nd Army, was arrested by the Germans before he could copy Miklos.

Far to the north following Finland's negotiations with Stalin in late August, two German mountain corps from the German 20th Mountain Army had withdrawn across Finland to Norway, leaving XIX Corps still on Soviet territory. The latter was preparing to withdraw just as Stalin struck. This was the tenth crushing blow of 1944 and the last of the series of strategic offensives conducted by the Red Army that year.

Some 97,000 troops from the Red Army's Karelian Front attacked the 56,000-strong German XIX Mountain Corps defending positions west of Murmansk on 7 October 1944. The Soviet 14th Army defeated them in the three phased, twenty-four-day Petsamo–Kirkenes operation. Although the Soviet 14th Army failed to destroy XIX Mountain Corps, as up to 18,000 escaped, it inflicted in total over 9,000 casualties on the Germans at a cost of 16,000 men.

In the meantime the Soviets reached the Baltic near Memel on 10 October, trapping Army Group North. Approximately 200,000 German troops, roughly twenty-six divisions, were to remain isolated in Latvia for the rest of the war in the Courland Pocket. The Soviets lost approximately 390,000 casualties, 2,700 tanks, 1,120 pieces of artillery and 720 aircraft trying to overrun it. By the time the renamed Army Group Courland surrendered on 7 May 1945 it was the only major German formation left intact.

Hitler Holds Budapest

After making a stand at Warsaw, in central Europe Hitler decided to hold Budapest against the Red Army using SS divisions and loyal Hungarian troops. Under pressure from the Red Army, by the end of 1944 the Hungarian 1st Army had withdrawn into Slovakia, while the Germans set up significant defences between Budapest and Lake Balaton to the south-west. By December 1944 these were being put to the test as the Soviets crossed the Danube and reached the lake. The Red Army having stretched its supply lines to the limit was unable to pierce the German defences, so switched its attentions east of Budapest. The 6th Guards Tank Army attacked from the north-east and the 46th Army from the south, encircling the city.

The IX SS Corps, consisting of the 8th SS and 22nd SS Kavallerie Divisions, was trapped in Budapest, while the 18th SS Panzergrenadier Division was forced to retreat. In an effort to raise the siege, IV SS Panzer Corps, comprising the 3rd SS and 5th SS Panzer Divisions, was diverted from Warsaw on 26 December. It moved to relieve the Hungarian capital on 2 January 1945; launching its counter-attack from the north-west, it came within 15 miles (24km) of the city.

By the 11th, IV SS Panzer had recaptured Budapest airport, and for the trapped 45,000 German defenders hope briefly flickered in their hearts. Redeploying to the Lake Balaton area they tried again on 17 January; this time the SS got to within 12 miles (19km) of the city, but soon found itself under attack. General Balck, commander of the 4th Army, seeking to trap ten Soviet divisions north of Lake Balaton, called IV SS to his assistance. Stiff Soviet resistance also thwarted this effort.

This diversion sealed the fate of Budapest's garrison, which on 11 February desperately attempted to break out. This ended in bloody disaster and only 700 men reached German lines; the vengeful Soviets annihilated the two SS divisions. Budapest capitulated the following day. The Red Army now expected a fairly trouble-free push through the rest of Hungary to the Austrian capital, Vienna. Elements of the Hungarian Army continued to fight alongside the Germans, but the Axis lay in ruins, and Hitler's dogs of war were now serving Stalin, intent on the final destruction of Hitler's Reich. Stalin's revenge was all but complete, save for the final assault on Berlin.

CHAPTER 12

Bagration: Stalin's Triumph?

By August 1944 Stalin must have felt a sense of smug satisfaction. The terrible shame of the summer of 1941 had been expunged and military honour restored, albeit at an appalling loss of lives and resources. Bagration cost the Red Army 178,000 casualties (60,000 dead, 110,000 wounded and 8,000 missing), and during the Lvov–Sandomierz Offensive it suffered an additional 198,000 casualties. The Red Army worked miracles throughout 1944, which became the year of ten victories – the pinnacle of which undoubtedly was Operation Bagration. By the end of the year the Red steamroller had to pause for breath after twelve months of continuous bloodletting.

With surprising understatement a Soviet Cold War era history of the 'Great Patriotic War' recorded modestly:

The first round of the furious battles in Byelorussia ended on 4 July. The main forces of the German Army Group Centre were destroyed in eleven-twelve days…

The great offensive in Byelorussia, started on 23 June, ended on 29 August, 1944. It was one of the Red Army's largest operations in the war…

This was an overwhelming victory. The Motherland fired thirty-six salvoes in honour of the four Fronts successfully advancing in to Byelorussia, Lithuania and Poland.

Stalin can only have been elated at the news of Minsk's liberation and the annihilation of Army Group Centre. In contrast three years before he had fallen into a depression for several days and then vented his anger on his hapless senior generals. Despite the warning signs he seemed dumbfounded at Hitler's attack and must also have feared a coup might topple him at his moment of crisis.

Zhukov flew from Baranovichi on 8 July 1944 to brief Stalin at Kuntsevo, his main Moscow residence. 'Stalin was in good humour and joked,' recalled Zhukov. After a telephone call from Vasilevsky he added, 'The news must have been good, for Stalin's gaiety increased.' They then ate a celebratory breakfast. Nine days later the victory parade with German prisoners was held in Moscow, but Stalin's sense of triumph was allegedly short-lived.

Stalin's good mood appeared to wilt in the face of the Warsaw rising, especially as he was under mounting pressure from the British and Americans to help out. Byelorussia became a distant memory. Zhukov and Rokossovsky arrived to see him, Beria and Molotov on 1 August, only to find their Supreme Commander in an agitated state. Stalin wanted to know if their armies could press on; both his generals were of the view that they must be rested.

Rokossovsky found himself reliving 22 May as he and Zhukov were ushered into the library to think things over. 'I know very well what Beria is capable of,' warned Rokossovsky in a hushed tone. 'I've been in his prisons.' They were left for twenty minutes before being informed Warsaw was on its own. In hindsight Zhukov suspected this discussion was a sham, for it would exonerate Stalin and the Red Army for not going that extra yard. Thanks to Bagration not only did Stalin get Byelorussia and the Baltic States back, but also complete dominance of Poland. This indeed was cause for 'gaiety'.

From Colonel Reinhard Gehlen's intelligence perspective he knew that all was lost for Hitler's cause on the Eastern Front:

> Right from the start we had sensed the growing Russian confidence in final victory, and now we could only agree that this confidence was justified. Early in October 1944 I told my more intimate colleagues that I considered the war was lost and that we must begin thinking of the future: we had to plan for the approaching catastrophe and turn minds to the question of what must be done when the final collapse became imminent.

The Right Decision

In the space of just six weeks in June/July 1944 the Red Army reached the Vistula, liberating Byelorussia, eastern Ukraine and eastern Poland. Within another four weeks it had rolled into the capitals of Romania and Bulgaria. In a further six weeks it had reached the Baltic and the Yugoslav capital.

Even Zhukov must have been astonished at the Red Army's massive gains and the enormous destruction it had wrought upon the German Army on the Eastern Front. He noted with some sense of achievement:

> In the summer of 1944 the Soviet troops carried out seven major operations to surround and smash groups of German troops. This was many more than in previous campaigns. The more important of them were the Byelorussian, Jassy-Kishinev and Lvov-Sandomierz operations in which 147 enemy divisions were crushed. As a result the German defensive front was broken over a 2,200km stretch from the Western Dvina to the Black Sea. On some sectors our troops advanced up to 700kms.

Despite the remarkable success of Bagration the war dragged on for almost another year. It would not be until the New Year that the Red Army was able to push from Bagration's high tide at Warsaw and the Vistula to the Oder just east of Berlin.

By December 1944 the Red Army had finally peaked: Stalin had exhausted his manpower reserves, and the army had reached the very limit of its supply lines. Stalin's 'tank riders' living off the land could press on for only so long; however, by this stage the back of the Wehrmacht had been broken. Even

Stalin appreciated that the Red Army would need to take stock before its final onslaught on Hitler's lair – Berlin.

Stalin knew that it would be folly to goad his exhausted armies on lest Hitler attempt a comeback on the Eastern Front. Stalin was spared this, as it was against the Western Allies that Hitler threw two rejuvenated panzer armies in the winter of 1944 when he desperately sought to regain the strategic initiative. By March 1945, when Hitler attempted to deliver a knockout blow against the Red Army in Hungary rather than on the Oder, it was too late. The Soviets were ready for him and already knocking on the very gates of Berlin.

While the Bagration offensive had positioned the Red Army ready to liberate Warsaw and push on to Berlin, the Lvov–Sandomierz offensive effectively unhinged Hitler's defences in the rest of central and eastern Europe and the Balkans. Hitler's attempts to draw a line in the sand before Budapest were too little and too late.

Did Stalin make the right decision to strike in Byelorussia first rather than continue liberating Ukraine? Shielded by the Carpathian mountains a Soviet drive south of the Pripyat marshes and north-west towards Warsaw and the Vistula could have forced Army Groups Centre and North to withdraw, or could have trapped them.

Stalin, though, wanted a grand gesture. Hitler's forces were to be not just driven back or defeated but destroyed wholesale. Events indicate that he made the right choice, especially as Army Group North Ukraine, though weakened by the loss of formations to Army Group Centre, still managed to avoid destruction on the same scale as the latter – but to be fair it was attacked by only a single Soviet front.

If Stalin had struck in Ukraine toward Hungary and Romania, Hitler's allies, feeling under threat, might have briefly rallied; Bagration clearly signalled that Hitler's cause was doomed, and the sort of treatment their armies could expect.

It is interesting that Stalin disagreed with Zhukov over trapping Army Group North with a thrust into East Prussia. It is doubtful that Stalin would have been greatly worried by heavy casualties, and it is unclear if he was really worried by the prospect of becoming bogged down there. In truth he had much bigger fish to fry than the Baltic States and East Prussia. He wanted to complete clearing Ukraine so that he could punish Hitler's wavering allies in Czechoslovakia, Bulgaria and Romania – not only that, but he had every intention of ensuring that once they were within the Soviet sphere of influence they stayed there.

Two Army Groups Smashed

Two of Hitler's Army groups were smashed in the summer of 1944: eighty-two divisions lost 70 to 80 per cent of their effectives, and at least twenty-six divisions were destroyed completely. German troops were successfully surrounded at Vitebsk, Bobruisk, Minsk and Brody, as well as Vilnius and Brest. In Byelorussia the Red Army advanced up to 400 miles (645km) and in Ukraine up to 200 miles (323km).

According to General Beloborodov, commander of the 1st Baltic Front's 43rd Army, over fifteen German divisions were destroyed and another fifty lost up to half their troops during Bagration. This, he said, made the liberation of France by the Western Allies easier. Alexander Werth observed:

> According to the Germans themselves, the Russian offensive in Byelorussia was the gravest defeat ever inflicted on the Wehrmacht on the Eastern Front. Between twenty-five and twenty-eight German divisions were destroyed, a loss of at least 350,000 men. In the words of the Official Journal of the OKW [armed forces high command] the rout of Army Group Centre (in Byelorussia) was 'a greater catastrophe than Stalingrad'.

During June and July 1944 Hitler's Wehrmacht suffered over 670,000 casualties, half of whom were lost by Army Group Centre. Wounded and missing accounted for almost half these losses, but many of them were hunted down by the Red Army around the lakes and through the forests of Byelorussia and annihilated.

In August alone the Allies had killed 64,000 German troops and wounded another 170,000, while some 407,000 men were unaccounted for. Following the German collapse in France, German losses there were nearing half a million. Germany's manpower had received a mortal blow. By this stage total German losses since the start of the Second World War, not including wounded, stood at 1,510,000 dead and a staggering 1,319,000 missing.

For the Wehrmacht Bagration was a vastly more serious deathblow than the catastrophes of Stalingrad or Falaise, both of which received vastly more publicity and as a result have left greater historical footprints. The destruction of Army Group Centre was a bigger and swifter disaster than the loss of Army Group B's 7th Army and 5th Panzer Army in mid-August 1944 at Falaise. Although overall total German losses in France were comparable to those in Byelorussia, the former occurred over a two and a half month period, not a matter of two weeks.

Following Falaise, Hitler's forces were still able to conduct a successful fighting withdrawal across France and then reconstitute their battered formations to such an extent that he was able to launch two panzer armies against the Americans at the end of the year. In Normandy very few of the lost divisions were total write-offs: a vital cadre of experienced officers and NCOs survived, and indeed all the lost panzer divisions were quickly rebuilt.

In Byelorussia one of the biggest blows to the German army was the loss of so many irreplaceable officers and NCOs. Hitler was already scraping the bottom of the barrel by calling up the old and young; now there would be no one to lead them. Of the forty-seven corps and divisional commanders caught up in Bagration, thirty-one were either captured or missing by the end of the fighting.

As a result of Bagration, Hitler's Army Group Centre reportedly lost twenty-seven divisions: the 6th, 12th, 14th, 31st, 36th, 45th, 57th, 78th, 95th, 110th, 134th, 197th, 206th, 246th, 257th, 260th, 267th, 296th, 299th, 383rd and 707th Infantry Divisions, the 20th Panzer, 18th, 25th and Feldherrnhalle Panzergrenadier

Divisions and Korps Abteilung D, and the 4th and 6th Luftwaffe Field Divisions. The 20th Panzer Division, 14th Infantry and Korps Abteilung D were mauled rather than destroyed; the 35th and 129th Infantry Divisions were reported as badly battered. In contrast the 201st, 221st and 286th Security Divisions were destroyed.

Certainly on account of their heavy losses in June–July 1944 nineteen Army Group Centre divisions were disbanded: the 6th, 12th, 31st, 36th, 45th, 78th, 110th, 134th, 206th, 246th, 267th, 296th, 383rd, 707th Infantry Divisions, the 4th and 6th Luftwaffe Field Divisions, and the 18th, 25th and Feldherrnhalle Panzergrenadier Divisions (though the panzergrenadier divisions were later formed anew). Some units were so tatty that they were amalgamated to form battalion-strength formations.

In addition the 57th, 260th, 299th and 337th Infantry Divisions were reorganized as the weak Korps Abteilung G, and the 95th, 197th, 256th Infantry Divisions as Korps Abteilung H. Both were later converted into 299th and 95th Infantry Divisions respectively. The Korps Abteilung D was disbanded and converted into the 56th Infantry Division.

According to Zhukov, in two months the 1st, 2nd and 3rd Byelorussian Fronts and the 1st Baltic Front routed some 70 German divisions; of these 30 were destroyed or captured. The 1st Ukrainian Front routed another 30 divisions, destroying 8. The 2nd and 3rd Ukrainian Fronts accounted for a further 24 divisions, of which 16 were forced to surrender. This means that at a conservative estimate in the summer of 1944 the Red Army drove back 124 German divisions (including allies), of which 54 were complete write-offs lost to Hitler's order of battle on the Eastern Front. A few were reconstituted but never regained their full combat potential.

Was Busch a Scapegoat?

Could Busch have done more to save his command? Certainly his forces did not really have the wherewithal to fend off Stalin's massive offensive. Nonetheless, had Busch not acted so slavishly to Hitler's dictates during the first few vital days of Bagration, a much greater number of divisions could have avoided encirclement and conducted successful fighting withdrawals.

Instead 133,000 troops were lost holding onto the *feste Plätze*; the sacrifice of 30,000 men of LIII Corps at Vitebsk, 48,000 men of XXXV and XXXXI Corps at Bobruisk, and another 55,000 men from XII and XXVII Corps at Minsk could have been avoided if Busch had acted swiftly. No doubt if he had ordered his commanders to act as they saw fit he would have been dismissed – this would have mattered little as he was still dismissed just six days into Bagration for adhering to Hitler's dictate of no retreat, no surrender.

Busch was cast into the wilderness for presiding over such a monumental military disaster. Reinhardt, who had succeeded Model as C-in-C Army Group Centre, wrote to Guderian on 10 September 1944 to quash rumours that Busch had taken his life or indeed defected to the Soviets.

The following month Busch was permitted to give the oration at General Rudolf Schmundt's funeral. The latter was head of the army personnel office, and had died of his wounds sustained during the 20 July bomb plot. Remarkably on 20 March 1945 Busch was appointed C-in-C Oberbefehlshaber or OB Northwest. Busch blustered that he would launch an offensive 'in the Hitler spirit'.

In reality hiding behind this grand command was just a Kampfgruppe, a few Labour Service (RAD) battalions, Senior Engineer Command XV, Hitler Youth and Volkssturm home guard; this ragbag of forces operated along the North Sea coast, Schleswig-Holstein and the edge of eastern Holland. In fact all that Busch wanted was the British to move in behind him, for although he was a loyal servant of Hitler's he was afraid of the SS.

Busch's final act of the war was to help oversee the German surrender to Field Marshal Montgomery on 4 May 1945. To assist the British administration Busch had under him generals Lindemann, commanding those German forces still in Denmark; Blumentritt, commanding those between the Baltic and the Weser; and Blaskowitz, controlling those between the Weser and western Holland.

Even this Busch mucked up with his attitude. Montgomery was displeased that those Germans saved from the Red Army expected to be treated as allies against the Russians. He found his orders being queried and delayed, and promptly summoned Busch on 11 May and reprimanded him. He also threatened to remove him if he did not cooperate. Montgomery recalled: 'After this I had no more trouble with Busch or with any other German commander.' Busch died in a prisoner of war camp in Aldershot, England, on 17 July 1945, and was buried at Cannock Chase German war cemetery, Staffordshire.

Could Army Group Centre have avoided defeat? Given the Red Army's concentrated strength it seems highly unlikely, but Hitler could have minimized the scale of its losses. If he had authorized a timely withdrawal those divisions tied up defending the *feste Plätze* could have provided valuable forces for local counter-attacks, albeit without much armour support, and the defence of the river lines.

While the lack of significant armoured forces would have greatly limited the effectiveness of such counter-attacks, they would have given the Soviet tank armies pause for thought. Similarly Hitler could have ordered a general withdrawal to the Berezina sooner: this could have rendered a Soviet crossing more costly.

The loss of most of Army Group Centre and a large portion of Army Group North Ukraine, as well as the entrapment of Army Group North, meant Hitler's forces had completely lost all strategic initiative. While this trend had commenced in 1943 the fate of Hitler's aspirations on the Eastern Front were finally sealed during the summer of 1944. Although the Germans often fought skilful retreats, the reality was that no matter what they did they could not fully arrest the Red Army's momentum or stave off the inevitable. Only the winter and logistical problems slowed the Red Army.

After Stalin's defeat in June 1941 the Soviet Union had the resources to recover from its staggering military losses. In contrast, following defeat in June 1944, Hitler simply did not have the manpower to retrieve the situation; from the start he had been reliant on his east European allies on the Ukrainian front. His industries, despite quite remarkable output, in 1944 were on the verge of collapse, in part because of dwindling raw materials and the Western Allies' unrelenting strategic air campaign. On top of this he had lost faith in his generals, especially after 20 July.

General von Mellenthin in his memoirs summed up the disaster succinctly and laid the blame firmly at the feet of Hitler:

> Generalfeldmarschall Busch, the Commander of Army Group Centre, had seen what was coming and had requested permission to step back to the line of the River Berezina, and throw the elaborate Russian preparations out of gear. Hitler of course imposed his veto and the unfortunate Army Group Centre, stretched out on far too wide a front, simply broke to pieces before the onslaught.

Guderian felt that Model and Harpe saved the situation after Bagration, stating: 'The outstanding performance and leadership of these two generals were primarily responsible for the re-establishment of an Eastern Front.'

Why did Hitler acquiesce in the destruction of Army Group Centre? He and his high command knew that a summer Soviet offensive in Byelorussia or Ukraine was to be expected, and yet they chose to ignore the dangers of Red Army encircling operations, despite the dire warnings of Stalingrad and Kursk. Time and again Hitler acquiesced to his troops being surrounded, time and again the Luftwaffe and the panzers had come to the rescue, but they could only keep this up for so long and with diminishing returns. Stalingrad had signalled that this was no longer a wise expedient and yet Hitler chose to ignore the warning signs.

In his defence, Hitler was preoccupied following the 6 June 1944 D-Day landings in Normandy and by subsequent British and American attempts to break out of their bridgehead. Also the Allies' deception plans had fooled him into believing that an attack across the Pas de Calais was imminent, which would have placed the Allies within striking distance of the industrial heartland of the Ruhr and then Berlin. Other deception plans also made Hitler apprehensive of invasions in the eastern Mediterranean and Scandinavia. In Italy, where Hitler had already been fighting a second front since September 1943, his successful attempts to arrest the Allies' expansion in the Mediterranean had received a blow with the loss of Rome.

Ultimately Hitler had no real way of knowing where the British and American centre of gravity lay until July/August when the American breakout signalled that this was clearly the real thing. The subsequent landings in the south of France were little more than a sideshow and had little bearing on Hitler's position in France, which was already beyond redemption by this stage. The swift destruction of Army Group Centre and the 20 July bomb plot must have convinced Hitler that he needed a miracle to retrieve the deteriorating situation.

Fighting On

Stalin's road to revenge, despite his success with Bagration and the subsequent offensives of 1944, was a long one, and the question remains: why?

Werth, witness to the appalling bloodletting, assessed:

Although in Byelorussia and eastern Lithuania the Russians had scored one of the greatest victories of the war – and one from which the Germans could never recover – their further progress from about 25 July to the end of August was much slower for a number of obvious reasons: long drawn out communications, fatigue among the troops, and the throwing in of heavy German reserves against the Russian attempt to advance both beyond the Niemen into East Prussia, and along the Narev and upper and middle Vistula into central Poland…

By this time Poland had become the scene of the most dramatic military and political events.

Frustratingly for Stalin, although Bagration hastened the end of the war, by inflicting huge irreplaceable losses in manpower and equipment on Germany, it did not deter Hitler from fighting on. Even after the destruction of Army Group Centre the Germans were able to carrying on resisting on the Eastern Front for almost a year.

Following Stalingrad and Kursk, Stalin faced a similar dilemma to Hitler: while Hitler had known Moscow was his goal, he had become distracted by military operations on his flanks. Stalin's ultimate prize was Berlin, but he still had to contend with the Vistula and Oder rivers. He also had to secure his flanks and in the wider scheme of things he wanted to punish Hitler's Axis allies and ensure that they never posed a threat to the Soviet Union again. This all took precious time and resources. It also diverted resources from the main central effort.

Geography was in the Germans' favour as they conducted a fighting retreat with numerous rivers to anchor their defences. The front contracted almost by half, shrinking from 2,500 to 1,300 miles (4,032 to 2,098). Additionally for all their strategic skill the Soviets relied on sheer weight of numbers, particularly artillery, to steamroller the Wehrmacht out of the way. Tactically the German army and Waffen SS were more adept.

The 1944 Soviet offensives cost Stalin 1.4 million killed; human suffering might not have affected him, but he had run out of manpower. While the Soviets had 14,000 tanks in the field, many still lacked radios, which greatly hampered coordination. They also lacked adequate transport, such as lorries and armoured personnel carriers, meaning the infantry often had to ride exposed on the tanks in order to keep up. The Soviet advances also kept outstripping available supplies and losing momentum.

By this stage too the Germans were the masters of defence. In particular East Prussia proved a hard nut to crack because the Germans were able to utilize the old border and city fortifications. Only Hitler's refusal to withdraw enabled the slower Soviet forces to conduct successful encircling operations.

The Appalling Byelorussian Toll
Not surprisingly, having been in the path of the German invasion in 1941 and the subsequent stubborn Red Army defence and bloody destruction of Army

Group Centre three years later, Byelorussia sustained losses during the war that were heavier than any other Soviet republic. It was also in Byelorussia that Hitler's demonic process of wholesale slaughter of the Jews was first tested.

The swiftness of the German invasion made it impossible for most of the Byelorussian Jews to flee, and no provision for the evacuation of the civil population had been made because of the Red Army's forward defence concept.

By the time Operation Bagration had liberated the republic its total population was 6,293,600, down from 10,528,000 in mid-1941. According to official data, population losses due to the depravations of war and genocide were in the region of 2 to 3 million people. The Nazi genocide was directed primarily against the Jewish Byelorussians. The total number of Holocaust victims in Byelorussia is still unclear, though estimates range from a quarter of a million to a million people.

The Nazis created over 270 ghettos in the four zones of occupation; over 150 of these existed in western Byelorussia. In the city of Vitebsk the Soviets discovered that over half of the 37,000-strong Jewish communities had gone. Mogilev had seen half of its 20,000 Jews exterminated. Gomel lost 4,000 out of a 40,000 population. The Nazis killed 2,035 Jews in the Borisov ghetto and in the surrounding region.

Another 404 Borisov Jews were killed serving the Red Army and the partisans. Of the 110,000 Byelorussian Jewish draftees or volunteers in the Red Army, 48,000 were killed.

Bagration's Legacy
Just before the end of the war a strange postscript to Operation Bagration occurred in April 1945, as British-born Byelorussian Nikolai Tolstoy recounts:

> Prince Irakly Bagration had knocked on the door of the British Embassy in Madrid, offering to arrange the surrender of 100,000 Georgians serving in the German Army, provided guarantees could be given that they would not be sent to the Soviet Union. The Foreign Office instructed the Embassy not to reply.

Under the Yalta Agreement the Western Allies had agreed any Soviet citizens serving the Nazis who surrendered to them would be returned to Stalin.

After Hitler's defeat Stalin's first act was to mould Eastern Europe in his image, and in the late 1940s there were purges and show trials in the satellite states. While Churchill spoke of an Iron Curtain descending on eastern Europe, Stalin saw it as appropriate punishment for the misery and suffering Hungary and Romania had helped inflict on Ukraine and Byelorussia. Even Bulgaria did not escape Stalin's wrath.

Soviet General Biryuzov, who had witnessed the effect of the purges on the Red Army, oversaw a purge of the Bulgarian army and was present when Bulgarian opposition leaders were hanged after show trials in 1947. In Hungary about 1,000 people suffered in these Soviet purges.

Stalin ensured that the real architects of Bagration and national war heroes, Zhukov and Rokossovsky, were no threat to him after the war. Rokossovsky's reward was to be appointed Polish defence minister, keeping him well away from Moscow. While he was in practice military governor of Poland, his death sentence was not revoked until after Stalin's death in 1953.

Zhukov, who perhaps foolishly stole the limelight during the Berlin victory parade, found himself subsequently sidelined while Stalin sought to take all the credit for victory in the 'Great Patriotic War'. Zhukov attempted to remedy this perception in his memoirs.

Just three months after Nazi Germany surrendered, Stalin's victorious Red Army invaded Japanese-held Manchukuo (Manchuria), and would eventually attack neighbouring Mengjiang, northern Korea, southern Sakhalin and the Kuril Islands as well. The invasion was conducted between the atomic bombs on Hiroshima on 6 August and Nagasaki on 9 August 1945. The Russians avenged themselves for Khalkin-Gol with Operation August Storm, launched on the 8th.

The scale of the assault was a vast repetition of Bagration, but this time the pincer movement enveloped an area the size of western Europe. The Soviets threw about 80 divisions, totalling 1.5 million men, over 5,000 tanks, over 28,000 artillery pieces and 4,300 aircraft at the Japanese.

In Manchukuo the Japanese Kwantung Army could field 600,000 men in 25 divisions equipped with 1,215 armoured cars and light tanks, 6,700 pieces of artillery and 1,800 aircraft, of which just 50 were front line; they were supported by the Chinese Manchukuo Defence Force, numbering 40,000 men. The fighting lasted about a week before the Japanese declared a ceasefire.

General von Mellenthin later attached Cold War significance to the success of Bagration, remarking: 'The destruction of our Army Group Centre, and the sweeping advance of Marshal Rotmistrov's tanks from the Dnepr to the Vistula marked a new stage in the history of the Red Army and one of ominous import to the West.' Certainly for forty years NATO lived in armed awe of the Soviet army, partly as a result of the Red Army's achievements in the summer of 1944, when it had demonstrated how easily it could overrun such vast areas.

Stalin's Cold War Shame

As the Cold War came to a close the triumphant liberation of Belarus, Ukraine, Poland and the Baltic States was marred by the admission of how Stalin had treated their people little better than had the Nazis. Indeed the deaths of so many people by the hand of their own government was a stain on Soviet history that could not remain concealed forever.

Before the coming of glasnost and President Gorbachev, Stalin was still largely hailed as a hero of the Great Patriotic War, and any executions were written off as errors, or political expediency. In the late 1980s a society called Memorial started a campaign to identify the burial places of the purged and to remember the dead.

This began a tide of admissions about the appalling treatment of the Soviet Union's own people. A four-hour demonstration organized by the Belarussian Popular Front in Kurapaty woods on 19 June 1988 called for an unofficial citizens' committee to examine Stalin's crimes. It was felt that the Byelorussian Council of Ministers' own investigation into the NKVD massacres in Kurapaty was inadequate.

The pressure continued, with mass demonstrations in Minsk. Finally the government gave in and on 24 January 1989 agreed to erect a monument to the 30,000 shot dead during the 1930s. Memorial claimed the figure was nearer 150,000.

Memorial also publicized a mass grave in Ukraine, near Kiev, estimated to hold 240,000 people. Ironically it was also revealed in 1988 that the NKVD itself had suffered 20,000 deaths during Stalin's purges. Then on 12 September 1989 Soviet television reported that up to 300,000 people shot in the 1930s had been found buried in an abandoned gold mine near Chelyabinsk in the southern Ural mountains.

The KGB (the NKVD's successor) initially made several announcements about the rehabilitation of hundreds of thousands of citizens groundlessly repressed in the 1930s–50s. But under growing pressure it set up a committee to look into the issue and announced in 1990 that 3,778,234 people had been sentenced without trial, of whom 786,098 were shot. During 1988–89 it reviewed 856,582 cases, of whom 844,740 were rehabilitated. It also examined 68,000 letters from the repressed and their families. This was just the tip of the iceberg.

The ghosts of thousands of Polish officers haunted Soviet-Polish relations for over fifty years. After the collapse of Communism in Poland the demands for the acknowledgement of Soviet guilt grew. President Gorbachev finally agreed in 1987 to set up a new commission to fill in this 'black spot'. It was not until three years later, on 13 April 1990, that Moscow finally admitted that it was responsible for the Katyn massacre and not the Nazis as it had always claimed.

Additionally *Moscow News* announced in mid-June 1990 that a second mass grave of Polish officers had been found in western Ukraine. Every year in a wood near Kharkov the spring thaw had brought human remains bearing Polish military buckles and decorations to the surface. The exact number of Poles lost in Kharkov was not known until then, although files showed that 3,891 had fallen into the hands of the local NKVD. The Ukrainian KGB admitted that 'Plot 6' contained 6,500 bodies, including 1,760 Soviet citizens.

Remarkable Revenge

The Russians had revered Stalin for so long as the leader who had brought order to chaos and so resolutely led them against Hitler; for many facing up to his purges and the consequences was abhorrent. In particular the systematic destruction of the loyal Red Army officer corps because of Stalin's political scheming and paranoia was appalling – especially in light of its subsequent unquestioning heroic defence of the Motherland and victories in 1944–45.

Even today some adamantly refuse to believe Stalin committed such wanton acts against his own people, while for others the sense of betrayal is palpable. The sad fact is that it was Stalin who dissipated his country's ability to resist Hitler and it was this state of affairs that contributed to his decision to invade.

Stalin's catalogue of mismanagement cost the Soviet people some 40 million dead, surely a legacy that would haunt any nation. Nonetheless, it was Stalin and his generals who galvanized the nation to expel the Nazi invader. In the final analysis there can be no denying Stalin's quite remarkable revenge on Hitler with Operation Bagration.

Appendix I: Stalin's New Tanks

Zhukov recalled that Stavka made its final decision on the 1944 summer campaign, including Byelorussia at the end of April, and that all the fronts were reinforced with additional tank corps:

The 1st Baltic Front was given the 1st Tank Corps, while the 3rd Byelorussian Front was reinforced by the 11th Guards Army and the 2nd Guards Tank Corps. The 28th Army, the 9th and 1st Guards Tank Corps, the 1st Mechanised and the 4th Guards Cavalry Corps were concentrated on the right wing of the 1st Byelorussian Front. The 5th Guards Tank Army – a reserve of the Supreme Command – was being concentrated in the area of the 3rd Byelorussian Front.

Soviet Tank Armies

After the shock of the German invasion in the summer of 1941, the Soviet high command sought to learn from its flawed Moscow counter-offensive in the winter of 1941–42. What was clear was that there was a shortage of tanks, and so tank production became a priority. By the spring of 1942 the Soviets began to form dedicated tank corps followed by mechanized corps.

Also in the spring of 1942 appeared the first tank armies, the 3rd and 5th, which were designed as breakthrough forces, or 'Stalin's armoured fist'. These new tank armies and corps were blooded at Kharkov, on the Bryansk front, the Voronezh front and on the approaches to Stalingrad. To start with their deployment was a case of trial and error; more often than not it was a case of error resulting in heavy losses. Eventually, though, this paid off, with notably spectacular results at Stalingrad.

At the beginning of 1943 the Soviets took the decision to create five standardized tank armies, all of which took part in the Battle of Kursk. Nikolai Yakovlevich Zheleznov started the war manufacturing anti-aircraft gun components in Moscow, but his factory was evacuated to Saratov, and he eventually found himself joining one of Stalin's new tank armies:

In the spring of 1943 we loaded onto a train that took us to a place near Moscow. The 4th Tank Army was being formed there, and our 30th Urals Volunteer Tank Corps, in whose ranks I spent the entire war, was a part of it. In the summer the army deployed to the southwest of Sukhinichi, and that's where I had my first battle.

It was not an auspicious start for the 4th Tank Army. The 62nd Tank Brigade led the attack to force the Ors River, followed by the 63rd Brigade, which Zheleznov was serving with. The river was crossed but the attackers could not penetrate German defences any further, so the 63rd was ordered to join the attack.

Zheleznov recalls things did not go according to plan:

> After forcing the Ors, they ran into German defences on, I believe, Hill 212, which they couldn't break through. The corps commander ordered our brigade to force its way through the enemy and advance towards the south, to capture Borilovo, then Masal'skoe. However, the brigade's engineering reconnaissance had been conducted poorly, and our tanks got stuck in the mud while crossing the Nugr' River – its basin was swampy, and the opposite bank was a vertical wall. So our first battle wasn't successful: our attack literally bogged down.

In January 1944 the 6th Tank Army was formed with about 600 tanks and self-propelled guns, 500 guns and mortars, and 30,000 men. The 6 tank armies had nearly 40 armoured corps. The tank corps now numbered 207 tanks and 63 self-propelled guns, while the mechanized corps could field 183 tanks and the same number of self-propelled guns. Also to reinforce the infantry they used separate infantry brigades, self-propelled artillery and heavy tank regiments.

Typically a Soviet Tank Army comprised two or three tank corps and an optional mechanized corps: with all the supporting arms this provided up to 50,000 men with 550–650 tanks and 650–850 guns and mortars. A tank corps was made up of three tank brigades and a motorized rifle brigade, plus supporting arms, fielding around 12,000 men, 270 tanks and self-propelled guns, and 180 guns and mortars. In a mechanized corps the mix of brigades was reversed, with three mechanized and one tank, giving a total of around 16,400 men supported by 250 tanks and self-propelled guns, and 230 guns and mortars.

A Soviet rifle army consisted of three rifle corps of up to twelve divisions, totalling 80,000–120,000 men equipped with up to 460 tanks and 2,000 guns and mortars. A rifle corps numbered three rifle divisions, totalling up to 30,000 troops. Rifle divisions could muster up to 9,000 men but were typically about half that number. A cavalry corps comprised three cavalry divisions with a total manpower strength of up to 15,000 (a cavalry division averaged about 4,700 men), supported by up to 100 tanks. It should be noted that Soviet organizational terminology was not the same as western armies': in the latter brigades make up a division; with the Soviets it was the reverse. In manpower terms a Soviet division was roughly equivalent to a western regiment or battalion.

Stalin's New Armour

While the Red Army was much better qualitatively than it had been in 1942, crucially it was now numerically stronger. Stalin's factories safely relocated to the Urals were now producing an increasing flow of armaments. Despite the Soviet Union's massive losses it had 7,700 tanks by the beginning of 1942 and

20,600 the following year. Soviet tank factories were churning out 2,000 a month, rising to almost 3,000 by the end of 1943.

By the beginning of 1944, despite massive losses sustained at Kursk and in Ukraine, thanks to Soviet industry the Red Army was still able to field 5,357 tanks and self-propelled guns. For the Byelorussian offensive the Soviets were to commit the bulk of their armoured forces, including five tank armies, ten separate tank and mechanized corps.

The cornerstone of Stalin's tank forces in 1941 was the T-34/76 and the KV-1, though the latter was quickly relegated to an infantry support role and then turned over to self-propelled gun production in the form of the 152mm armed SU-152. During the opening stages of the war the Soviets quickly discovered that their range of light tanks (T-40, T-60 and T-70) and medium tanks (T-26 and BT-7) were wholly inadequate and stopped producing them except as self-propelled gun chassis, most notably the SU-76 using the T-70, mounting a 76.2mm anti-tank gun which appeared in 1943. Intended as a tank destroyer it was soon employed in the assault gun role. The Soviets' cumbersome heavy tanks such as the KV-1 and KV-2 were also phased out by 1944.

In contrast the new T-34/76, also armed with the 76.2mm anti-tank gun, was not found wanting, and caused an acceleration in German tank designs to try to counter it. The T-34 was well suited to Russia's weather: in particular its wide tracks and low ground pressure gave it good traction and speed. Although the first T-34s had transmission problems and during the German invasion more broke down than were knocked out, the German Panther, which appeared in 1943, copied many of its features.

During 1943 the Red Army lost over 14,000 T-34/76s, almost fifty per cent during the second half of the year to Army Group South, equipped with the new Panther. The Germans lost almost 500 of these, half of which had been destroyed by their crews when forced into flight. By 1944 the general view was that the Soviet Union's tanks were as good as anyone else's, indeed many Germans felt they were in fact better. Although lacking frills such as crew comfort and radios, they had the armament, the endurance and the performance to match Hitler's panzers.

Following Kursk, future Soviet premier Lieutenant General Nikita Khrushchev recalled in his memoirs:

Later I saw an order we captured from a demolished German armoured unit. It contained a message addressed to German troops which went something like this: 'You are now waging an offensive with tanks far superior to the Russian T-34s. Until now the T-34 has been the best tank in the world, better even than our own. But now you have our new Tiger tanks. There is no equal to them. With such a weapon you warriors of the German army cannot fail to crush the enemy.'

Their new tanks were very menacing indeed, but our troops learned quickly how to deal with them.

The Soviets introduced new up-gunned tanks in 1944 that finally gave them parity with the best of the German heavy and medium tanks, namely the T-34/85 and the IS-1 and IS-2 (for Iosif Stalin, the Cyrillic alphabet being without the western J for Joseph). At the end of 1943 a variant of the KV-85 turret was adapted for the T-34, and the new up-gunned T-34/85 went into production in mid-December. The T-34/85's introduction was not before time because the T-34/76's gun could not tackle the Tiger.

Zheleznov noted that the new T-34 finally gave his side some parity:

In essence, until we got the 85mm gun we had to run from Tigers like rabbits, and look for an opportunity to turn back and get at their flanks. It was difficult. If you saw a Tiger 800–1,000 metres away and it started 'crossing' you, while it moved its gun horizontally you could stay in your tank, but once it started moving it vertically you'd better jump out, or you could get burned! It never happened to me, but other guys bailed out. But when the T-34/85 entered service, we could stand up against enemy tanks one on one.

The larger calibre armament of the T-34/85, providing greater ballistic range, granted combat parity with the Germans' heavy tanks: this and its ever-growing numbers was a war-winning combination. It was capable of penetrating the frontal armour of the Tiger at 1,000 metres, though accuracy remained a problem. The T-34/85 was heavier than the T-34/76, but overall its performance was not greatly affected.

During the spring of 1944 Soviet Guards' armoured brigades were issued with the very first new T-34s. Once production was in full swing it became the standard medium tank in all armoured units, although the T-34/76 remained in general service. While many units were re-quipped for the coming Bagration offensive, they did not get the T-34/85, instead having to make do with the earlier 76.2mm armed version. Almost 11,800 of the newer variant were produced during 1944.

Another improved variant developed that year was known as the T-44, but it did not see service until the early post-war years.

A tank destroyer variant of the T-34 known as the SU-85 was produced in late 1943, and production was ramped up during 1944. This was issued to replace the SU-76, which was relegated to infantry support. Assault gun regiments were formed mainly to fight alongside the armoured forces, and the T-34/85 was deployed in conjunction with the SU-85. This heavily armoured assault gun appeared in the battles in Ukraine in 1944 and was subsequently replaced by the SU-100 mounting the powerful 100mm M-1944 field gun.

Following the German invasion the Soviets sought to outgun German armour: the challenge for the designers was to marry the gun to the mount, which was easier said than done. The Red Army had been particularly impressed by the German Sturmgeschütz assault gun and sought to emulate it.

An early attempt at this was the SU-122 self-propelled gun, based on the T-34 chassis, which went into production in January 1943. Employed in platoons of three they provided fire support for the tank divisions, though from late 1943 this vehicle was superseded by the SU-152. The latter was nicknamed *Zveroboi* or Animal Hunter and consisted of a 152mm howitzer based on the KV-1 chassis. This was to prove particularly successful against the Tiger, Panther and Elefant. The Germans dubbed it the 'can opener' because of its ability to tear a Tiger's turret off.

At the end of 1943 the ISU-152, based on the KV-2 heavy tank chassis, was produced, also armed with a 152mm howitzer. This was intended for a dual role as an anti-tank gun and heavy assault gun. While an effective weapon its lack of storage restricted ammunition and therefore its tactical flexibility as it was reliant on ammunition carriers.

To counter the German Tiger tank, which first appeared on the Russian front in 1943, the Soviets adapted their 85mm Model 1939 anti-aircraft gun for anti-tank use. Once modified this had an effective range of 1,000m (1,100 yards) and could penetrate 100mm of armour, so constituted a very real threat to the Panther and Tiger, although it was far from accurate at long range. At the end of the summer of 1943 the gun was installed into a heavy cast turret and fitted to the KV-1 chassis that became the KV-85. This was produced as a stopgap until the IS tank was ready for production.

Although classed as a heavy tank the IS was actually roughly the same weight as the German Panther medium tank. Initially equipped with the 85mm gun, then a 100mm, this was replaced with a 122mm, enabling Soviet tank crews to engage any German tank at extremely long ranges. This capability was a deathblow to the panzers already struggling to fend off superior Soviet tank numbers. The IS-1 went into production in late 1943, though only 102 were made; the following year Soviet factories churned out 2,250. The IS-2 had an improved hull with contour castings, and up-gunned with a 122mm proved to be one of the most powerful tanks to go into service with any army during the Second World War. About 1,000 had been built by June 1944.

The Stalin chassis also provided the basis for the ISU-122 and ISU-152 self-propelled guns: both entered service in 1944 superseding the SU-122 and SU-152 mounted on the KV chassis. Their commonality proved useful as they were mainly employed with the heavy tank regiments equipped with the Stalin tanks.

Stalin also viewed artillery as the god of war, and guns of all calibres rolled from his factories thick and fast. Even more dedicated artillery divisions were created, eventually numbering over 40 of them. In support of Soviet offensives the Red Army was able to put down massive and devastating bombardments.

After 1941 the Soviets took the prudent view that any guns capable of direct fire should be issued with anti-tank ammunition. The combination field and anti-tank gun was epitomized by the M1942 76.2mm field gun, a development of the M1939, which was produced in greater numbers than any other gun during the war. The M1942 was supplemented by the 152mm M1943 howitzer and the M1937 gun-howitzer and the 122mm M1938.

Lend-Lease Armour

The Red Army was also equipped with huge quantities of tanks provided under the Lend-Lease arrangements. Major General F.W. von Mellenthin saw the equipment provided by Britain and America playing a vital role in Stalin's summer offensive:

> From the Russian point of view the most important items were the aircraft and motor vehicles. These greatly enabled the Russians to speed up the whole tempo of their operations. The dramatic advance from the Dnepr to the Vistula in June and July 1944, and subsequent rapid breakthroughs in Hungary and Poland can be attributed directly to the Anglo-American aid. Thus did [President] Roosevelt ensure that Stalin would make himself master of Central Europe.

During 1941 and 1942 Britain and the Commonwealth supplied almost 3,300 tanks, as well as 24,400 other vehicles and 2,600 aircraft. America stepped in from 1942 to 1945, providing Stalin with 7,000 tanks, 436,500 wheeled vehicles and 14,800 aircraft.

Walter Kerr recalled:

> Every three weeks or so large convoys of American and British ships arrived in the Arctic ports of Murmansk and Archangel. They moved through waters controlled by German torpedo bombers, in winter when the days were short and in the summer when the days were long. Sometimes they suffered terrible losses. Sometimes they got through intact.

Two other supply routes were opened up through Iran and Alaska.

By 1944 the main Allied tank in evidence with the Red Army was the American M4A2 Sherman, which had a diesel engine and all-steel tracks, and usually included extra fuel drums and ditching beams. The Soviet tankers nicknamed it *Emcha*, after the first letter and number – 'M four' being *M chetyre* in Russian.

The Soviets had mixed feelings about this Lend-Lease armour; on the whole their attitude was negative. Tanker A.V. Bodnar noted:

> I had a look at an American M4A2 Sherman. My God! It was like a hotel inside! It was all lined with leather so that you didn't smash your head! There was also a medical kit with condoms and sulphidin – they had everything! But at the same time they weren't fit for war. Because of their two diesel engines, their earth fuel cleaners, their narrow tracks – all these things didn't last in Russia.

Nor were the tankers impressed with its propensity to burn – even the Germans had dubbed it the 'Tommy cooker'. For the coming Bagration offensive the 3rd Guards Tank Corps was one of the Soviet units equipped with the ubiquitous Sherman.

Until mid-1943, when the Germans had a greater proportion of 50mm to 75mm anti-tank guns, the sloping armour of the T-34 had been a distinct advantage, and this reassured Soviet crews of its merits. Only British tanks had any advantages, as battalion commander Bryokhov recalled: 'If a shell had gone through the turret of a British tank the commander and the gunner could have stayed alive, because there were virtually no splinters, while in a T-34 the armour would spall a lot and the crew had few chances of survival.'

As Alexay Isaev explains: 'This was because the medium hardness of Britain's Matilda and Valentine tanks have a very high nickel content (3–3.5 per cent), whereas Soviet 45mm high hardness armour contained only 1–1.5 per cent nickel, resulting in much lower ductility.'

The only tank the Red Army seemed to have any time for was the Canadian-built British Valentine. Zheleznov's verdict after his training at Saratov was: 'It was a very successful tank, low to the ground, with a powerful gun and quiet engine.' His comments on the gun are a little generous in light of its being armed variously with a 2-pounder, 6-pounder or 75mm gun. Even so the Soviets were even known to use the Valentine to stalk the Tiger tank. On one such occasion, on 23 or 24 March 1944 near Kamenets-Podolsk, Nikolai Zheleznov recounts:

> Then the brigade commander, Colonel Fomichev…sent two of the low profile Valentine tanks from our 7th Motorcycle Battalion, and they, using the bushes as cover, approached the Tigers to within 300–400 metres. By firing at their sides they destroyed two tanks, and then the third one. A fourth Tiger was on the slope of the hill and didn't see what was happening to his left. Then it crawled away somewhere.

British tanks were also used for training purposes, as Aleksandr Sergeyevich Burtsev, who received instruction at the 1st Saratov Tank Military Academy, experienced:

> We spent a long time at the school – eighteen months. For about a year we learned on the Matilda and Valentine tanks, then on the T-34s. We were taught well. We studied theory in classes and practised on the artillery range, where we were trained for weeks – we drove, fired, analysed tactics for individual tanks and for tank units. At the same time we also learned infantry tactics, for we were required to be able to interact with motorised troops.

America also supplied the Red Army with over 400,000 military vehicles. About 25 per cent of the trucks were 2½ ton 6 × 4 and 6 × 6 Studebakers; the rest were Jeeps, Dodge Weapons Carriers, Chevrolet and Dodge 4 × 4 1½ tonners. Many Lend-Lease trucks were assembled in Iran and then driven northward. Canada also supplied General Motors trucks, and Britain sent Albion, Austin, Bedford and Ford vehicles. GAZ and ZIS were the USSR's two most important lorry manufacturers; JAG and JAS also built trucks for the Red Army but in fewer numbers.

Despite American generosity with Lend-Lease, motor transport remained a problem. The infantry were often obliged to hitch a ride dangerously exposed on the tanks. It was only Hitler's insistence on not giving up ground and therefore consigning his generals to static defence that enabled the relatively slow-moving Red Army to conduct successful encircling movements.

The food sent by the Western Allies was particularly welcome. 'I also recall the 1.5 kilo cans of smoked pork fat we received via Lend-Lease,' said Zheleznov. 'It was cut into ten centimetre long and one centimetre wide strips, with paper in between. You'd take two or three slices, put them on a piece of bread, drink half a cup of alcohol, chase it with that sandwich, and life was beautiful!'

Appendix II: Stalin's Revitalized Air Power

By 1944 the turning point in the fortunes of the Red Air Force (or VVS, *Voenno-vozdushnye sili*, Air Forces) had been reached after much toil and loss of life and machines. The battles for Moscow, Stalingrad, the Kuban and Kursk had witnessed its transformation from a shambles into an experienced, well-organized and well-run force that could match the Luftwaffe. It was now ready to assist the Red Army to push the Wehrmacht out of Mother Russia.

Stalin had mastery of the air by the time of Operation Bagration. Guy Sajer who claimed to have served with the Grossdeutschland Panzergrenadier Division in Ukraine, recalled in the summer of 1944:

> The pale blue sky belonged to the Russians, whose air power had grown enormously. The Luftwaffe, whose numbers had been seriously reduced by the necessity of defending German cities and dealing with the increasing demands of the Western front, flew daily sorties which amounted to suicide flights against overwhelming enemy strength on the ground and in the air. Our few victories were the product of absolute heroism. The sky belonged to the enemy.

Zhukov took a key role in planning the air attacks on Army Group Centre:

> I also proposed that all the long-range aviation be employed in the Byelorussian action, and its operation against targets on German territory be put off until a later time. The Supreme Commander agreed, and immediately ordered Air Marshal A.A. Novikov and Air Marshal A.E. Golovanov, who was in charge of the long-range aviation, to report to me. I had worked with both these capable commanders in all major previous operations, and they had given the ground troops valuable assistance.
>
> Novikov, Golovanov, Rudenko, Vershinin and I thoroughly discussed the situation – the tasks and the operational plans of the various air armies and their cooperation with the long-range aviation, which was to strike at enemy headquarters, communication centres of operational formations, reserves and other key targets. We also discussed the manoeuvres of the air forces of the individual Fronts in the common interest. Vasilevsky was given 350 heavy long-range aircraft to support the actions of the 3rd Byelorussian Front.

In contrast in June 1941 the Red Air Force in the Western Military District had lost 1,200 aircraft, 800 of which had been destroyed while still on the ground. From then till November 1942 it focused on rebuilding its ground-attack force. Subsequently from November 1942 to December 1943 it had worked hard to improve its air-ground system by centralizing one air army per front. It also developed the aviation offensive, which involved forward air command posts that would be used to some effect during Bagration. From 1944 to 1945 this close air support liaison greatly expanded, and air support and air control involved highly detailed planning.

During the second half of 1943 with about 8,500 deployable aircraft the Red Air Force remained static, but over the first six months of 1944 it rapidly expanded to 13,500 planes. That year a new tactical bomber was introduced into service, the Tu-2, which was to play a key role in the Red Army's final offensives. The Soviets' dabbling with strategic bombers was half-hearted at best and dogged by engine problems. Production of the Pe-8 strategic bombers, which had played a limited role at Kursk, was ended in 1944 after just seventy-nine had been built.

By far the Red Air Force's best ground-attack weapon was the famous Ilyushin 'Flying Tank' or Il-2 Shturmovik, which first appeared in 1941. This was designed as a low-level close-support aircraft capable of defeating enemy armour and other ground targets. Following early teething problems it developed into one of the world's most potent ground-attack aircraft, armed with 23mm cannons, machine guns, rockets and bombs, including anti-tank bomblets; with good cause the Germans dubbed it the *Schlächter* or Slaughterer.

The Il-2 pilots developed the 'circle of death' for attacking panzers. They would circle around the enemy armour and peel off to make individual attack runs. When the run ended, they would rejoin their formation to wait for another turn. This kept the Germans under constant fire for as long as the Il-2s had ammunition left.

Notably during the summer of 1943 and the Battle of Kursk the Shturmovik finally came into its own, severely mauling the 2nd and 3rd Panzer Divisions. By 1943–44 some 12,000 were in service and the Soviets were flying the Il-2M3 variant, which included a rear gunner. Similarly the improved La-5FN and Yak-3 fighters that appeared in 1943 helped the Red Air Force wrest air superiority from the Luftwaffe. By May 1944 the Soviet fighter squadrons were being equipped with an improved version of the La-5, the La-7. That year aircraft production reached 40,300.

Stalin also received new ground-attack aircraft in 1944 courtesy of the Americans, principally the Bell P-63 Kingcobra (an upgrade of the earlier P-39 Airacobra), the P-40 and the P-47. The Soviets had received about 2,000 P-40s by March 1944, but they did not like them, considering them cast-offs, and the aircraft were largely relegated to a training role. Only 200 P-47s were sent during 1944–45; in contrast 2,421 P-63s were received, which were based on a proven and well-liked design.

However, by this stage in the war the Soviets were keener on bombers and transports, as their factories were producing fighters equal or superior in quality and in plentiful numbers. During 1944 aircraft production reached 40,300 machines.

The Soviets were already equipped with the P-39 Airacobra and the British Hurricane and Spitfire. They found the Airacobra armed with a 37mm cannon to be an excellent ground-attack aircraft, and received 4,750 of them. The Soviets nicknamed it *britchik* or 'little shaver'. Britain and the Commonwealth supplied in total 4,770 aircraft, while from 1942 until the end of the war America provided another 14,800, of which 9,438 were fighters. To supplement the Soviet bomber force the Americans provided 2,908 A-20 Havoc light bombers and 862 B-25 Mitchell medium bombers.

By the time of Bagration the Soviets had got the hang of their American-supplied fighters. Two years earlier for fear of American spies or simply national pride Stalin had refused offers of American pilots and mechanics. The consequences, as American journalist Walter Kerr recalled, were predictable:

> One result was that in the early months when they used our Airacobras and B-25 medium bombers, many were damaged through inexperienced handling. Both planes have a nose wheel, which has led to their being called planes with a tricycle landing gear. In fact, they should be landed on two wheels, then nosed over on to the front wheel as the pilot taxis across the field. The Russians, however, tried to land them on three wheels, and the relatively weak forward wheel frequently broke.

The Americans also secured agreement with Stalin for their air force to operate from the Soviet Union in 1944. Apart from the RAF fighter squadron based at Murmansk to help protect the Arctic convoys, this was Stalin's only concession to the Western Allies' desire to operate from his territory.

Khrushchev recalled:

> I got my first glimpse of Americans in the late spring or early summer of 1944 near Kiev. It was a bright, warm day. Suddenly we heard a rumbling noise in the distance. We scanned the sky and saw a large formation of airplanes flying toward us. I'd never seen this type of plane before. I realised they must be Americans because we didn't have anything like them in our own air force. I certainly hoped they were American; the only other thing they could have been was German. I later found out that these planes were B-17 'flying fortresses' and were based outside Poltava as part of our agreement with Roosevelt. They used our territory to rearm and refuel after bombing missions over Germany. We would often see them flying overhead at night, on their way to targets in Germany, and then returning at daybreak.

With Operation Frantic the Americans had considerable expectations of this shuttle bombing of Germany; however, the success was short-lived, thanks to the Luftwaffe. Khrushchev continued: 'Somehow the Germans were able to track the American bombers back to Poltava and bomb their base. I received a report that many planes had been destroyed and many lives had been lost. Most of the casualties were our own men whom we had provided as maintenance personnel at the base.'

This retaliatory raid took place on 21–22 June 1944. Only eighteen American missions were flown, the whole operation largely being stymied by Stalin, who suspected American motives.

Appendix III: Hitler's New Panzers

The brutal struggle fought on the Eastern Front between 1941 and 1945 was largely one of who could build the most tanks, but Hitler failed to grasp the urgency of the looming tank race. In 1940 he had produced just over 1,500 panzers; by 1944 he was turning out almost 8,000, but by then it was too few too late. Total German tank production amounted to about 25,000, plus another 12,000 assault guns and assault artillery. The upshot was that the panzers could not sustain their momentum on the Eastern Front and the initiative passed over to the Red Army. Additionally the Germans seemed unable to stick to one tank type, instead producing a vast variety of platforms for different roles.

Once Stalin had recovered from the shock of the invasion his factories were able to produce enough tanks to eventually swamp Hitler's panzers. When the Germans launched Operation Barbarossa they had over 3,000 tanks, which ranged from the largely useless Panzer I up to the Panzer IV. Production of the Panzer I and II had ceased, although the chassis continued to be used for self-propelled guns. Most of the Panzer IIIs were upgraded from a 37mm gun to a 50mm, while the Panzer IV had the short 75mm. These proved inadequate against the Red Army's T-34 and KV-1. Subsequently both the Panzer III and IV were produced with thicker armour, and the latter was rearmed with a longer 75mm anti-tank gun.

Those Panzer IVs lost during the invasion were replaced by April 1942, but there was no increase in overall numbers. In terms of production the Germans could not compete: in November 1942 they managed 100 Panzer IVs compared to 1,000 Soviet T-34s. Hitler, determined the war should not affect the civilian population, resisted stepping up production. The following month Panzer III assembly was turned over to the StuG III assault gun. By February 1943 the Germans had just 495 tanks in eighteen panzer divisions on the Eastern Front. The writing was on the wall.

Hitler sought to offset Stalin's growing numerical superiority by introducing new armour designs. However, the later German armour, while first-class tank killers, were big and heavy, rendering them a tactical liability, if they were not supported adequately.

Notably 1943 saw the introduction of the famed Panther and Tiger I. Like the famous 8.8cm Flak 18 and Flak 36 guns, the Tiger was armed with the KwK 36 anti-tank gun, the main differences being the addition of a muzzle brake and electric firing trigger. The latter was able to stand off and kill Soviet tanks at ranges of over 1,500m (12,000 yards), thus out of range of Soviet tank guns. Fortunately for the Red Army the Tiger was slow, difficult to recover when disabled and expensive to build. The Germans also produced limited numbers of the Elefant, a turret-less Tiger.

The Panther Ausf D and A, essentially T-34 wannabes, combined armament, armour and mobility. Early models proved mechanically unreliable, in part because of being rushed into production too soon. Armed with the 7.5cm L/70 gun, an improved version of that in the Panzer IV, they could knock out Soviet tanks almost as easily as the Tiger.

The appearance of the Panther Ausf G in March 1944 addressed some of the mechanical problems experienced by the early models, but it was heavy on the fuel and by mid-1944 was facing much more capable Soviet 85mm and 122mm anti-tank guns. While limited numbers of Panthers had claimed about 500 T-34s, only about two dozen were lost to enemy armour. In contrast what the T-34/76 had lacked in punch it made up for in reliability, endurance and numbers.

The Henschel Tiger I was undoubtedly the finest quality tank ever put into mass production, but it required elaborate machine tools and was labour intensive. The result was that it could not be churned out in any great numbers. In 1944 the German army had taken receipt of the Tiger II, also variously known as the King Tiger or Royal Tiger, and Jagdtiger (based on the Tiger II). Limited numbers of both were deployed on the Eastern and Western Fronts. Fortunately for the Allies the Tiger II, while better armed than the initial Tiger, was much heavier and mechanically unreliable, and only 485 in total were built.

The Jagdtiger, armed with the largest anti-tank gun of the war, a 12.8cm, in a straight shooting match was unstoppable, but its weight to mobility ratio meant that it could not cope with the fluid armoured warfare of 1944 either in the east or the west. Also, like its predecessor it was not manufactured in significant numbers. Under ninety were produced, and it did not go into action until September.

German self-propelled gun variants based on the Panzer IV included the Brummbär or Grizzly Bear, Nashorn or Rhinoceros, and Hummel or Bumblebee. Hitler's Hungarian, Slovak and Romanian allies were equipped with the Czech LT-35 and LT-38 and Hungarian Toldi and Turan light tanks; all of these were more a liability than an asset.

Also in 1944 the Germans produced the Jagdpanzer IV and Hetzer (based on the Czech LT-38 tank chassis). Although seen as an unnecessary diversion of tank production, the Jagdpanzer was ideal for Germany's many defensive battles of 1944–45. None of this equipment, though, was able to stave off the inevitable.

Appendix IV: The Enfeebled Luftwaffe

Britain and America's greatest contribution to Stalin's war effort was the strategic air campaign against Germany's cities and industries; as the battles over the Reich increased in tempo so the fighter units were siphoned off from the Eastern Front. Also, the stepping up of production of anti-aircraft artillery affected the production of other weapons, especially artillery. Despite the massive bomber effort during 1943 German aircraft production had achieved over 24,800 planes, of which 11,730 were fighters; it was to peak the following year with 39,800, of which a staggering 28,900 were fighters.

In fact the strategic bomber offensive made a huge contribution to the Soviets' advances because it forced the Luftwaffe to withdraw 80 per cent of their fighter squadrons and anti-aircraft batteries from the Eastern Front, and that enabled the vast Soviet victories and advances of 1943, and above all 1944. The destruction of Army Group Centre would never have been possible without that withdrawal of so many Luftwaffe squadrons.

By the end of May 1944 the Luftwaffe on the Eastern Front consisted of General der Flieger Kurt Pflugbeil's Luftflotte 1, Generaloberst Otto Dessloch's Luftflotte 4 and Generalfeldmarschall Robert Ritter von Greim's Luftflotte 6, which between them had a total of 2,199 aircraft, though only 1,624 were listed as available for combat. The Luftwaffe's senior command authority was the XXV Field Luftgau Command with its HQ in Minsk.

Bearing in mind that the Germans were fighting in France, Italy, the Soviet Union and over Germany, the inadequate strength of the Luftwaffe fighter force was such by mid-1944 it was incapable of covering the entire Eastern Front effectively. Growing Allied air superiority in the west and east meant that the best the Luftwaffe could achieve was temporary air superiority over combat zones. By 1944 this was no longer possible over France or Italy.

In particular the air war over the German Reich now precluded sending any large-scale reinforcements to bolster the Eastern Front. To make matters worse, once pilots had accumulated some combat experience over Russia they were transferred back to Germany for home defence against the bombers. The young replacements were inevitably inexperienced trainees. The Germans refused to mount standing flying patrols, instead holding their pilots poised to scramble, and as a result interception of low-flying Soviet ground-attack aircraft was poor. Only during offensive operations could the panzers hope for continuous fighter cover.

In 1943, because major offensives were no longer possible, the Luftwaffe's tactical air commands were disbanded. Instead each air corps had to support two or three armies. It was not feasible to support the ground forces and conduct a counter-air campaign at the same time. The air forces became the servant of their allotted army group. Their role was to attack ground targets directly in front of the ground forces, and this tied up about 80 per cent of the bomber force. Each month, for all theatres of operation, for tactical support employing short-range bombers the Luftwaffe could put into the air about twenty *Gruppen* (with a nominal strength of thirty aircraft each).

The Luftwaffe usually conducted during the operational planning phase the 'pre-planned mission' for close air support. Once the operation had started this was supplemented by 'independent commitment' that allowed for additional sorties against pre-planned or new targets. On the Eastern Front the Luftwaffe also conducted 'free commitment' sorties, allowing for attacks on targets of opportunity on the flanks as well as the front of the spearhead force. These were effectively combat air patrols. During 1942–43 they were increasingly the type of missions flown.

As well as acting as flying artillery the Luftwaffe was also acting as the eyes of the German army, as providing long-range reconnaissance for the ground forces had become a Luftwaffe mission. German aerial intelligence-gathering was far from adequate. In total the Luftwaffe's tactical reconnaissance units had available thirty *Staffeln* (smallest combat flying unit, with a nominal strength of nine aircraft) on a monthly basis, which was not a great increase from 1941. Similarly strategic reconnaissance units operating with the army numbered only twenty-eight *Staffeln* per month.

General von Tippelskirch felt that Hitler's 'hedgehog' or strongpoint policy had been the death knell of the Luftwaffe on the Eastern Front as early as the winter of 1941–42:

> That winter ruined the Luftwaffe – because it had to be used for flying supplies to the garrisons of the 'hedgehogs', the forward positions that were isolated by the Russian flanking advances. The II Corps [under which Tippelskirch was serving] required 200 tons of supplies a day, which called for a daily average of 100 transport aircraft. But as bad weather often intervened, the actual number had to be considerably larger, so as to make full use of an interval of passable weather – on one day as many as 350 aircraft were used to reprovision this single corps. The overall strain of keeping up supplies by air to all the isolated positions on such a vast front was fatal to the future development of the Luftwaffe.

Also, Stalingrad had been a disaster for the Luftwaffe; its success at Demyansk saving part of 16th Army had set a dangerous precedent. In keeping 6th Army resupplied at Stalingrad the Luftwaffe lost 490 transport planes and bombers: this was equivalent to more than an entire air corps, and was a blow from which it could never recover.

Tank Busting

Not all was doom and gloom for the Luftwaffe on the Eastern Front: it was still more than capable of protecting the ground forces, mainly because of the superiority of its pilots and aircraft. Indeed up until 1944 it was notable that German road and rail traffic moved in the Soviet Union largely unhindered by the Red Air Force, whereas the Red Army avoided the railways and roads during the day except when a major offensive was being prepared. This situation was to change dramatically in the summer of 1944.

German efforts to completely destroy the Soviet rail system were partly thwarted by the Americans, who during the course of the war shipped in almost 2,000 locomotives and over 11,000 rail cars. Furthermore, by 1944 Soviet tactics for defending trains had greatly improved.

Nonetheless, in the summer of 1944 specially trained Luftwaffe units, principally the 9th Staffel of Bomber Geschwader 3, equipped with Ju 88s, and the 14th Staffel of Geschwader 27 and 55, equipped with He 111s assigned to Air Corps IV, resumed attacking Russian railways, particularly the depots. These raids continued until the end of 1944, when fuel shortages forced their deactivation. This tactic was largely a reflection of the lack of a strategic bomber force that could have ranged further into the Soviet rear.

A crucial failure was in building up a strong heavy bomber force, which meant many Soviet weapons factories were out of range of the twin-engined bombers, and those attacks that did reach them did not disrupt production sufficiently. This left the German armed forces having to destroy Soviet armour bit by bit on the battlefield.

Indeed, combating Soviet tanks had become a primary mission for the Luftwaffe by 1944. The German army, lacking overwhelming numbers of panzers and anti-tank guns, needed the Luftwaffe's support, and following the failure at Kursk all German ground-attack forces of the Stukagruppen, Schlachtgruppen and Schnellkampfgruppen were combined into a separate ground-attack command under a *General der Schlachtflieger*.

Once it had become evident that the Stuka Ju 87 was too slow to survive combat conditions, units were re-equipped with the Focke-Wulfe 190. The latter, designed to supplement the Messerschmitt Bf 109, soon proved itself to be an able ground-attack aircraft. During the second half of 1942 four fighter wings or *Gruppen* had converted to the Fw 190: I and III/JG 51 and I and II/JG 54.

Because of shortages of the Fw 190, the Ju 87 units did not begin converting until the spring of 1944. Initially II/SG 2 and I/SG 77 were the only ground-attack units equipped with the Fw 190. Remarkably by May there were seven Fw 190 equipped Schlachtgruppen on the central and southern sectors of the Eastern Front, totalling 197 aircraft, although most of these were in Poland and Romania. Only one *Gruppe*, III/SG 1, had been re-equipped on the central sector.

While the growing ground-attack fleet was cause for cautious optimism, there were just thirty-one Fw 190 fighters available by June, at a time when the Soviet air force stood at nearly 13,500. Production of the Fw 190 could not keep pace with demand, and in early 1944 I and III Gruppen of JG 51 were forced to re-equip with the Bf 109G. I/JG 51 returned to Bobruisk on the central sector from Deblin-Irena in March having completed the process.

In addition the loss of the Ju 87 in 1944 meant that the SD 4HI anti-tank bomb, capable of piercing 5 inches of armour, could not be delivered as regularly as before. This was an unwelcome degradation of capabilities especially as the bomb also had a fragmentation effect and, carried in a container holding seventy-eight, had been used to good effect against infantry.

Once Soviet armour became increasingly invulnerable to air attack, new ways had to be found to destroy it. In 1943 the Ju 87 and Ju 88 were fitted with a 37mm cannon, and conducted operational tests in the Bryansk area. The Ju 88 did not prove to be a good platform, and though the Ju 87 produced good results the Luftwaffe were unable to form large anti-tank air units. In July 1944, out of desperation, Göring dispatched Heinkel He 177 heavy bombers to deliver low-level attacks on Soviet armour.

In a rare example of the Eastern Front taking precedence over home defence, in June 1944 IV/JG 54 redeployed to the Eastern Front equipped with Fw 190A-8s. This Bf 109 Gruppe had retired through Romania to Germany to re-equip, but was sent to the Soviet-Polish border with sixty-four Fw 190s to cover the retreating ground troops. With JG 54 in the Baltic States and later Poland, the only Fw 190s on the main sectors of the Eastern Front were ground-attack variants numbering some 300 aircraft.

By early 1944 the Germans had only three Flak Corps: I and II Flakkorps were on the southern sector of the Eastern Front, while the III Flakkorps was in France. Two new corps came into being in the second half of the year, but these were deployed to defend Germany. By 1944 the Luftwaffe had a total of twenty-six flak divisions.

Appendix V: Göring's Luftwaffe Field Divisions

After the intoxicating success of the summer of 1941, Hitler's plans soon began to become horribly unstuck. By the close of the winter fighting of 1941–42, German casualties had reached over 1.6 million, not including the sick, and Hitler simply did not have enough replacements. To make matters worse the numerous components of the Wehrmacht, Heeres (army), Kriegsmarine (navy) and Luftwaffe, plus the Waffen SS and the *Reichsarbeitsdienst* (RAD or Reich Labour Service), were all competing for recruits.

Reichsmarschall Hermann Göring, C-in-C of the Luftwaffe, had it in his grasp to help Army Group Centre and Army Group North, but in the name of safeguarding his own personal power base chose not to. The German air force, like the Waffen SS, had far greater recruiting appeal for the more proficient and politically motivated Nazi youngsters. Once the Battle of Britain was over in 1940 the Luftwaffe found itself with more ground crew than it really needed. In the summer of 1942 the German army tried to secure them for retraining as vital infantry replacements.

Göring was having none of it, and reasoned persuasively with Hitler that transferring these 'genuinely Nationalist Socialist' young men would expose them 'to an army which still has chaplains and was led by officers steeped with the traditions of the Kaiser.' He got his own way and instead created twenty-two Luftwaffe field divisions using 170,000 surplus ground support personnel. Similarly the Waffen SS would raise thirty-eight divisions, totalling 800,000 men by the end of the war.

Generalfeldmarschall von Manstein was aghast at Göring's actions:

> To form these excellent troops into divisions within the Luftwaffe was sheer lunacy. Where would they get the necessary close-combat training and practice in working with other formations? Where were they to get the battle experience so vital in the east? And where was the Luftwaffe to find divisional, regimental, and battalion commanders?

These men could have been used as desperately needed infantry replacements to replenish Army Groups Centre and North; instead under Luftwaffe control they added very little to the combat capabilities of the German army on the Eastern Front and further muddled the chain of the command. Indeed reliance on the 2nd Luftwaffe Field Division resulted in the loss of Nevel on 6 October

1943, and combat around the town continued into December, involving all the Luftwaffe field divisions. The net result was that they were left in a very vulnerable position around Vitebsk, and the survivors from the 2nd Luftwaffe Field Division were merged with the 3rd and 4th divisions.

After their indifferent performance the army was finally allowed to assume control of Göring's ground forces in November 1943. The first thing the army did was to replace nearly all the air force officers with regular army officers, and they were reorganized as regular army infantry divisions. By June 1944 the 4th and 6th Luftwaffe Field Divisions were the only ones left in the central zone. The 1st and 3rd had been disbanded in January, and the 5th and 15th were largely non-existent.

The 4th and 6th under Generalleutnant Robert Pistorius and Generalmajor Rudolf Peschel respectively were to play a key if brief role in defending Vitebsk in June 1944. No one believed that they were up to much, with one air force officer commenting on these two units noting:

> They have the best morale. The soldiers are good, the weapons and equipment are excellent. But the training is insufficient. How can they gain experience? The division commanders were company commanders in their last assignment with the Army. The majority of officers are as good as untrained in ground combat. Certainly the divisions will bravely defend their positions. But if they have to attack then it is over.

Another two Luftwaffe units, the 12th and 21st, were assigned to Army Group North. These four divisions, though, were but a fraction of the manpower available. Other Luftwaffe field divisions assigned to Army Group B in France were to fight the Western Allies during June 1944.

Appendix VI:
Soviet Order of Battle,
June–August 1944

Soviet Order of Battle, 23 June 1944

1st Baltic Front
General Army I.Kh. Bagramyan

4th Assault Army
General Lieutenant P.F. Malyshev
Army Artillery
8th Gun Artillery Division
21st Breakthrough Artillery Division

83rd Rifle Corps
General Major N.L. Soldatov
16th Rifle Division
119th Rifle Division
360th Rifle Division

6th Guards Army
General Lieutenant I.M. Chistyakov

2nd Guards Rifle Corps
General Lieutenant A.S. Ksenofontov
9th Guards Rifle Division
46th Guards Rifle Division
166th Rifle Division

22nd Guards Rifle Corps
General Major A.I. Ruchkin
90th Guards Rifle Division
47th Rifle Division
51st Rifle Division

23rd Guards Rifle Corps
General Lieutenant A.N. Yermakov
51st Guards Rifle Division
67th Guards Rifle Division
71st Guards Rifle Division

103rd Rifle Corps
General Major I.F. Fedyunkin
29th Rifle Division
270th Rifle Division

43rd Army
General Lieutenant A.P. Beloborodov

1st Rifle Corps
General Lieutenant N.A. Vasilyev
179th Rifle Division
306th Rifle Division

60th Rifle Corps
General Major A.S. Lyukhtikov
235th Rifle Division
334th Rifle Division
357th Rifle Division

92nd Rifle Corps
General Lieutenant N.B. Ibyansky
145th Rifle Division
204th Rifle Division

1st Tank Corps
General Lieutenant V.V. Butkov
89th Tank Brigade
117th Tank Brigade
159th Tank Brigade

3rd Air Army
General Lieutenant N.F. Papivin

11th Fighter Aviation Corps
General Major G.A. Ivanov
5th Guards Fighter Aviation Division
190th Fighter Aviation Division

Independent Air Units
211th Fighter Aviation Division
259th Fighter Aviation Division
314th Night Bomber Aviation Division
332nd Strike Aviation Division
335th Strike Aviation Division

3rd Byelorussian Front
General Colonel I.D. Chernyakovsky

5th Artillery Corps
2nd Guards Breakthrough Artillery Division
4th Guards Gun Artillery Division
20th Breakthrough Artillery Division

11th Guards Army
General Lieutenant K.N. Galitsky
Army Artillery
7th Guards Mortar (Multiple Rocket) Division

8th Guards Rifle Corps
General Major M.N. Zavodovsky
5th Guards Rifle Division
26th Guards Rifle Division
83rd Guards Rifle Division

16th Guards Rifle Corps
General Major Ya.S. Vorobyev
1st Guards Rifle Division
11th Guards Rifle Division
31st Guards Rifle Division

36th Guards Rifle Corps
General Major P.G. Shafranov
16th Guards Rifle Division
18th Guards Rifle Division
84th Guards Rifle Division

2nd Tank Corps
General Major A.S. Burdeyny
4th Tank Brigade
25th Guards Tank Brigade
26th Guards Tank Brigade

5th Army
General Lieutenant N.I. Krylov
Army Artillery
3rd Guards Breakthrough Artillery Division

45th Rifle Corps
General Major S.F. Gorokhov
159th Rifle Division
184th Rifle Division
338th Rifle Division

65th Rifle Corps
General Major G.N. Perekrestov
97th Rifle Division
144th Rifle Division
371st Rifle Division

72nd Rifle Corps
General Major A.I. Kazariev
63rd Rifle Division
215th Rifle Division
277th Rifle Division
2nd Tank Brigade
153rd Tank Brigade

31st Army
General Lieutenant V.V. Glagolev

36th Rifle Corps
General Major N.N. Oleshev
173rd Rifle Division
220th Rifle Division
352nd Rifle Division

71st Rifle Corps
General Lieutenant P.K. Koshevoy
88th Rifle Division
192nd Rifle Division
331st Rifle Division

113th Rifle Corps
General Major K.I. Provalov
62nd Rifle Division
174th Rifle Division
213th Tank Brigade

39th Army
General Lieutenant I.I. Lyudnikov

5th Guards Rifle Corps
General Major I.S. Bezugly
17th Guards Rifle Division
19th Guards Rifle Division
91st Guards Rifle Division
251st Guards Rifle Division

84th Rifle Corps
General Major Yu.M Prokofiev
158th Rifle Division
164th Rifle Division
262nd Rifle Division
28th Tank Brigade

5th Tank Army
Marshal P.A. Rotmistrov

3rd Guards Tank Corps
General Major I.A. Bobchenko
3rd Guards Tank Brigade
18th Guards Tank Brigade
19th Guards Tank Brigade

3rd Guards Cavalry Corps
General Lieutenant N.S. Oslikovsky
5th Cavalry Division
6th Guards Cavalry Division
32nd Guards Cavalry Division

3rd Mechanized Corps
General Lieutenant V.T. Obukov
7th Guards Mechanized Brigade
8th Guards Mechanized Brigade
35th Guards Tank Brigade

1st Air Army
General Lieutenant T.T. Khryukin

1st Guards Bomber Corps
General Lieutenant V.A. Ushakov
3rd Guards Bomber Aviation Division
4th Guards Bomber Aviation Division
5th Guards Bomber Aviation Division

6th Guards Bomber Aviation Division
113th Guards Bomber Aviation Division
213th Night Bomber Aviation Division
334th Guards Bomber Aviation Division

3rd Strike Aviation Corps
General Major M.I. Gorlachenko
307th Strike Aviation Division
308th Strike Aviation Division

1st Guards Fighter Aviation Corps
General Major Ye.M. Belitsky
3rd Guards Fighter Aviation Division
4th Guards Fighter Aviation Division

2nd Fighter Aviation Corps
General Major A.S. Blagoveshchensky
7th Guards Fighter Aviation Division
322nd Fighter Aviation Division

3rd Fighter Aviation Corps
General Lieutenant Ye.Ya. Savitsky
265th Fighter Aviation Division
278th Fighter Aviation Division

2nd Byelorussian Front
General Colonel G.F. Zakharov

33rd Army
General Lieutenant V.D. Kryuchenkin

70th Rifle Division
157th Rifle Division
344th Rifle Division

49th Army
General Lieutenant I.T. Grishin

62nd Rifle Corps
General Major A.F. Naumov
64th Rifle Division
330th Rifle Division
369th Rifle Division

69th Rifle Corps
General Major H.N. Multan
42nd Rifle Division
222nd Rifle Division

76th Rifle Corps
General Major M.I. Glukhov
49th Rifle Division
199th Rifle Division
290th Rifle Division

81st Rifle Corps
General Major V.V. Panyukhov
32nd Rifle Division
95th Rifle Division
153rd Rifle Division
42nd Guards Tank Brigade
43rd Guards Tank Brigade

50th Army
General Lieutenant I.V. Boldin

19th Rifle Corps
General Major D.I. Samarsky
324th Rifle Division
362nd Rifle Division

38th Rifle Corps
General Major A.D. Tereshkov
110th Rifle Division
139th Rifle Division
385th Rifle Division

121st Rifle Corps
General Major D.I. Smirnov
238th Rifle Division
307th Rifle Division
380th Rifle Division

4th Air Army
General Colonel K.A. Vershinin

229th Fighter Air Division
230th Strike Air Division
233rd Strike Air Division
309th Fighter Air Division
325th Night Bomber Aviation Division

1st Byelorussian Front
Gen. Army K.K. Rokossovsky

(Excludes armies held back for the Lublin–Brest operation, including the 8th, 47th, 70th, 1st Polish and 2nd Tank.)

4th Artillery Corps

3rd Army
General Lieutenant A.V. Gorbatov
Army Artillery
5th Guards Mortar (Multiple Rocket) Division

35th Rifle Corps
General Major V.G. Zholudev
250th Rifle Division
323rd Rifle Division
348th Rifle Division

40th Rifle Corps
General Major V.S. Kuznetsov
120th Guards Rifle Division
269th Rifle Division

41st Rifle Corps
General Major V.K. Urbanovich
129th Rifle Division
169th Rifle Division

46th Rifle Corps
General Major K.M. Erastov
82nd Rifle Division
108th Rifle Division
413th Rifle Division

80th Rifle Corps
General Major I.L. Ragulya
5th Rifle Division
186th Rifle Division
283rd Rifle Division

9th Tank Corps
General Major B.S. Bakharov
8th Mechanized Brigade
23rd Tank Brigade
95th Tank Brigade
109th Tank Brigade

28th Army
General Lieutenant A.A. Luchinsky
Army Artillery
5th Breakthrough Artillery Division
12th Breakthrough Artillery Division

3rd Guards Rifle Corps
General Major F.I. Perkhorovich
50th Guards Rifle Division
54th Guards Rifle Division
96th Guards Rifle Division

20th Rifle Corps
General Major N.A. Shvarev
20th Rifle Division
48th Guards Rifle Division
55th Guards Rifle Division

128th Rifle Corps
General Major P.F. Batitsky
61st Rifle Division
130th Rifle Division
152nd Rifle Division

48th Army
General Lieutenant P.L. Romanenko
Army Artillery
22nd Breakthrough Artillery Division

29th Rifle Corps
General Major A.M. Andreyev
102nd Rifle Division
217th Rifle Division

42nd Rifle Corps
General Lieutenant K.S. Kolganov
137th Rifle Division
170th Rifle Division
399th Rifle Division

53rd Rifle Corps
General Major I.A. Gartsev
17th Rifle Division
73rd Rifle Division
96th Rifle Division
194th Rifle Division

61st Army
General Lieutenant P.A. Bedov

9th Guards Rifle Corps
General Major M.A. Popov
12th Guards Rifle Division
212th Rifle Division

89th Rifle Corps
General Major A.Ya. Yanovsky
23rd Rifle Division
55th Rifle Division
397th Rifle Division
415th Rifle Division

65th Army
General Lieutenant P.I. Batov
Army Artillery
26th Artillery Division

18th Rifle Corps
General Major I.I. Ivanov
37th Guards Rifle Division
69th Rifle Division
44th Guards Rifle Division

105th Rifle Corps
General Major D.F. Alekseyev
15th Rifle Division
75th Guards Rifle Division
193rd Rifle Division
354th Rifle Division
356th Rifle Division

1st Guards Tank Corps
General Major M.F. Panov
1st Guards Mechanized Brigade
15th Guards Tank Brigade
16th Guards Tank Brigade
17th Guards Tank Brigade

1st Mechanized Corps
General Lieutenant S.M. Krivoshein
19th Mechanized Brigade
35th Mechanized Brigade
37th Mechanized Brigade
219th Tank Brigade

Front Units
2nd Guards Cavalry Corps
General Lieutenant V.V. Kryukov
3rd Guards Cavalry Division
4th Guards Cavalry Division
17th Guards Cavalry Division

4th Guards Cavalry Corps
General Lieutenant I.A. Pliyev
9th Guards Cavalry Division
10th Guards Cavalry Division
30th Guards Cavalry Division

7th Guards Cavalry Corps
General Major M.P. Konstantinov
14th Guards Cavalry Division
15th Guards Cavalry Division
16th Guards Cavalry Division

Dnepr Combat Flotilla
Capt. 1st Rank V.V. Grigoryev
1st Riverine Brigade
2nd Riverine Brigade
3rd Riverine Brigade

6th Air Army
General Lieutenant F.P. Polynin
3rd Strike Air Division
242nd Night Bomber Aviation Division
336th Fighter Aviation Division

16th Air Army
General Colonel S.I. Rudenko

3rd Bomber Aviation Corps
General Major A.Z. Karavatsky
241st Bomber Aviation Division
301st Bomber Aviation Division

4th Strike Aviation Corps
General Major G.F. Baydukov
196th Strike Air Division
199th Strike Air Division

6th Fighter Aviation Corps
General Major I.M. Deusov
273rd Fighter Aviation Division
279th Fighter Aviation Division

8th Fighter Aviation Corps
General Major F.F. Zherebchenko
215th Fighter Aviation Division
323rd Fighter Aviation Division

6th Mixed Aviation Corps
Col. M.Kh. Borisenko
221st Bomber Aviation Division
282nd Fighter Aviation Division

Interdependent units
1st Guards Fighter Aviation Division
2nd Guards Fighter Aviation Division
132nd Bomber Aviation Division
234th Fighter Aviation Division
283rd Fighter Aviation Division
286th Fighter Aviation Division
299th Strike Aviation Division
300th Strike Aviation Division

Lublin–Brest Offensive

Soviet Order of Battle, 18 July 1944
1st Byelorussian Front
General K.K. Rokossovsky

70th Army
47th Army
8th Guards Army
Polish 1st Army
69th Army
2nd Tank Army

Lvov–Sandomierz Offensive

Soviet Order of Battle, 18 July 1944
1st Ukrainian Front
Marshal I.S. Konev

3rd Guards Army
1st Guards Tank Army

13th Army
60th Army
38th Army
3rd Guards Tank Army
4th Tank Army
1st Guards Army
5th Guards Army
18th Army
2nd Air Army
8th Air Army (elements deployed to 2nd Air Army)

Jassy–Kishinev Offensive

Soviet Order of Battle, 20 August 1944
4th Ukrainian Front
1st Guards Army
18th Army
17th Guards Infantry Corps
8th Air Army (reconstituted)

2nd Ukrainian Front
40th Army
Mechanized Cavalry group
6th Tank Army
7th Guards Army
27th Army
52nd Army
53rd Army
18th Tank Corps
4th Guards Army
5th Air Army

3rd Ukrainian Front
5th Shock Army
57th Army
37th Army
46th Army
7th Motorized Corps
4th Guards Motorized Corps
17th Air Army

Appendix VII: German Order of Battle, June–July 1944

Army Group Centre (HQ Minsk)
Generalfeldmarschall Ernst Busch

Army Group Reserves
20th Panzer Division
Panzergrenadier Feldherrnhalle
14th Infantry Division (formerly a panzergrenadier division)
707th Security Division (command post Bobruisk)

3rd Panzer Army (HQ Beshenkovichi)
Generaloberst Georg-Hans Reinhardt

Sturmgeschütz-Brigade 28 (VI Corps)
Sturmgeschütz-Brigade 232 (XXVI Corps mid-July 1944)
Sturmgeschütz-Brigade 245 (IX Corps)
Sturmgeschütz-Brigade 277 (XXVI Corps mid-July 1944)
Sturmgeschütz-Brigade 909 (mid-July 1944)

VI Corps
General der Artillerie Georg Pfeiffer
197th Infantry Division
256th Infantry Division
299th Infantry Division

IX Corps
General der Artillerie Rolf Wuthmann
252nd Infantry Division

LIII Corps
General der Infanterie Friedrich Gollwitzer
206th Infantry Division
246th Infantry Division
4th Luftwaffe Field Division
6th Luftwaffe Field Division

4th Army (HQ Orsha)
General der Infanterie Kurt von Tippelskirch

Sturmgeschütz-Brigade 185 (XXXIX Panzer Corps)
Leichte-Sturmgeschütz-Brigade 190
286th Security Division (command post south of Orsha)

XII Corps
Generalleutnant Vincenz Müller
18th Panzergrenadier Division
57th Infantry Division
267th Infantry Division

XXVII Corps
General der Infanterie Paul Völckers
14th Infantry Division
25th Panzergrenadier Division
78th Sturm (Assault) Division
260th Infantry Division

XXXIX Panzer Corps
General der Artillerie Robert Martinek
12th Infantry Division
31st Infantry Division
110th Infantry Division
337th Infantry Division

9th Army (HQ Bobruisk)
General der Infanterie Hans Jordan

Sturmgeschütz-Brigade 189 (XXIII Corps attached to 78th Sturm Assault Division)
Sturmgeschütz-Brigade 244

XXXV Corps
Generalleutnant Kurt-Jürgen Freiherr von Lützow
6th Infantry Division
45th Infantry Division
134th Infantry Division
296th Infantry Division
383rd Infantry Division

XXXXI Panzer Corps
General der Artillerie Helmuth Weidling
35th Infantry Division
36th Infantry Division
129th Infantry Division

LV Corps
General der Infanterie Friedrich Herrlein
102nd Infantry Division
292nd Infantry Division

2nd Army (HQ Petrikov)
Generaloberst Walter Weiss

VIII Corps (5th Jäger Division & 211th Infantry Division)
General der Infanterie Gustav Höhne
XX Corps (3rd Cavalry Brigade)
General der Artillerie Rudolf Freiherr von Roman
XXIII Corps (7th Infantry Division & 203rd Security Division)
General der Pionere Otto Tiemann

Plus:
Sturmgeschütz-Brigade 237 (VIII Corps)
Sturmgeschütz-Brigade 904 (VIII Corps)

201st Security Division (command post Lepel)
221st Security Division
391st Security Division
390th Field Training Division

Army Group North
Generaloberst Georg Lindemann

Army Group Reserves
12th Panzer Division
Field Training Division North

16th Army
General der Artillerie Christian Hansen

Reserves:
24th Infantry Division
69th Infantry Division
281st Security Division
285th Security Division (elements)

I Corps
87th Infantry Division
205th Infantry Division

X Corps
263rd Infantry Division
290th Infantry Division
389th Infantry Division (bulk)

II Corps
23rd Infantry Division
81st Infantry Division
329th Infantry Division

VI SS Corps
15th SS-Grenadier Division
19th SS-Grenadier Division
93rd Infantry Division

L Corps
83rd Infantry Division
132nd Infantry Division
218th Infantry Division

18th Army
General der Artillerie Herbert Loch

Reserves
215th Infantry Division

XXXVIII Corps
21st Luftwaffe Field Division
32nd Infantry Division
121st Infantry Division

XXVIII Corps
12th Luftwaffe Field Division
21st Infantry Division
30th Infantry Division
126th Infantry Division
212th Infantry Division
300 zur besonderen Verwendung or z.b.V. (for special use) Division:
1st (Estonian) Grenzschutz Regiment
2nd and 3rd (Estonian) Grenzschutz Regiments (attached to 227th Infantry
    Division)
4th (Estonian) Grenzschutz Regiment
5th (Estonian) Grenzschutz Regiment (attached to 207th Security Division)

Army ABT Narva
Reserves
61st Infantry Division

XXVI Corps
170th Infantry division
225th Infantry Division
227th Infantry Division and 2nd and 3rd (Estonian) Grenzschutz Regiments

XXXXIII Corps
11th Infantry Division
58th Infantry Division
122nd Infantry Division

III SS Panzer Corps
11th SS-Panzergrenadier Division Nordland and SS-Grenadier Brigade Nederland
20th SS-Grenadier Division Estonian
Küstenverteidigung Ost:
2nd Luftwaffe Flak Division staff and 5 Estonian battalions
Küstenverteidigung 'West':
285th Security Division and 4 (Estonian) battalions

Army Group North Ukraine
Generalfeldmarschall Walter Model

Army Group Reserves
II SS-Panzer Corps
9th SS Panzer Division Hohenstaufen
10th SS Panzer Division Frundsburg
16th SS Panzergrenadier Division Reichsführer-SS

1st Hungarian Army
Lieutenant General Károly Beregfy
Army Reserves
2nd (Hung) Tank Division
19th (Hung) Reserve Division

VI (Hungarian) Corps
Major General Ferenc Farkas
27th (Hungarian) Light Division
1st (Hungarian) Mountain Brigade
2nd (Hungarian) Mountain Brigade
Schlebrügge Brigade

XI Corps
General der Infanterie Rudolf Bünau
18th (Hungarian) Reserve Division
24th (Hungarian) Infantry Division
25th (Hungarian) Infantry Division
101st Jäger Division

VII (Hungarian) Corps
Major General Géza Vörös
16th (Hungarian) Infantry Division
68th Infantry Division

1st Panzer Army
Generaloberst Erhard Raus
Reserves
Stab III Panzer Corps
1st Panzer Division
7th Panzer Division
8th Panzer Division

17th Panzer Division
20th Panzergrenadier Division

XXXXVI Panzer Corps
Generalleutnant Fritz Becker
1st Infantry Division
168th Infantry Division
367th Infantry Division

LIX Corps
General der Infanterie Edgar Röhricht
20th (Hungarian) Infantry Division
208th Infantry Division
254th Infantry Division

XXIV Panzer Corps
General der Panzertruppen Fritz-Hubert Gräser
75th Infantry Division
100th Jäger Division
371st Infantry Division

XXXXVIII Panzer Corps
General der Panzertruppen Hermann Balck
96th Infantry Division
349th Infantry Division
359th Infantry Division
357th Infantry Division

4th Panzer Army
General der Panzertruppen Walther Nehring
Reserves
4th Panzer Division
5th Panzer Division
28th Jäger Division
454th Security Division

XIII Corps
General der Infanterie Arthur Hauffe
Korps Abteilung C (Division Groups 183-217-339)
340th Infantry Division
361st Infantry Division

XXXXII Corps
General der Infanterie Hermann Recknagel
72nd Infantry Division
88th Infantry Division
214th Infantry Division
291st Infantry Division

LVI Panzer Corps
General der Infanterie Johannes Block
1st Ski-Jäger Division
26th Infantry Division
253rd Infantry Division
342nd Infantry Division

Army Group South Ukraine
Generalfeldmarschall Ferdinand Schörner

Army Group Reserves
Stab: 17th Army
Stab V Corps
Stab XXXXIX Gebirgskorps
153rd Field Training Division
1st Slovenian Infantry Division
8th Romanian Cavalry Division
1st Romanian Armoured Division (elements)

Army Group 'Dumitrescu'
HQ: 3rd Rumanian Army
Reserves:
HQ: II (Rumanian) Corps
Stab LXXII z.b.V. Korps

3rd Romanian Army
Reserves:
9th Romanian Infantry Division
Romanian Kdt. d. 'Donau-Mündung'

III Romanian Corps
110th Romanian Infantry Brigade
2nd Romanian Infantry Division
15th Romanian Infantry Division
Stab 685 z.b.V. Regiment

XXIX Corps
304th Infantry Division
21st Romanian Infantry Division
4th Romanian Mountain Division
9th Infantry Division

6th Army
Reserves:
3rd Panzer Division
13th Panzer Division

XXX Corps
306th Infantry Division
15th Infantry Division
257th Infantry Division
302nd Infantry Division
384th Infantry Division

LII Corps
Korps Abteilung D (Division Groups 161-293-355)
17th Infantry Division
320th Infantry Division
97th Jäger Division
294th Infantry Division
4th Mountain Division

XXXXIV Corps
335th Infantry Division
282nd Infantry Division
10th Panzergrenadier Division
Korps Abteilung F (Division Groups 38-62-123)
258th Infantry Division

VII Corps
14th Romanian Infantry Division
106th Infantry Division
370th Infantry Division

Army Group 'Wohler'
Stab: 8th German Army
Reserves: XXXX Panzer Corps
18th Romanian Mountain Division (elements)

8th Army
IV Romanian Corps
Romanian Fast Brigade 'Cojucaru'
102nd Romanian Mountain Brigade
5th Romanian Cavalry Division

Group Gen. Mieth (Stab IV Corps):
376th Infantry Division
11th Romanian Infantry Division
23rd Panzer Division
79th Infantry Division
3rd Romanian Infantry Division

4th Romanian Army
Reserves
1st Romanian Cavalry Division

Group 'D'
24th Panzer Division
3rd SS-Panzer Division
8th Romanian Infantry Division
198th Infantry Division (Kampfgruppe)

Group Knobelsdorff (Stab LVII Panzer Corps)
Reserves
14th Panzer Division
(Units under LVII Panzer Corps Command)

VI Romanian Corps
7th Romanian Infantry Division
76th Infantry Division
18th Romanian Mountain Division (part)
5th Romanian Infantry Division
101st Romanian Mountain Brigade

V Romanian Corps
4th Romanian Infantry Division
1st Romanian Guard Division

LVII Panzer Corps
1st Romanian Infantry Division
46th Infantry Division
13th Romanian Infantry Division

I Romanian Corps
6th Romanian Infantry Division
20th Romanian Infantry Division

VII Romanian Corps
104th Romanian Infantry Brigade
103rd Romanian Infantry Brigade

XVII Corps
3rd Gebirgs Division and elements of the Romanian army
8th Jäger Division (most) and elements of the Romanian army

Appendix VIII: Principal Soviet Armoured Fighting Vehicles Deployed on the Eastern Front

Tanks
T-34/76
T-34/85
IS-1
IS-2
Valentine I
Matilda II
M4 Sherman

Tank Destroyers
SU-85
SU-100

Self-Propelled Guns
SU-76
SU-122
SU-152

Appendix IX: Principal German Armoured Fighting Vehicles Deployed on the Eastern Front

Panzers
PzKpfw IV Ausf H and Ausf J Medium Tank
PzKpfw V Panther Ausf A and Ausf G Heavy Medium Tank
PzKpfw VI Tiger I Ausf E Heavy Tank
PzKpfw VI Tiger II Ausf B Heavy Tank

Assault Guns
Sturmgeschütz III Ausf G Assault Gun
Jagdpanzer IV Tank Destroyer
Jagdpanzer Heavy Tank Destroyer

Self-Propelled Guns
Hummel Heavy Howitzer
Wespe Light Field Howitzer
Marder III Anti-tank Gun

Source Notes

Chapter 1. Debate, Deception and Deployment

p. 1   'Aboard a Moscow-bound plane...', Zhukov, 1985, vol. 2, p. 258
p. 2   'These will not be...', ibid., p. 261
p. 2   'In outlining my suggestions...', ibid.
p. 2   'But our tasks cannot end with...', Merridale, p. 243
p. 3   'The defence must be breached...', K. Nepomniaschii, cited by Bialer,
          pp. 459–60
p. 3   'Go out and think...', Montefiore, pp. 483–84, and Bialer, p. 461
p. 4   'It must be pointed out...', Zhukov, 1985, vol. 2, p. 267
p. 6   'By the Spring of 1944...', Gehlen, p. 110
pp. 6–7 'All these movements...', Zhukov, 1985, vol. 2, p. 269
p. 7   'It was... with the possible exception...', Werth, p. 771
p. 9   'Partisan units and detachments...', Zhukov, 1985, vol. 2, p. 269
p. 10   'General Tippelskirch, Commander of the...', Tippelskirch, cited by
          Werth, p. 773

Chapter 2. Red Storm Rising

p. 13   'In the last two years, despite...', Werth, pp. 768–69
p. 13   'This quantitative advantage, coupled...', Zhukov, 1985, vol. 2, p. 230
p. 13   'After an indepth and comprehensive...', ibid., p. 231
p. 15   'After Kursk I was...', Khrushchev, p. 211
p. 16   'You can rely on me...', Zhukov, 1985, vol. 2, p. 243
pp. 16–17 'According to information received...', ibid.
p. 17   'Capabilities of III Panzer Corps...', US Department of the Army,
          Operations of Encircled Forces, ch. 5, section III
p. 18   'After the Orel offensive...', Zheleznov, cited by Drabkin and Sheremet,
          p. 159
p. 18   'We got held up...', ibid., p. 160
p. 18   'At dawn on 25 March...', Bessonov, p. 69
p. 19   'the scale and...', Manstein, p. 535
p. 19   'Four days after the bombing...', Sebastian, p. 589
p. 19   'It will remain one of...', Werth, pp. 746–47
p. 21   'Even though throughout...', Zhukov, 1985, vol. 2, p. 257

Chapter 3. Where Will Stalin's Blow Fall?

pp. 24–25 'Hitler's remaining allies...', Werth, p. 769
p. 25   'Despite persistent attacks...', Mellenthin, p. 335

p. 68   'Not less than two...', Moynahan, p. 175
p. 69   '383rd Infantry Division is in...', Haupt, p. 202
p. 69   'When we entered Bobruisk...', Grossman, 1989
p. 70   'Generalleutnant Lützow does...', Beevor and Vinogradova, p. 274
p. 71   'In view of these...', Guderian, p. 336
p. 71   'Harpe was a former...', ibid.

Chapter 8. Minsk Freed from the Nazi Yoke
p. 75   'Today, for the first time in...', Haupt, p. 203
p. 77   'The Byelorussian partisans...', Zhukov, 1985, vol. 2, p. 279
p. 77   'The capital of Byelorussia was...', ibid.
p. 80   'In this region...', Allen and Muratoff, p. 119
p. 81   'Slutsk [between Baranovichi and...', Batov, cited by Bialer, p. 419
p. 82   'Vasilevsky is nearing Vilnius...', ibid., p. 420
p. 83   'On 26 July the...', Rogers and Williams, p. 70
p. 86   'Particularly striking was the...', Werth, pp. 772–73

Chapter 9. Lvov–Sandomierz: The Second Blow
p. 87   'By 13 July the Russians had...', Mellenthin, p. 339
p. 90   'Are you in cahoots...', Zhukov, 1985, vol. 2, p. 283
p. 90   'When the preparations were...', ibid., pp. 290–91
p. 90   'In early July our battalion...', Bessonov, p. 95
p. 90   'Wireless intercepts and...', Mellenthin, p. 338
p. 91   'At dawn on 14 July...', Bessonov, p. 96
p. 92   'At 0820 on 14 July...', Mellenthin, p. 341
p. 92   'I set my command post...', Zhukov, 1985, vol. 2, p. 284
p. 93   'The next operation in which...', Drabkin and Sheremet, p. 162
p. 93   'There were motorcycles and...', ibid., p. 163
p. 94   'We were hit hard...', Bessonov, p. 96
p. 95   'Two days later the bulk of...', Mellenthin, p. 343
p. 95   'On the evening of...', Scheiderbauer, cited by Rogers and Williams, p. 72
p. 96   'It must be said...', Gersdorff, p. 26
p. 96   'When I was compelled to...', Guderian, p. 352
p. 97   'We approached Lvov from...', Bessonov, p. 122

Chapter 10. Rokossovsky: Defeat at the Gates of Warsaw
p. 101   'After the defeat of Army Group...', Davies, 2003, p. 373
p. 104   'Together with a group...', ibid., p. 165
p. 105   'As was established later...', Zhukov, 1985, vol. 2, p. 301
p. 106   'The fighting value of...', Bruce, p. 183
p. 108   'When General [Bor] met my...', Davies, 2003, p. 374

Chapter 11. Konev: To the Vistula and Beyond
p. 110   'When we reached the...', Drabkin and Sheremet, p. 165
p. 112   'We were to advance...', Konev, cited by Bialer, p. 481

p. 112 'On 9 January I had a...', ibid.
p. 113 'Finally, the big day...', Bessonov, pp. 153–54
p. 115 'A parade of Soviet heavy tanks...', Sebastian, pp. 609–10

Chapter 12. Bagration: Stalin's Triumph?
p. 118 'The first round of the...', Minasyan, pp. 269–74
p. 118 'Stalin was in good humour...', Zhukov, 1985, vol. 2, p. 281
p. 119 'I know what Beria is capable...', Montefiore, p. 485
p. 119 'Right from the start we...', Gehlen, pp. 114–15
p. 119 'In the summer of 1944...', Zhukov, 1985, vol. 2, p. 296
p. 121 'According to the Germans...', Werth, p. 774
p. 123 'After this I had...', Montgomery, p. 357
p. 124 'Generalfeldmarschall Busch...', Mellenthin, p. 338
p. 124 'The outstanding performance...', Guderian, p. 337
p. 125 'Although, in Byelorussia and...', Werth, p. 775
p. 126 'Prince Irakly Bagration had...', Tolstoy, p. 193
p. 127 'The destruction of our Army Group...', Mellenthin, p. 361

Appendix I. Stalin's New Tanks
p. 129 'The 1st Baltic Front was given...', Zhukov, 1985, vol. 2, p. 266
p. 129 'In the spring of 1943 we...', Drabkin and Sheremet, p. 158
p. 130 'After forcing the Ors...', ibid.
p. 131 'Later I saw an order we...', Khrushchev, pp. 210–11
p. 132 'In essence, until we got the...', Drabkin and Sheremet, p. 160
p. 134 'From the Russian point of view...', Mellenthin, p. 333
p. 134 'Every three weeks or...', Kerr, 1944, p. 127
p. 134 'I had a look at...', Drabkin and Sheremet, p. 16
p. 134 'If a shell had gone...', ibid., pp. 23–24
p. 135 'This was because...', ibid., p. 24
p. 135 'It was a very successful...', ibid., p. 17
p. 135 'Then the brigade commander...', ibid., p. 160
p. 135 'We spent a long time...', ibid., p. 119
p. 136 'I also recall...', ibid., pp. 164–65

Appendix II. Stalin's Revitalized Air Power
p. 137 'The pale blue sky...', Sajer, p. 441
p. 137 'I also proposed that all...', Zhukov, 1985, vol. 2, p. 273
p. 139 'One result was that in...', Kerr, 1944, pp. 129–30
p. 139 'I got my first glimpse of...', Khrushchev, p. 217

Appendix IV. The Enfeebled Luftwaffe
p. 143 'That winter ruined...', Liddell Hart, p. 292

Appendix V. Göring's Luftwaffe Field Divisions
p. 146 'to an army which...', Manstein, p. 269
p. 146 'To form these excellent...', ibid., p. 268
p. 147 'They have the best morale...', Ruffner, pp. 36–37

Bibliography

Note on Sources

The following is far from an exhaustive catalogue of the key/related works on the Eastern Front, nor is it intended to be, but simply lists those studies that have helped shape this volume. However, as fellow military historians will appreciate, producing a coherent narrative and analysis on such a broad canvas requires considerable research. For the more academically minded I must crave your indulgence over the absence of more detailed references, but to do these justice would have required almost a book in itself.

In general there is little appreciation of the vast battles fought on the Eastern Front (beyond Leningrad, Stalingrad, Kursk and Berlin) in comparison to those fought in the west. In recent years this has been partly rectified by a number of fine scholarly studies on the battles for Moscow, Berlin, Budapest and Warsaw, in particular the Beevor and Braithwaite works.

Those seeking an overview of the 'Great Patriotic War' are recommended to consult David Bellamy's comprehensive study *Absolute War*, or Alan Clark's classic *Barbarossa*. John Erickson's in-depth *The Road to Berlin* provides one of the most comprehensive guides covering the 1943–45 campaigns (though a third of the book is references).

Bagration should be as well known as D-Day, but it is not. While there is a wealth of studies on the general aspects of the 'Great Patriotic War' and indeed certain campaigns, Bagration, despite its overwhelming significance and size, remains surprisingly neglected or subsumed in broader studies. The focus has long been on what happened on the flanks, i.e. Leningrad and Stalingrad. There are very few English-language volumes that deal specifically with this operation: works by Paul Adair, Ian Baxter, David Glantz and Steven Zaloga are the most obvious.

Despite the secrecy and paranoia surrounding the machinations of Stalin's Red Court, a surprisingly clear picture of Soviet motives and actions can be drawn from the numerous memoirs of senior Soviet leaders. German accounts are much less comprehensive and coherent.

For non-Russian speakers the most accessible and comprehensive primary Soviet sources are Zhukov's memoirs. Seweryn Bialer's collection of Soviet military memoirs also provides useful insight into the psyche of the Soviet generals, especially Zhukov's blunt if not downright bullying style of generalship. American war correspondents Alexander Werth and Walter Kerr reported from the Soviet Union from 1941 to 1948 and from 1942 to 1943 respectively, providing frank western assessments of the Red Army's development. The work of Artem

Drabkin has also made Soviet infantryman and tanker recollections more accessible in recent years.

The National Archives of Belarus in Minsk and Ukraine in Kiev hold the occupation archives for 1941–44; the former provides frank insight into local collaboration, especially in documenting the creation and activities of the pro-Nazi Byelorussian Regional Defence force, the partisan war and the effects of the Holocaust.

German first-hand accounts of Bagration are rare as so many of those involved were killed or captured and subsequently died in the Soviet Gulag. The archives of the US Army's Center of Military History, Combat Studies Institute and Military History Institute hold useful material, including copies of the debriefs conducted in the 1950s of German generals who fought on the Eastern Front. Also, the Fort Leavenworth papers and US Department of the Army pamphlets are valuable in highlighting the evolution of German strategy and tactics on the Eastern Front.

One can never be too confident in the post-war figures provided by the Soviet authorities; inevitably the scale of their victories is tainted by self-inflated propaganda and aggrandisement. Order of battle figures and casualties will always be open to question. Nonetheless what they do illustrate is a gathering trend and in no way detract from the Red Army's heroic feat of arms.

In contrast on the whole German figures are probably more frank, as is their generals' appreciation of the situation. Although Hitler's refusal to give ground often sealed the fate of the Wehrmacht, his generals in many instances are culpable for acquiescing to his wishes and ultimately in effect signing the death warrants of their own men.

Those generals who insisted on withdrawing and chose to ignore Hitler's orders usually found themselves dismissed. Heinz Guderian and Erich von Manstein are prime examples of Hitler's policy of 'I know best' regardless of the reality of the situation on the ground, and in this instance the known quality and skills of his generals. Their understandable bitterness over this treatment is reflected in their detailed memoirs.

Contemporary Sources and Memoirs

Allen, W.E.D., and Muratoff, P., *The Russian Campaigns of 1944–45* (Harmondsworth, 1946)

Beevor, A., and Vinogradova, L., *A Writer At War: Vasily Grossman with the Red Army, 1941–45* (London, 2006)

Bessonov, E., *Tank Rider into the Third Reich with the Red Army* (London, 2003)

Bialer, S. (ed.), *Stalin and His Generals: Soviet Military Memoirs of World War II* (London, 1970)

Chuikov, V.I., *The End of the Third Reich* (London, 1967)

Deichmann, P., General der Flieger, *Spearhead for Blitzkrieg, Luftwaffe Operations in Support of the Army, 1939–1945* (London, 1996)

Drabkin, A. (ed.), *Red Road from Stalingrad: Recollections of a Soviet Infantryman, Mansur Abdulin* (Barnsley, 2004)

Drabkin, A., and Sheremet, O., *T-34 in Action* (Barnsley, 2006)

Gehlen, R., General, *The Gehlen Memoirs* (London, 1972)

Grossman, V., *Forever Flowing* (New York, 1972)

Grossman, V., *Life and Fate,* (Geneva, 1985)

Grossman, V., *The War Years* (Moscow, 1989)

Guderian, H. General, *Panzer Leader* (London, 1982)

Kerr, W., *The Russian Army, Its Men, Its Leaders and Its Battles* (London, 1944)

Kerr, W., *The Secret of Stalingrad* (London, 1979)

Khrushchev, N., *Khrushchev Remembers,* ed. S. Talbott (London, 1971)

Liddell Hart, B.H., *The Other Side of the Hill: Germany's Generals, Their Rise and Fall, with Their Own Account of Military Events, 1939–45* (London, 1983)

Manstein, E. von, Field Marshal, *Lost Victories* (Elstree, 1987)

Mellenthin, F.W. von, Major General, *Panzer Battles* (London, 1984)

Montgomery, B.L., Field Marshal, *The Memoirs of Field Marshal Montgomery* (London, 1958)

Muñoz, A.J. (ed.), *Wehrmacht Rear Guard Security in the USSR 1941–1945,* Department of the Army Pamphlet 20–240 Washington, DC, 1951 (New York, undated)

Sajer, G., *The Forgotten Soldier* (London, 1999)

Sebastian, M., *Journal, 1935–44* (London?)

Solzhenitsyn, A., *The Gulag Archipelago* (Glasgow, 1974)

Stalin, Marshal, J., *On the Great Patriotic War of the Soviet Union* (London, 1943)

Trevor-Roper, H.R. (ed.), *Hitler's War Directives 1939–1945* (London, 1983)

Werth, A., *Russia at War, 1941–1945* (London, 1965)

White, D.F., *The Growth of the Red Army* (Princeton, 1944)

Zhukov, G., *Marshal Zhukov's Greatest Battles* (London, 1969)

Zhukov, G., Marshal of the Soviet Union, *Reminiscences and Reflections,* vols 1 and 2 (Moscow, 1985)

Fort Leavenworth Papers

Armstrong, Colonel R.N., *Soviet Operational Deception: The Red Cloak,* Combat Studies Institute (Fort Leavenworth, Kansas, 1989)

Connor, Lieutenant Colonel W., *Analysis of Deep Attack Operations: Operation Bagration, Belorussia, 22 June – 29 August 1944,* Combat Studies Institute (Fort Leavenworth, Kansas, 1987)

Gebhardt, Major, J., *The Petsamo-Kirkenes Operation: Soviet Breakthrough and Pursuit in the Arctic, October 1944,* Leavenworth Papers no. 17 (Fort Leavenworth, Kansas, 1990)

Samuel, Dr J. Lewis, *German Counterartillery Measures on the Eastern Front 1944–45: Operation Bagration, Tactical Responses to Concentrated Artillery,* Combat Studies Institute Report no. 13 (Fort Leavenworth, Kansas)

Sasso, Major C.R., *Soviet Night Operations in World War II,* Leavenworth Papers no. 6 (Fort Leavenworth, Kansas, 1982)

Steadman, Lieutenant Colonel, K.A., *A Comparative Look at Air-Ground Support Doctrine and Practice in World War II,* Combat Studies Institute Report no. 2 (Fort Leavenworth, Kansas, 1982)

Wray, Major T.A., *Standing Fast: German Defensive Doctrine on the Russian Front during World War II – Prewar to March 1943,* Combat Studies Institute, Research Survey no. 5 (Fort Leavenworth, Kansas, 1985)

US Army Military History Institute

Gersdorff, F.R.C. von, Generalmajor, *History of the Attempt on Hitler's Life (20 July 1944)*, MS A-855

US Department of the Army Pamphlets

German Defense Tactics against Russian Breakthroughs, no. 20–233 (Washington, DC, 1951)

Military Improvisations during the Russian Campaign, no. 20–201 (Washington, DC, 1951)

Night Combat, no. 20–236 (Washington, DC, 1953)

Operations of Encircled Forces: German Experiences in Russia, no. 20–234 (Washington, DC, 1952)

Rear Area Security in Russia: The Soviet Second Front Behind the German Lines, no. 20–240 (Washington, DC, 1951)

Small Unit Actions during the German Campaign in Russia, no. 20–269 (Washington, DC, 1953)

Other Published Sources

Abbot, P., and Pinak, E., *Ukrainian Armies, 1914–55* (Oxford, 2004)

Abbott, P., and Thomas, N., *Germany's Eastern Front Allies, 1941–45* (London, 1982)

Abbott, P., and Thomas, N., *Partisan Warfare, 1941–45* (London, 1983)

Adair, P., *Hitler's Greatest Defeat: The Collapse of Army Group Centre, June 1944* (London, 2004)

Ailsby, C., *SS Hell on the Eastern Front: The Waffen-SS War in Russia, 1941–1945* (Staplehurst, 1998)

Applebaum, A., *Gulag: A History of the Soviet Camps* (London, 2003)

Axell, A., *Russia's Heroes, 1941–45* (London, 2001)

Baxter, I., *Operation Bagration: The Destruction of Army Group Centre, A Photographic History* (Solihull, 2007)

Bean, T., and Fowler, W., *Russian Tanks of World War II: Stalin's Armoured Might* (Hersham, 2002)

Beevor, A., *Stalingrad* (London, 1999)

Bekker, C., *The Luftwaffe War Diaries* (London, 1972)

Bellamy, C., *Absolute War: Soviet Russia in the Second World War* (London, 2008)

Bergstrom, C., *Bagration to Berlin: The Final Air Battles in the East, 1944–1945* (Hersham, 2008)

Boyd, A., *The Soviet Air Force since 1918* (London, 1977)

Braithwaite, R., *Moscow, 1941* (London, 2006)

Brett-James, A., *1812: Eyewitness Accounts of Napoleon's Defeat in Russia* (London, 1967)

Bruce, G., *The Warsaw Uprising, 1 August – 2 October 1944* (London, 1974)

Bullock, A., *Hitler: A Study in Tyranny* (Harmondsworth, 1979)

Chandler, D.G., *Dictionary of the Napoleonic Wars* (Ware, 1999)

Chaney, O.P., Jr, *Zhukov* (Newton Abbot, 1972)

Clark, A., *Barbarossa: The Russian German Conflict, 1941–1945* (London, 2001)

Collier, R., *The War That Stalin Won* (London, 1983)

Colvin, J., *Zhukov: The Conqueror of Berlin* (London, 2004)

Cornish, N., *Images of Kursk: History's Greatest Tank Battle, July 1943* (Staplehurst, 2002)

Cornish, N., *Armageddon Ost: The German Defeat on the Eastern Front, 1944–5* (Hersham, 2006)

Craig, W., *Enemy at the Gates: The Battle for Stalingrad* (London, 1973)

Davies, N., *Rising '44: The Battle for Warsaw* (London, 2003)

Davies, N., *Europe at War, 1939–1945: No Simple Victory* (London, 2006)

Duffy, P., *Brothers in Arms* (London, 2003)

Einsiedel, H.G., von, *The Onslaught: The German Drive to Stalingrad* (London, 1984)

Erickson, J., *The Road to Stalingrad* (London, 1975)

Erickson, J., *The Road to Berlin* (London, 1983)

Forczyk, R., *Panther vs T-34: Ukraine, 1943* (Oxford/New York, 2007)

Forty, J., *Tanks in Detail, 1: Panzer IV PzKpfw IV Ausf A to J* (Hersham, 2002)

Forty, J., *Tanks in Detail, 3: Panzer V Panther PzKpfw V Ausf A, D and G* (Hersham, 2003)

Gander, T.J., *Tanks in Detail 5: Panzer VI Tiger I and II PzKpfw E and B* (Hersham, 2003)

Gladkov, T.K., *Operation Bagration* (Moscow, 1984)

Glantz, D.M., *Barbarossa: Hitler's Invasion of Russia 1941* (Stroud, 2001)

Glantz, D.M., *The Siege of Leningrad, 1941–1944: 900 Days of Terror* (London, 2001)

Glantz, D.M., and House, J.M., *When Titans Clashed: How the Red Army Stopped Hitler* (Kansas, 1995)

Glantz, D.M., and Orenstein, H.S. (trans. and ed.), *Belorussia, 1944: The Soviet General Staff Study* (Abingdon, 2004)

Gunter, G., *Last Laurels: The German Defence of Upper Silesia, January–May 1945* (Solihull, 2002)

Hastings, M., *Armageddon: The Battle for Germany, 1944–45* (London, 2004)

Haupt, W., *Army Group Centre: The Wehrmacht in Russia, 1941–1945* (Atglen, PA, 1997)

Haupt, W., *Army Group North: The Wehrmacht in Russia, 1941–1945* (Atglen, PA, 1997)

Hooton, E.R., *Eagle in Flames: The Fall of the Luftwaffe* (London, 1997)

Humble, R., *Hitler's Generals* (St Albans, 1976)

Infield, G.B., *The Poltava Affair* (London, 1974)

Irving, D., *The Rise and Fall of the Luftwaffe: The Life of Luftwaffe Marshal Erhard Milch* (London, 1973)

Jacobsen, H.A., and Rohwer, J. (ed.), *Decisive Battles of World War II: The German View* (New York, 1965)

Jukes, G., *The Eastern Front, 1941–1945* (Oxford, 2002)

Jurado, C.C., *Foreign Volunteers of the Wehrmacht, 1941–45* (London, 1983)

Kirchubel, R., *Operation Barbarossa, 1941 (3) Army Group Center* (Oxford and New York, 2007)

Kurowski, F., *Deadlock before Moscow Army Group Center, 1942/1943* (West Chester, PA, 1992)

Kurowski, F., *Panzer Aces* (Mechanicsburg, PA, 2004)

Lucas, J., *War on the Eastern Front: The German Soldier in Russia, 1941–1945* (London, 1998)

Lucas, J., *Hitler's Enforcers: Leaders of the German War Machine, 1933–45* (London, 1999)

Lucas, J., *Hitler's Commanders: German Bravery in the Field, 1939–1945* (London, 2000)

Lucas, J., *Last Days of the Reich* (London, 2002)

Mathews, R., *Hitler, Military Commander* (London, 2003)

Merridale, C., *Ivan's War: The Red Army, 1939–1945* (London, 2005)

Messenger, C., *The Art of Blitzkrieg*, 2nd edn. (Shepperton, 1991)

Minasyan, M.M. (ed.), *Great Patriotic War of the Soviet Union, 1941–45* (Moscow, 1974)

Mitcham, S.W., Jr, *Hitler's Field Marshals and Their Battles* (London, 1988)

Montefiore, S.S., *Stalin: The Court of the Red Tsar* (London, 2004)

Morgan, H., *Soviet Aces of World War 2* (Madrid, 1999)

Moynahan, B., *The Claws of the Bear* (London, 1989)

Myers, S., et al., *Slaughterhouse: The Handbook of the Eastern Front* (Bedford, PA, 2005)

O'Balance, E., *The Red Army* (London, 1964)

Overy, R., *Russia's War* (London, 1998)

Quarrie, B., *Hitler's Samurai: The Waffen-SS in Action* (London, 1985)

Quarrie, B., *Hitler's Teutonic Knights: SS Panzers in Action* (London, 1986)

Reitlinger, G., *The SS Alibi of a Nation, 1922–1945* (London, 1985)

Riasanovsky, N.V., *A History of Russia* (New York, 1993)

Ripley, T., *Steel Storm: Waffen-SS Panzer Battles on the Eastern Front, 1943–1945* (Stroud, 2000)

Rogers, D., and Williams, S. (eds), *On the Bloody Road To Berlin* (Solihull, 2005)

Ruffner, K.C., *Luftwaffe Field Divisions, 1941–45* (Oxford, 1990)

Salisbury, H.E., *The 900 Days: The Siege of Leningrad* (London, 2000)

Seaton, A., *Stalin as Warlord* (London, 1976)

Seaton, A., *The Fall of Fortress Europe, 1943–1945* (London, 1981)

Seaton, A., *The Battle for Moscow* (New York, 1983)

Seaton, A., *The German Army, 1933–45* (London, 1983)

Sharpe, M., and Davis L., *Grossdeutschland: Guderian's Eastern Front Elite* (Hersham, 2001)

Slepyan, K., *Stalin's Guerrillas: Soviet Partisans in World War II* (Kansas, 2006)

Spick, M., *Luftwaffe Fighter Aces: The Jagdflieger and their Combat Tactics and Techniques* (London, 1996)

Suvorov, V., *Inside The Soviet Army* (London, 1982)

Taylor, B., *Barbarossa to Berlin*, vol. 2 (Staplehurst, 2004)

Thomas, N., and Abbott, P., *Partisan Warfare, 1941–45* (London, 1983)

Tolstoy, N., *Victims of Yalta* (London, 1979)

Tucker-Jones, A., *Hitler's Great Panzer Heist* (Barnsley, 2007)

Tucker-Jones, A., *Falaise: The Flawed Victory* (Barnsley, 2008)

Tucker-Jones, A., 'Hitler's Cossacks', *Military Illustrated* (November 2002)

Tucker-Jones, A., 'Berlin Runners', *Classic Military Vehicle* (April 2005)

Tucker-Jones, A., 'Echoes of the Eastern Front', *Classic Military Vehicle* (June 2005)

Tucker-Jones, A., 'How Stalin Crippled the Red Army', *Military Illustrated* (September 2005)

Tucker-Jones, A., 'Tankograd', *Classic Military Vehicle* (November 2005)

Tucker-Jones, A., 'Disaster at Stalingrad', *Military Illustrated* (May 2006)

Tucker-Jones, A., 'The Führer's Last Gasp', *Military Illustrated* (September 2006)

Tucker-Jones, A., 'Horthy's Hungarian Horrors', *Classic Military Vehicle* (January 2007)

Tucker-Jones, A., 'King Boris's Panzers', *Classic Military Vehicle* (April 2007)

Tucker-Jones, A., 'Antonescu's Armour', *Classic Military Vehicle* (June 2007)

Tucker-Jones, A., 'Clash of the Titans', *Military Illustrated* (February 2008)

Tucker-Jones, A., 'Stalin's Armour 1941', *Classic Military Vehicle* (June 2008)

Tucker-Jones, A., Hitler's Dogs of War', *Military Illustrated* (June 2008)

Weal, J., *Focke-Wulf Fw 190 Aces on the Eastern Front* (Madrid, 2000)

Williamson, G., *German Military Police Units, 1939–45* (Oxford, 1989)

Williamson, G., *The SS: Hitler's Instrument of Terror* (London, 2002)

Williamson, G., *Waffen-SS Handbook, 1933–1945* (Stroud, 2003)

Willmott, H.P., *June 1944* (Poole, 1984)

Winchester, C., *Ostfront: Hitler's War on Russia, 1941–45* (Oxford, 1998)

Wood, A., *Stalin and Stalinism* (London, 1997)

Zaloga, S., *Bagration, 1944: The Destruction of Army Group Centre* (Oxford, 1996; Westport, Connecticut, 2004)

Websites

In researching this book I must also acknowledge a debt to the *Axis History Factbook* (axishistory.com) and Feldgrau.com. These websites are invaluable reference tools that greatly assist the military historian to navigate their way around the organizational complexities of the German armed forces and individual generals' service records.

Index